Military Thought in Early China

Military Thought in Early China

Christopher C. Rand

SUNY PRESS

Published by State University of New York Press, Albany

Printed in the United States of America

For information, contact State University of New York Press, Albany, NY
www.sunypress.edu

Production, Eileen Nizer
Marketing, Anne M. Valentine

Library of Congress Cataloging-in-Publication Data

Names: Rand, Christopher C. (Christopher Clark), 1950– author.
Title: Military thought in early China / by Christopher C. Rand.
Description: Albany, NY : State University of New York Press, [2017] | Includes bibliographical references and index.
Identifiers: LCCN 2016031409 (print) | LCCN 2016044927 (ebook) | ISBN 9781438465173 (hardcover : alk. paper) | ISBN 9781438465166 (pbk. : alk. paper) | ISBN 9781438465180 (ebook)
Subjects: LCSH: Military art and science—China—History. | China—Intellectual life—History. | Militarism—China—History.
Classification: LCC U43.C6 R44 2017 (print) | LCC U43.C6 (ebook) | DDC 355.001—dc23
LC record available at https://lccn.loc.gov/2016031409

10 9 8 7 6 5 4 3 2 1

Contents

Preface

The writing of this brief history of military thought in early China began more than forty years ago as the topic of my doctoral dissertation in the Department of East Asian Languages and Civilizations at Harvard University. At that time, in the mid-1970s, the Cultural Revolution in the People's Republic of China was drawing to a close and archeological excavations throughout China were just beginning to reveal entirely new facets of cultural life in the early Sinitic realm. It was an exciting time to be studying early Chinese intellectual history (as it continues to be today), and I was eager to examine how these new findings, particularly regarding military affairs, fit with our previous knowledge of how early Chinese philosophers thought about their world and society.

Under the guidance of Professors Benjamin I. Schwartz, Yu Ying-shih, Yang Lien-sheng, and others at Harvard, I succeeded in completing my PhD thesis in May 1977 on the role of military thought in early Chinese intellectual history. I began writing journal articles based on my thesis and looked forward to obtaining a suitable position in academia where I could teach Chinese history and literature, as I had already done as a teaching fellow for Professors John K. Fairbank and James R. Hightower, and continue my research into Chinese intellectual developments. However, destiny changed that hoped-for trajectory. Rather than obtaining an academic position, I became an employee of the United States government, where I continued to work on Chinese affairs for most of the next thirty years.

After retirement, I decided to resume my study of China in the role of an independent scholar. One of my projects has been to reassess my dissertation of long ago to see whether my conclusions were still valid in the wake of continuing archeological revelations in the intervening years and new examinations by other researchers of the development of military thought in China. There have undoubtedly been many excellent achievements in this field in the decades since I left Harvard, including publications by those who were my fellow graduate students in the 1970s, such as Professor Robin D.S. Yates at McGill University and Professor Victor H. Mair at the University of Pennsylvania. Nevertheless, I felt that the approach and conclusions of my forty-year-old study, if thoroughly updated and succinctly recast, might still make a small contribution to a general understanding of this unique strain of Chinese philosophical inquiry. For that reason I proceeded with a total revamping of my earlier work, sharpening my arguments and adding new evidence in order to make a more complete history of the ideas underpinning military strategy in early China.

I can only hope that the reader will find my efforts worthwhile.

Prologue

For a long time, both inside and outside China, relatively little scholarly attention was given to military thought in early China beyond consideration of the best known of Chinese military treatises, *Sunzi's Military Methods* (*Sunzi bingfa* 孫子兵法). This was chiefly because of the Chinese traditional bias in the imperial era against the value of military affairs in comparison to civil affairs, as well as a limited number of extant primary source materials on warfare from the early period of China's history. Scholars have long been aware from the fifty-three titles compiled by Liu Xiang 劉向 (79–8 BCE) and his son, Liu Xin 劉歆 (ca. 50 BCE–23 CE), and placed by Ban Gu 班固 (32–92 CE) in the military book section ("Bingshu lüe" 兵書略) of the "Treatise on Literature" ("Yiwen zhi" 藝文志) of the *Hanshu* 漢書 that there was a wealth of works devoted to martial affairs in the Han and earlier periods of Chinese history. However, most of these works were presumed permanently lost.[1]

Since the 1970s, however, several previously unavailable documents devoted to military strategy and tactics or related lore—some perhaps versions of works listed in the *Hanshu* "Treatise on Literature"—have been unearthed from widely dispersed archeological sites dating to the Western Han 西漢 dynasty (202 BCE–8 CE) and earlier. The most prominent of these are works addressing military lore and theory that were found in Western Han tombs in Yinqueshan 銀雀山, Shandong Province, in 1972–1973; Mawangdui 馬王堆, Hunan Province, in 1972–1974; Dingxian 定縣, Hebei Province, in 1973; Shangsunjiazhai 上孫家寨, Qinghai Province, in 1978; and Zhangjiashan 張家山, Hubei Province, in 1983. In addition, the Shanghai Museum acquired in 1994 a previously unknown political-military treatise centered on the state of Lu 魯.[2]

As a result of these finds, scholars are now in a position to build a more comprehensive picture of military thinking in the Han and pre-Han periods than has hitherto been possible. We now have enough primary sources at our disposal to trace a line of development for Chinese military philosophy from earliest times through the early Han dynasty and to perceive how this development fits with other intellectual trends of the period.

The present study partakes of this impetus, and also adopts the view—now widely held among specialists—that military thought in early China, like other intellectual strands of that era, should not be described as the output of a discrete school of military philosophers (*bingjia* 兵家).[3] The development of philosophy in the pre-Han and Western Han periods occurred not in separate compartments or lineages but in an interactive way, producing new amalgams and hybrids of ideas as the sociopolitical problems to which they were applied changed. One has only to note the Legalist predilections of Xunzi 荀子 (fl. third century BCE), a Ruist (Confucian), or the development of Yin-Yang 陰陽 theory by Dong Zhongshu 董仲舒 (ca. 179–ca. 104 BCE), also a Ruist, to see this common willingness by philosophical exponents to borrow from different intellectual streams of thought when the objective conditions demanded a new permutation of ideas. This is not to say that one should dismiss the importance of clusters of Chinese thinkers who held similar opinions on current issues; indeed, it will be necessary to refer to such groups in the course of this study. But for China, where social, political, and economic institutions have evolved slowly over many centuries, it is possible to shift the writing of early intellectual history from analyzing the relationships among separate schools of philosophers to assessing the interplay of recurring problems faced by a changing society and the different solutions forwarded by various thinkers, whatever their nominal affiliations, to deal with those problems.[4]

This problem-centered approach is especially useful in studying military thought in early China because, despite the traditional designation of a military school, opinions and information on military affairs appear in numerous sources, philosophical and otherwise, which were often considered by Chinese scholars in later times as being the outgrowths of specific school traditions. Accordingly, this study intends to construct a history of military thought in early China that is focused not on a military school but on the perennial debate, as it evolved from earliest times through the Western Zhou 西周 (ca. 1045–771 BCE), Chunqiu 春秋 (771–ca. 475 BCE), and Zhanguo 戰國 (Warring States) (ca. 475–221 BCE) periods, and into the Western Han, regarding the proper uses of civility (*wen* 文) and martiality (*wu* 武) to preserve cultural stability—what I call the *wen*/*wu* problem.

Because of this focus on the development of a philosophy of war in early China, I will not attempt, except in isolated instances, to recount the details of individual battles fought in early China. Indeed, as other scholars have noted, writing such a history is significantly hindered by a lack of sources on the actual prosecution of battles in these periods. The large majority of battle accounts available to us from ancient times through Western Han emphasize the situation leading up to a battle, the qualities of the rival generals and their political masters, the preparations by each side for waging a potential offense or defense, and the impact of the battle's outcome on subsequent events. In only a few cases, such as the Battle of Chengpu 城濮 in 632 BCE and the Battle of Jingxing 井陘 in 205 BCE, do we have enough data from the early histories to chart the movements of troops on the battlefield and describe the precise tactics used in fighting an engagement.[5] Thus, my examination will concentrate on the principles used in early China to prosecute war, with the aim of showing how these ideas were used to help resolve the *wen/wu* problem.

In analyzing the various strands of the development of early military thought in China, I have discerned three major solutions to the *wen/wu* problem that had their antecedents in the Western Zhou period and before, became fully formed during the late Chunqiu and Zhanguo periods, and continued to be argued following imperial unification in the Qin 秦 dynasty (221–206 BCE) and during the Western Han. I refer to these three solutions as *militarism*, *compartmentalism*, and *syncretism*. In addition, I have identified three applications or perspectives that were variously used by commentators or advocates of these three solutions to explain and/or justify their respective positions. These I have named *metaphysical*, *pragmatic*, and *ethical*. Each of these six elements will be discussed in depth in succeeding chapters. To ensure clarity, the names of these elements, or grammatical variations thereof, are italicized throughout the study.

Also, for reasons of clarity and convenience, when the term "military treatises" appears in the study, this term is meant to refer to the following texts, all of which existed in a variety of written versions during the Zhanguo period and were available during the Western Han as well: the *Sunzi bingfa*, traditionally ascribed to Sun Wu 孫武, said to have flourished in the sixth century BCE; the *Sun Bin bingfa* 孫臏兵法, traditionally ascribed to Sun Bin 孫臏 (ca. 380–316 BCE); the *Wuzi* 吳子, traditionally attributed to Wu Qi 吳起 (440–381 BCE); the *Weiliaozi* 尉繚子, traditionally credited to Wei Liao 尉繚 (fl, late fourth century BCE); the *Liutao* 六韜 (also known as the *Tai Gong liutao* 太公六韜); and the *Simafa* 司馬法, traditionally imputed to Marshal Tian Rangju 田穰苴 (fl. sixth century BCE).[6]

With the above as prologue, I begin this philosophical history with a consideration of the emergence of the *wen/wu* problem in the quasi-legendary period before the Western Zhou.[7]

Chapter 1

The Emergence of the *Wen/Wu* Problem

The dominance of the civil over the martial in most Chinese historical and philosophical texts of the imperial era has tended to obscure the essential importance of *wu* in the Sinitic (*Huaxia* 華夏) realm during the pre-Qin period. In the compiling of China's standard histories (*zhengshi* 正史), for example, military affairs were largely restricted to incidental treatment in the basic annals (*benji* 本紀) and biographical accounts (*liezhuan* 列傳), and garnered only uneven coverage in the treatises (*shu* 書 or *zhi* 志). Generally speaking, if military matters were considered at all in the official accounts of Chinese regimes, institutional evolution and penal administration were the principal interests of traditional scholars, not the broader significance of martiality in Chinese culture and society.[1]

And yet, as shown in the *Hanshu* "Treatise on Literature," there was a sizable and diversified stratum of general and specialized works in the Han and pre-Han eras dealing wholly or in part with martial affairs as an ingredient of government policy and intellectual discourse. The volume of these titles bespeaks keen interest in the early imperial era and before in resolving a set of compelling sociopolitical, philosophical, and practical questions centered on martiality and its proper relation to civility—that is, the *wen/wu* problem. This chapter will explore the conditions that led initially to the consideration of this problem and the major solutions proposed to resolve the issue in the pre-Han period.

The Achievement of Balance

Repeatedly one finds in pre-Qin writings the notion that war is a natural, evolving attribute of the human community, and that martial activity allowed, paradoxically, for the advancement of civilized life. In a number of works from the period, the origins of war are said to coincide with the drive to survive and with the demands of the natural environment. Following the way of Heaven and Earth, the sages of Chinese antiquity, according to tradition, did not exclude violence but rather stipulated it as an outlet for hostile feelings, much as those manifested by armed beasts. War was perceived as an impetus for positive change rather than a negative feature of social life. Harkening back to earliest times, the "Wu zheng" 五正 section of the *Jing* 經—one of the *Huangdi sijing* 黃帝四經 dating from the pre-Han era—uses an anecdote about preparations for battle between the legendary sovereign Huangdi 黃帝 and his rival, the tribal leader Chiyou 蚩尤, to illustrate the necessity of martiality in maintaining harmony.

> Huangdi [asked Yanran 閹冉], "I want to show myself to be humble. What is your opinion?"
>
> [Yanran] replied: "Those who share the Way share the same affairs and those who differ from the Way differ in their affairs. Today the world is in great conflict and the time has come [to take action]. Can you therefore be so cautious that you will not engage in combat?"
>
> Huangdi said, "What if I did not engage in combat?"
>
> [Yanran] responded, "Anger is a matter of blood and vital energy (*qi* 氣), while combat is a matter of exterior fat and flesh. If anger is not released, its fluid will collect into pustules, which can then ruin your [other] four [vital organs]. How would dry bones be capable of fighting?"
>
> Huangdi then withdrew from his state ministers, and going up to the Bowang 博望 mountains, he lay back and communed [with himself] for three years, searching himself [for the answer]. Shancai 單才 and Yanran then went up for Huangdi, roused him and said: "It must be done. To engage in combat may be inauspicious, but not to fight is also lacking in merit. How can you refuse?" Huangdi then produced his *qiang* 鏘 halberd, prepared his battle weapons, and, taking drumsticks in hand, [led his army] to meet Chiyou, whom he subsequently captured.[2]

The therapeutic release of vital energy being a positive function of war, martiality was viewed in antiquity as a cultural *sine qua non*. Even in Western Han times, Sima Qian 司馬遷 (ca. 145–ca. 86 BCE), author with his father, Sima Tan 司馬談 (ca. 165–110 BCE), of the first general history of China, the *Shiji* 史記, seemed to recognize the hygienic attributes of combat:[3]

> Now, music is the means by which the former kings embellished their happiness, and armies and battle weapons were the means by which the former kings embellished their anger. Hence the happiness and anger of the former kings each attained its meet [expression]. With happiness the world was harmonized, and with anger the violent and disorderly were overawed.[4]

In similar organic fashion, warfare was seen in Chinese antiquity as an extension of hunting practices. The *Shi* 詩 (*Odes*), an anthology of verse dating from about 1000 to about 600 BCE, provides an example of this in the ode "Shu yu tian" 叔于田, in which Shu 叔 the huntsman is hailed not only as "admirable and kind" and "admirable and good," but "admirable and martial" (*mei qie wu* 美且武).[5] Another *Shi* ode, "Qi yue" 七月, tells us that certain times of the year were set aside in ancient times for aristocratic hunting exercises that served concurrently as war games.[6] Also, the *Chunqiu Zuozhuan* 春秋左傳 (hereafter *Zuozhuan*), composed perhaps during the fourth century BCE, gives a description of a custom practiced since earliest times of combining hunting expeditions and martial training.[7] In a remonstration in 718 BCE with Lord Yin 隱公 of Lu (r. 723–712 BC), Zang Xibo 臧僖伯, a noble in Lu, is quoted to say:

> The frequent indulgence in a government of disorder is the way to ruin. In accordance with this there are the spring hunting, the summer hunting, the autumn hunting, and the winter hunting—all in the intervals of husbandry to address affairs [of state]. Then every three years there is the [grand] military review (*zhibing* 治兵). When it is over, the troops are all led back (*zhenlü* 振旅),[8] and their return is announced by the cup of spirits in the temple—all to take reckoning of the accouterments and spoils, to display the various blazonry, to exhibit the noble and the mean, to distinguish the observance of order and ranks, to show the proper difference between the young and the old, and to practice the various observances of discipline.[9]

In comparable fashion, warfare and agriculture were seen in early texts as complementary activities, contributing together to social harmony. The

Guoyu 國語, a work whose contents were composed variously in the fifth and fourth centuries BCE, recounts an ancient tradition of devoting three seasons to agriculture and one season—the autumn—to military instruction. The ruler may thus be "awe-inspiring" in conducting punitive expeditions and have the resources when in defense. "He is able to be pleasing to the spirits and bring harmony to the people."[10] In the Zhanguo period, one of the military treatises, the *Liutao*, likewise draws a close linkage between martial warfare and civil agriculture by pointing out the double utility of agricultural implements:

> The equipment for offensive and defensive warfare is entirely within the scope of people's [everyday] affairs: plows and plowshares become their *chevaux de frise* (*xingma* 行馬) and [blocking] spiked rods (*jili* 蒺藜); horses and oxen, carts and carriages become their encampment ramparts and covered turrets; hoes and harrows become their spears and halberds (*ji* 戟); wild ginger and marsh grass, bamboo umbrellas and rain hats become their armor, helmets and shields; mattocks, spades, cleavers, saws, pestles and mortars become their instruments for assaulting fortress walls. Oxen and horses become means for transporting provisions and equipment; cocks and dogs become lookouts; wives' weaving [techniques are used for] banners and flags; husbands' land-clearing [techniques are used for] assaulting fortresses. [The techniques for] slashing down grass and brambles in spring become [the means for] fighting chariots and cavalry; [the techniques for] weeding fields in summer become [the means for] fighting infantry; [the techniques for] cutting grain and firewood in autumn become [the means for] collecting provisions and stores; and [the techniques for] filling granaries and warehouses in winter become [the means for] making a solid defense.[11]

In short, martial activities were considered integral to early Sinitic society. Far from being an aberration, war was thought to be a normal feature of the yearly cycle of life. Moreover, both martial and civil activities were part of the descriptions of China's earliest cultural heroes. As we have seen, while the legendary Huangdi was hailed for his civil accomplishments, he also had to excel in martial affairs if he was to maintain harmony in his realm. In similar fashion, Lord Liu 公劉, a leading member of the Ji 姬 clan that founded the Zhou dynasty, is described in the *Shi* as making proportional use of martial force even as he moved his clan away from hostile northern tribes and established agricultural lands in a new territory.

> Of generous devotion to the people was Lord Liu.
> Unable to rest or take his ease [where he was],
> He divided and subdivided the country into fields;
> He stored up the produce in the fields and in barns;
> He tied up dried meat and grain,
> In bottomless bags and in sacks—
> That he might hold [the people] together, and glorify [his tribe].
> Then with bows and arrows all ready,
> With shields and spears, and axes, large and small,
> He commenced his march [to a new settlement area].[12]

In this fashion, the praiseworthy leaders of China's antiquity were, by necessity, warriors as well as creators of civilization.[13] And, as suggested above, intercultural conflict in ancient China was, at least in its early stage, seen as progressive: war constituted a means for societal consolidation and dialectical advancement, and the arts of peace and war for the early cultures in the river valleys of north China were mutually supportive, synergistic.

Yet there was impending danger in the continued practice of occasional, random conflict. As populations in north China grew closer to one another and internal frictions grew, the benefits of unregulated warfare diminished.[14] Probably as early as late Shang 商 times (ca. 1100 BCE), if one can extrapolate back from Western Zhou sources, there was a realization that war, though still useful for expansion and cultural enrichment, had to be balanced carefully with the pacific arts of government, with internal ordering, and with social stabilization. Differentiation and hierarchies under absolute authority could not be maintained with continual exposure to destruction and debilitating war levies. It may have been at this time that civility and martiality first began to be recognized among Chinese thinkers as important and perennial factors in Chinese cultural change.

Evidence for this recognition of tension between *wen* and *wu*, and the problem of resolving this tension, can be gleaned from the earliest known literature. The "Chang fa" 長發 ode in the *Shi*, for instance, expresses an indirect admiration for *wu* in its description of the moving splendor of a soldier's garb and bearing. Similarly, the "Yi jie" 猗嗟 ode in the *Shi* expresses delight in the martial prowess and awesome appearance of a now-dead archer.

Alas for him, so handsome and accomplished!
How grandly tall!
With what elegance in his high forehead!
With what motion of his beautiful eyes!
With what skill in the swift movements of his feet!
With what mastery of archery!
. . .
Alas for him, so beautiful!
His bright eyes and high forehead how lovely!
His dancing so choice!
Sure to send his arrows right through!
The four all going to the same place!
One able to withstand rebellion![15]

Other verses in the *Shi*, however, tell of an aversion to the wrongful byproducts of war. The "Bo xi" 伯兮 ode, for example, combines wonder and pride in military events with sadness in the separation and loss that war brings. Likewise, many *Shi* verses like "Cai wei" 采薇 tell of soldiers' toils and regrets during seemingly interminable marches. And yet a few odes in the *Shi* reveal an affinity for both the warlike and the peaceful. The "Pan shui" 泮水 ode, for example, integrates the martial and civil virtues into a single exemplary figure. A marquis of Lu is described throughout the ode as a dashing figure, bristling with martial splendor, leader of victorious armies. But at times in the ode he is also described as one who appreciates civil qualities and desires to institute such qualities in his realm:

Very admirable is the marquis of Lu,
Reverently displaying his virtue,
And reverently watching over his deportment,
The pattern of the people.
With great qualities truly civil and martial,
Brilliantly he affects his meritorious ancestors.
In everything entirely filial,
He seeks the blessing for himself.[16]

Thus, in the airs and encomiums of the *Shi* one can find ambivalence about civility and martiality. On the one hand, the glories of potential combat are conspicuously admired, but on the other hand, the trauma of participation in actual combat and its attendant marches is emotionally on display. The modern China scholar C.H. Wang once pointed out that the actual clash of arms in battle is largely undescribed in the *Shi*. The emphasis instead is on the effects that grandly intimidating formations of men and equipment, especially particular personalities in military costume, have on the minds of friend and foe alike. In Wang's view, this lack of expressed violence was due to the overweening stress on civility in this collection of verses. But it is also possible to say that the *Shi*'s lack of Homeric battle gore was the result of an emphasis on the potency of martiality, rather than its violent effects.[17]

The Western Zhou Solution

To further examine this matter, we turn to the events surrounding the overthrow of Shang by Zhou and the results of this overthrow on thought regarding the *wen/wu* problem. In this momentous transition to a new regime there was a father-son combination of talents, King Wen 文王 (d. 1086 BCE) and King Wu 武王 (d. 1043 BCE), whose posthumous names became eponyms for model culture builders.[18] Even before the integrity and strength of the Zhou ruling house began to falter under King Li 厲王 (d. 828 BCE) and later King You 幽王 (r. 781–771 BCE), a nostalgia for the august progenitors of the dynasty was evoked in documents and song to commemorate those heroic, spring-like years of the kingdom and the leaders that made that kingdom possible. We see this in several *Shi* odes, including the "Bi gong" 閟宮, "Lai" 賚, "Wu" 武, and "Huan" 桓 odes. Of particular note is the "Da Ming" 大明 ode, which describes the crucial Battle of Muye 牧野 that spelled the end of the Shang dynasty at the hands of King Wu, following the establishment of the Zhou dynasty by King Wen:

> The favoring mandate was from Heaven,
> Giving the throne to our King Wen,
> In the capital of Zhou.
> The lady-successor was from Xin,
> Its eldest daughter, who came to marry him.
> She was blessed to give birth to King Wu,
> Who was preserved and helped, and received also the appointment,
> And in accordance with it smote the great Shang.

The troops of Shang
Were collected like a forest,
And marshaled at Muye.[19]
We rose [to the crisis]—
"God is with you," [said Shangfu 尙父 to the king],[20]
"Have no doubts in your heart."

Muye spread out extensive;
Bright shone the chariots of sandalwood;
The teams of bays, black-maned and white-bellied, galloped along;
Was like an eagle on the wing
Assisting King Wu,
Who at one onset smote the great Shang.
That morning's encounter was followed by a clear bright [day].[21]

Finally, there is the "Shi mai" 時邁 ode, which not only depicts a triumphant progress by King Wu after the establishment of Zhou, but also describes the king's evident success in shifting from the martial battlefield where he won victory to the cultivation and display of "admirable virtue" (*yi de* 懿德) to bring civil peace to the kingdom.

Now is he making a progress through the states,
May Heaven accept him as its son!
Truly are the honor and succession come from it to the House of Zhou.
To his movements
All respond with tremulous awe.
He has attracted and given rest to all spiritual Beings,
Even to [the spirits of] the Yellow River and the highest hills.
Truly is the king the sovereign lord.
Brilliant and illustrious is the House of Zhou.
He has regulated the positions of the princes;
He has called in shields and spears;
He has returned to their cases bows and arrows.
I will cultivate admirable virtue,
And display it throughout these great regions—
Truly will the king preserve the mandate.[22]

From this body of verse many later Chinese scholars judged that the aftermath of the Battle of Muye—disarmament and pacification—was more important than the martial actions taken to overwhelm the Shang. In their eyes, *wen* metaphorically overtook *wu* in importance. Herrlee G. Creel (1905–1994), in his work on the origins of statecraft in China, supported this traditional view, in part by pointing out the larger number of references in the *Shi* to King Wen as compared to King Wu by a ratio of three to one.[23] However, those genuine portions of the Zhou-era *Shu* 書 or *Shangshu* 尚書 (*Documents*) that deal with the Shang-Zhou transition fail to lend solid support to this interpretation.[24] It is true that the "Kang gao" 康誥 document speaks of King Wen as the principal actor in the Zhou's takeover of Shang. However, as Creel pointed out, since the Song 宋 dynasty (960–1279) there was general agreement among Chinese scholars that King Wu was the author of the "Kang gao."[25] If so, then filial deference would probably have prevented him from inserting into the declaration his own contributions to the Zhou success, which were clearly substantial. Thus, it is probably not warranted to place King Wen over King Wu in importance, and therefore of symbolically ranking *wen* over *wu*. Based on the evidence available, it seems more reasonable to infer that, at a time of Shang dynastic weakness when war seemed imminent, King Wen and King Wu must have realized the necessity for both military preparedness and civil stability. As we have seen earlier, such had been the attitude ascribed to the early cultural heroes, and such would also be the case for King Cheng 成王 of Zhou (d. 1021 BCE) and his regent, the Duke of Zhou 周公 (brother of King Wu), at least until after the failed rebellion fomented by Wu Geng 武庚, a son of the last Shang king.

Accordingly, it would seem more appropriate to say that Kings Wen and Wu approached the problem of conquest and pacification in two different phases of the takeover of the Shang, but with the same essential balance of martial and civil. King Wen, as founder of the Zhou dynastic line, had already consolidated a degree of power during the reign of King Zhou 紂王 of Shang (d. 1046 BCE), in hopes of carrying out a coup d'état. However, he died before consummating his plans. King Wu therefore inherited the responsibility for continuing the buildup of military and ideological strength King Wen had created and for leading the decisive attack on Shang. The "Wu cheng" 武成 document of the *Shangshu* illustrates King Wu's strategy as seen in the prosecution and aftermath of the Battle of Muye:

> On the *wuwu* 戊午 day the army crossed Meng Ford (Mengjin 孟津), and on the *guihai* 癸亥 day it drew up in array on the outskirts of Shang, waiting for the mandate of Heaven. On the *jiazi* 甲子 day, at early dawn, Shou 受 [i.e., King Zhou of

> Shang] led forward his hosts like a forest and assembled them at Muye. But they would offer no opposition to our army. Those in the front inverted their spears and attacked those behind them until they fled, and the blood flowed until it floated pestles. Thus did [King Wu] but once don his arms and the world was greatly settled. He overthrew the government of Shang and made it resume its old course. He released Jizi 箕子 from captivity, performed sacrifices at the grave of Bi Gan 比干, and bowed in his carriage at the gate of Shang Rong's 商容 village.[26] He disbursed the [accumulated] treasures in Lu Tower 鹿臺 and distributed the [stored] grain at Juqiao 鉅橋, conferring great gifts throughout the realm.[27] As a result, the people joyfully submitted.[28]

Not by sheer force of arms did King Wu cause the grisly demise of King Zhou of Shang and his hapless army, but rather by the will of Heaven. With that spiritual assistance there was no need for total war; instead, King Wu emphasized economy of force. As King Wu is quoted in the "Mu shi" 牧誓 document of the *Shangshu*:

> Now I, Fa 發 [i.e., King Wu], am simply executing respectfully the punishment appointed by Heaven. In today's business do not advance more than six or seven steps, and then stop and adjust your ranks—my brave men, be energetic! Do not exceed four blows, five blows, six blows, or seven blows; and then stop and adjust your ranks—my brave men, be energetic! If you are not thus energetic, you will bring destruction on yourselves.[29]

Indulgent toward the fallen, King Wu was concerned with the neutralization of power, not bloody retribution. In reflection of his father's intentions, King Wu sought to preserve the essential cultural traits of Shang civilization in the wake of his conquest of the Shang royal house. Militaristic policies were, from his viewpoint, the least effective means to conquer the Shang while retaining the values of what had been a constructive, vibrant society. Thus, in conjunction with martial potency, Kings Wen and Wu together championed the notion of virtue (*de* 德) to legitimize in civil terms Zhou's rise to leadership. At the same time, the co-founders realized that virtue alone was not sufficient to unify and retain their captive empire; *de* had to be coupled with a complementary martial notion of due punishment (*xing*

刑) to justify Zhou's military consolidation efforts. In tandem, these moral entities served to transform the idea of *wen/wu* balance shared by Kings Wen and Wu into a workable policy.

It is possible to illustrate this moral linkage of *wen* and *wu* by observing that in the conquest legend King Wu did not attack when he had the military wherewithal to do so. Instead, as suggested in the "Zhuo" 酌 ode of the *Shi*, he bided his time:

> Oh! powerful was the king's army,
> But he nursed it in obedience to circumstances while the time was yet dark.
> When the time was clearly bright,
> He thereupon donned his grand armor.[30]

Not only was King Wu waiting for the militarily advantageous time to attack, he was waiting for the proper moral opportunity when King Zhou's malfeasances were no longer bearable. He thereby set an important precedent for future martial planning. He saw the wisdom of timing his attack to accord with objective conditions, whether they were human or environmental power relationships or accepted standards of moral legitimacy. Here, clearly, the evidence is weighted toward the latter, for King Wu was acting on the basis of the words in the "Zhonghui zhi gao" 仲虺之誥 document of the *Shu*, which advocated "showing favor to the able and right-principled" and "aiding the virtuous," while "punishing the willfully blind" and "dealing summarily with those going to ruin."[31]

Thus, through their chroniclers, Kings Wen and Wu came to represent a synthesis of values necessary for the success of the Zhou regime at a time when the former benefits of warfare had become obsolete. *Wu* was now viewed as an expedient for rapid, decisive change when conditions, moral and otherwise, demanded it. Once administered, *wu* must properly retreat into dormancy, allowing *wen* to manifest itself.

This Western Zhou solution to the *wen/wu* problem, calling for reciprocal use of martiality and civility based on the situation at hand, became one of the fundamental axioms in a developing philosophy of war in early China. Though reliable textual sources are still few, it is nevertheless reasonable to suggest that during Western Zhou the complementarity of *wen* and *wu*, and its derivative, the complementarity of virtue (*de*) and punishment (*xing*), had already entered the realm of political ideology. By the time the legends of Kings Wen and Wu had been formalized in the later Western Zhou period, the concepts of martiality and civility had become primary causative factors in the founding and maintenance of a harmonious realm: *Wu* was that force necessary to punish (*xing*) those who failed to submit to a ruler's *de*; *wen* was the exercise of *de* for social well-being. Together these moral imperatives represented the principal means for assuring cultural equilibrium and vigorous growth.

The Duke of Zhou seems to have continued this advocacy of martial/civil balance during King Cheng's reign. Because of his prototypal position as a wise advisor, later Ruist and other philosophers aspiring to comparable government power in the Zhanguo period hailed the duke as the creator of several Zhou institutions and as virtuous minister *par excellence*. No solid evidence exists for most of these ascriptions, but on the basis of genuine documents in the *Shangshu*, it was plausibly the duke who standardized the Heavenly mandate (*tianming* 天命) ideology. Moreover, it was probably he who directed the suppression of the Shang counterattack and, with the establishment of Luo 洛, consolidated the eastern territories under Zhou rule. Like Kings Wen and Wu, of whom he was continually mindful in his proclamations, the duke combined conqueror and administrator into a single vocation. In addition, by promoting the rationale of a Heavenly mandate, he strengthened the key intellectual hinge connecting martial and civil activities into a balanced whole.[32]

Evolution in Chunqiu Times

During Chunqiu times, the Western Zhou solution to the *wen*/*wu* problem still retained much of its original vitality. The *Guoyu* describes Lord Huan 桓公 of the state of Qi 齊 (r. 686–643 BCE), who became the first hegemon (*ba* 霸) of the lords of the realm (*zhuhou* 諸侯), as adopting policies that closely followed the Western Zhou solution regarding martiality and civility. As a result, we are told in the *Guoyu*, "none of the lords of small states all over the empire dared to oppose him." They "put trust in his humaneness and were overawed by his martiality."[33] The *Zuozhuan* provides comparable evidence in its description of an incident of 558 BCE, when the then marquis of Jin 晉侯 consulted a Jin noble, Zhonghang Xianzi 中行獻子, about a possible attack on the state of Wei 衞. Zhonghang Xianzi's reply is drawn directly from the "Zhonghui zhi gao" document of the *Shangshu*: " 'Deal summarily with states that are going to ruin, and take their states from the disorderly. To overthrow the perishing and strengthen what is being preserved is the way in which to administer a state.' Let Your Lordship now settle Wei, and wait the time [for a different course]."[34]

While adherence to the Western Zhou solution was evident during the Chunqiu period, the *wen/wu* nexus was also being interpreted in new ways, which served to give *wu* more definition. Martiality and civility became less general descriptions of punitive or pacifying behavior and more a set of clearly defined characteristics and mutual relationships.

At the conclusion of the Battle of Bi 邲 between the states of Jin and Chu 楚 in 597 BCE, the viscount of Chu 楚子 was encouraged to construct a monument out of the soldiers of Jin who had been killed in combat. He rejected the idea, saying: "You do not know what you are talking about. The character for 'prowess' (*wu*) is formed by those for 'stay' (*zhi* 止) and 'spear' (*ge* 戈)."[35] After citing the virtues of King Wu of Zhou as expressed in the *Shi*, the viscount continued:

> Thus military prowess is seen in the repression of cruelty, the calling in of the weapons of war, the preservation of the great appointment, the firm establishment of one's merit, the giving of repose to the people, the harmonizing of all [the states], and the enlargement of the general wealth; and King Wu took by those stanzas that his posterity should not forget this. Now, I have caused the bones of the soldiers of two states to lie bleaching on the earth—an act of cruelty; I display my weapons of war, how can I preserve the great appointment? And while still the state of Jin remains, how can I firmly establish my merit? There are many things by which I oppose what the people desire, and how can they get repose from me? Without the practice of virtue, striving by force for supremacy among the states, how can I produce harmony among them? I have made my gain from the perils of others, and found my safety in their disorders—these things are my glory, but what enlargement of the general wealth is there in them? Not one of the seven virtues belonging to military prowess attaches to me—what have I to display to my posterity? Let us simply make here a temple for the tablets of my predecessors and announce to them our success. The merit of military prowess does not belong to me!"[36]

Once again King Wu is esteemed as the source of true martiality—military power that has its effect in a state of latency. Indeed, the viscount of

Chu sees his ideal in a figure such as the marquis of Lu in the "Pan shui" ode of the *Shi*, who combined *wen* and *wu* but manifested them in paradoxical ways. Civility must be open, visible to all, for it to be effective; martiality, on the other hand, must remain awe-inspiring but unconsummated. It might appear from the viscount's description that martiality is actually civility in disguise, but this is only to emphasize the concealed nature of *wu*. While acts of *wen* appear clearly to all, *wu* lies in a state of potentiality, giving force to *wen*'s inner power. The *Guoyu* has the following illustrative passage:

> King Wu was preparing to chastise the Quanrong 犬戎 [an ethnic group to the north of the Zhou], when Moufu 謀父, lord of Ji 祭公, admonished him, saying, "It must not be done. The former kings manifested their virtue, but did not display their weapons. If weapons are stored away and only used on timely occasions, then when they are used, they will be awe-inspiring. But if they are displayed, then they will [tend to] be overused. And if they are overused, then they will hold no terror."[37]

According to this notion, true power—the ability to motivate others to fulfill your wishes—lies not in coercion but in a concerted application of manifest *wen* and latent *wu*. Consequently, though *wen* may appear dominant, *wu* also has utility in potency. Based on the tradition invoked by the viscount, *wu* cannot exist without manifest *wen*, and as implied by the above *Guoyu* passage, *wen* without the opportune display of *wu* cannot be effective. The *Zuozhuan* similarly highlights this truth in an anecdote set on the eve of the Battle of Bi in 597 BCE. In the passage, Zhizi 彘子 (Xianhu 先穀), adjutant to the commander of the Jin army, advises an attack against Chu despite the danger of a defeat. He reasoned that a failure to attack would be to dismiss the tradition of military prowess (*wu*) that had made Jin first among the states of the realm.[38] Rather than being an example of bravery in the face of danger, however, the parable is intended to show a misapprehension of power and its uses. Zhizi's concept of *wu* is taken in the *Zuozhuan* to be an incautious advocacy of brute strength and a brash show of chauvinism, which in the end led to a debacle for Jin. Even in waging a battle, martiality must be applied sparingly to achieve the best outcome.

Another strain of Chunqiu-era thinking on *wen*/*wu* expands on the reciprocality of civility and martiality seen in the Western Zhou era. This is evident in the *Zuozhuan* description of the events surrounding the nonaggression covenant conference of 546 BCE, which was hosted by the state of Song 宋 and succeeded in temporarily halting the repeated military incursions by the principal state rivals of the time, Jin and Chu, and their respective allies. In the wake of the conclave, Xiang Xu 向戌, Song's master of the left, asked the lord of Song to reward him for his efforts in managing the conference, saying, "Please grant me some towns for arresting the occasion of death." After the lord issued an edict rewarding Xiang Xu sixty towns, Xiang Xu showed the grant document to Zihan 子罕 (Yue Xi 樂喜), a senior minister in Song. Zihan replied by underscoring the importance of martiality, even as attempts were being made to arrest its use in favor of civility:

> "It is by their arms that Jin and Chu keep the small states in awe. Standing in awe, the high and low in them are loving and harmonious; and through love and harmony they can keep their states in quiet, and thereby serve the great states. In this is the way of preservation. If they were not kept in awe, they would become haughty. That haughtiness would produce disorder, and that disorder would lead to their extinction. This is the way of ruin. Heaven has produced the five materials (*wu cai* 五材), all of which may be dispensed with, but who can do away with the instruments of war? They have long been in requisition. It is by them that the lawless are kept in awe and accomplished virtue is displayed. Sages have risen to their eminence by means of them and men of confusion have been removed. The courses which lead to decline or growth, to preservation or ruin, to blindness, on the one hand, and intelligence, on the other, are all to be traced to these instruments, and yet you have been seeking to do away with them. Is not your scheme a delusion? No offense can be greater than to lead the states astray by such a delusion. You have escaped without a great punishment, and yet you have sought reward with extreme insatiableness." With this Zihan cut to pieces the grant document and cast it away.[39]

Zihan's vigorous defense of the ineluctability of *wu* is later complemented in the *Zuozhuan* by commentary from Shen Shushi 申叔時, a noble of Chu, in speaking to the Chu general Zifan 子反 before Jin's attack on the state of Zheng 鄭, an ally of Chu, in the Battle of Yanling 鄢陵 in 575 BCE. After learning of Jin's intentions, Zheng alerted Chu, whose viscount sent an army in relief, with Zifan commanding the army of the center. As the Chu army passed by Shen 申, Zifan entered the city to see Shen Shushi and ask him what he thought of the expedition. According to the *Zuozhuan*, Shen Shushi replied:

> "Virtuous goodness, punishments, religion, righteousness, propriety, and good faith, all are the appliances of war. Virtuous goodness appears in the exercise of kindness; punishment in the correction of what is wrong; religion in the service of the spirits; righteousness in the establishment of what is beneficial; propriety in doing things at the proper times; and good faith in the watchful keeping of everything. [When these things obtain,] the people live well off and their virtue is correct; all movements are with advantage and affairs are rightly ordered; the seasons are all accorded with and everything is prosperous; harmony prevails between superiors and inferiors; all movements are made without insubordinate opposition; whatever the superiors require is responded to; everyone knows his duty. Hence it is said in the ode, 'Thou didst establish [and nourish] the multitudes of our people, / The immense gift of thy goodness.'[40] In consequence of this, [in that ancient time] the spirits sent down their blessing, and the seasons all passed without calamity or injury. The wants of the people were abundantly supplied, and with consenting harmony they received the orders of their superiors. They all did their utmost to obey those orders and would devote themselves to death to supply the places of any that were lacking. This was the way to secure victory in battle."[41]

Here Shen Shushi eloquently states the case seen elsewhere in Chunqiu writings that *wen* and *wu* are tandem elements, one depending on the other, and that their apposite application leads to a harmonious result.

An additional indication of the continued reciprocality seen in Chunqiu times between martiality and civility appears in other *Zuozhuan* passages addressing the close connection between warfare and ritual—a connection that existed as far back as the Shang era. Battles described in the *Zuozhuan* were typically preceded by a whole series of prescribed rites (*li* 禮) designed to ascertain the ancestors' and/or Heaven's purposes and desires.[42] The "Wang zhi" 王制 chapter of the *Liji* 禮記, despite its later compilation, probably gives what may have earlier become a standardized procedure:

> When the sovereign was about to go forth on a punitive expedition, he sacrificed especially, but with the usual forms, to the Lord on High (*Shangdi* 上帝), offered the *yi* 宜 sacrifice at the altar of the Earth, and then performed the *zao* 造 sacrifice in the temple of his deceased father. He offered sacrifices also to the Father of War (*ma* 禡) [on arriving] at the state which was the object of the expedition. He had received his charge from his ancestors and the complete [plan] for the execution of it in the Jade Academy (*biyong* 辟雍).[43] He went forth accordingly, and seized the criminals; and on his return he set forth his offerings in the Jade Academy and announced [to his ancestors] how he had questioned [his prisoners], and cut off the ears [of the slain].[44]

Referring to such spiritual proceedings for prosecuting martial expeditions, the *Zuozhuan* quotes the viscount of Liu 劉子 as saying in 578 BCE: "The great affairs of state are sacrifice and war. At sacrifices [in the ancestral temple, officers] receive the roasted flesh; in war they receive that offered at the altar of the soil—these are the great ceremonies in worshiping the spirits."[45] While the viscount was restating a tradition of antiquity, the religious rituals of war of which he spoke were being expanded during the Chunqiu period to include rites of a purely military nature.

This change may be illustrated by a dramatic incident in 569 BCE, in which Yanggan 揚干, a brother of the marquis of Jin, after having thrown the ranks of his military unit into confusion, was executed by his military superior, Wei Jiang 魏絳. Angered by the killing of his brother, the marquis called for Wei Jiang to be put to death. Wei subsequently appeared before the marquis to present his explanation in writing and to demonstrate his willingness to die for having offended his lord. However, after reading Wei's statement, the marquis realized he had been too quick to demand retribution. Running out barefoot to speak to Wei in person, the marquis admitted that he had responded to Yanggan's death out of brotherly love and had not considered that Wei, as Yanggan's military superior, was correct in punishing Yanggan in accordance with military rites (*junli* 軍禮). "I was not able to instruct my brother, which made him violate your great orders. That was my fault; do not you render it still heavier." As concluded in the

Zuozhuan, Wei Jiang, by using proper military punishments, had proven "capable of aiding in the government of the people" and therefore was qualified for promotion to assistant commander of the Jin army.[46]

In this passage we have clear evidence that military rites were being recognized as essential to both internal army discipline and civil justice, and that disorder either in ranks of soldiers or in communities of civilians was considered preventable through the potential application of *wu*'s correlate—*xing*. As the frequency of war increased during the latter part of the Chunqiu period, rites to the ancestral spirits as part of military activity were being adapted for internal military order and discipline.

New Solutions in the Zhanguo Era

Thus we see that during the Chunqiu period the idea of *wen/wu* reciprocality in the Western Zhou began to change as warfare became more frequent between the lords of the realm. Each of the two elements acquired greater texture, a clearer intention, and a more definitive relationship with the other as the problems of interstate strife, social-cultural changes, and royal house decline intensified. After the mid–fifth century BCE, when the Warring States period is generally said to begin, new solutions were needed to deal with these stresses and, as a result, there was a surge in discourse on the roles of martiality and civility and the means for applying these elements in real-world situations.

Three new solutions for the *wen/wu* problem appeared during the late Chunqiu and Zhanguo eras that built on Western Zhou ideas and came to the fore as violence increased, social order broke down, and the political-religious values inherited from the Western Zhou went into decline. These solutions were *militarism, syncretism,* and *compartmentalism.*

Militarism

The first of the three solutions placed high value on martiality, as opposed to civility, to secure social stability and to build a lasting political order. For many commentators looking back on the roots of the Qin reunification, the generators of a militaristic ideology to unify the realm were members of the Legalist school (*fajia* 法家). However, as various scholars and analysts of the *Huangdi sijing* have demonstrated, Legalists were an often misconstrued, artificial assemblage of thinkers who would not have agreed on any one body of ideas, including a single thesis on the problem of martiality and civility.[47] That is, authors who held traditionally Legalist notions about the worthiness of penal law and administrative discipline had different views on the *wen/wu* relationship from those represented by Huang-Lao 黃老 philosophers, who combined these same legalistic beliefs with the Daoist idea of nonassertion (*wuwei* 無為) and a naturalistic cosmology. Consequently, the idea of promoting a solution to the *wen/wu* problem that emphasized martiality at the expense of civility—what I am calling *militarism*—can be currently observed in only two sources from the Zhanguo period, namely, the *Shangjunshu* 商君書 and the *Hanfeizi* 韓非子, which conventionally have been labeled Legalist.[48]

In the *Shangjunshu*, the putative author, Shang Yang 商鞅 (ca. 390–338 BCE; also known as Wei Yang 衛鞅), and his followers asserted that it was not only acceptable but imperative in a period of constant strife such as Zhanguo that war become a premier instrument of political action.[49] But more than punitive measures, war was for Shang Yang the only means for assuring national wealth and sustained sovereignty.

> From antiquity to the present time, it has never happened that one attained supremacy without conquest, or that one came to ruin without defeat. If the people are brave, one conquers in war, but if they are not brave, one is defeated in war. If one can unify the people for war, they are brave, but if one cannot unify the people for war, they are not brave. A sage-king obtains the kingship through the efforts of his soldiers. Therefore, he rouses the country and charges it with the obligation of military service. If one enters a state and sees its administration, it is strong if its people are of use. How does one know that the people are of use? If they, on perceiving war, behave like hungry wolves on seeing meat, then they are of use. Generally, war is a thing that people hate; he who succeeds in making people delight in war attains supremacy.[50]

Even for those advocating *militarism*, however, a nominally civil complement to war existed in the guise of agriculture. Again, from the *Shangjunshu*:

> When the army is mobilized for an offensive, rank is given according to military merit, and, reliance being placed upon the military, victory is certain. When the army is in reserve and

> agriculture is pursued, rank is given according to the production of grain, and, reliance being placed upon farming, the country will be rich. If in military enterprises the enemy is conquered and if, when the army is in reserve, the country becomes rich, then it attains supremacy.[51]

This recognition of the necessity of agriculture notwithstanding, elements of civility that had been cited since the days of Kings Wen and Wu of Western Zhou as positive forces were considered by Shang Yang and his disciples as lethal to a country's deterrent strength:

> If in a country there are the following ten things: odes and history, rites and music, virtue and cultivation thereof, humaneness and integrity, sophistry and intelligence, then the ruler has no one whom he can employ for defense and warfare. If a country is governed by means of these ten things, it will be dismembered, as soon as an enemy approaches, and even if no enemy approaches, it will be poor. But if a country banishes these ten things, enemies will not dare to approach, and even if they should, they would be driven back. When it mobilizes its army and attacks, it will gain victories; when it holds the army in reserve and does not attack, it will be rich.[52]

The *Hanfeizi*, probably authored by Han Fei 韓非 (ca. 280–ca. 233 BCE), expresses a *militarist* opinion in terms similar to those in the *Shangjunshu*. Like Shang Yang, Han Fei links a legalistic devotion to agriculture and war as critical to state power, and he describes the absence of such dedication as dangerous:

> Now, the people of the state all discuss good government, and everyone has a copy of the works on law by Shang Yang and Guan Zhong 管仲 in his house,[53] and yet the state gets poorer and poorer, for though many people talk about farming, very few put their hands to a plow. The people of the state all discuss military affairs, and everyone has a copy of the works of Sun Wu and Wu Qi in his house, and yet the armies grow weaker and weaker, for though many people talk about war, very few buckle on armor. Therefore, an enlightened ruler will make use of men's strength but will not heed their words, will reward their accomplishments but will prohibit useless activities. Then

> the people will be willing to exert themselves to the point of death in the service of their sovereign.[54]

Perhaps it was the simplicity of this program of strict, legal adherence to military might and agriculture that led the Qin unifiers to adopt *militarism* as a key part of their ideology, even though its success in post-conquest Qin proved limited. As Kings Wen and Wu of Western Zhou had discovered centuries before, a state could not be established with but one of the reciprocal elements, *wen* and *wu*; some kind of mean was necessary. However, in the more complex society emerging in the Zhanguo period, it was questionable whether the old balance or this new *militarism* could deal satisfactorily with the increased conflict inside the fractured Zhou kingdom as well as the threat of nomadic peoples from the north and west.

Compartmentalism

A second alternative forwarded to resolve the *wen/wu* problem in the Zhanguo era posited a clear separation between martial and civil. According to the advocates of this approach, *wen* and *wu*, though theoretically complementary, in fact pertain to two distinct modes of political action. Moreover, martiality and civility represent such different facets of political practice that they should not be allowed to intersect for fear that one might disrupt the proper functions of the other. Moreover, the *compartmentalist* view posits that martial activity is necessarily subordinate to civility and must be applied only *in extremis*. The *Daodejing* 道德經, a Daoist work probably compiled in the third and/or second centuries BCE, exemplifies this view by speaking of warfare as an activity to be segregated from civil matters and avoided unless absolutely necessary.[55]

> It is because arms are instruments of ill omen and there are spirits that detest them that one who has the ways does not abode by their use. The gentleman gives precedence to the left when at home, but to the right when he goes to war. Arms are instruments of ill omen, not the instruments of the gentleman. When one is compelled to use them, it is best to do so without relish.[56]

Thus a man of war does not prance to battle as described in the *Shi*, with stunning chariot fittings and an awesome mien, welcoming the approaching battle. Rather, generalship is the occupation of a doomed man, who, because he deals in death and destruction, must be separated from vital, pacific government.[57] War, in this view, must be divided from civil affairs and entrusted to certain devoted men, so that the ill effects of war are minimized and the benefits are maximized.[58]

One explanation for this conception of a strict division between the realms of *wu* and *wen* is that such separation attempts to protect the high status of the civil ruler, while not interfering with the war-making duties of the military leader. After the hostilities of war have ended and military commanders cease to have immediate usefulness, whatever successes they enjoyed on the battlefield should not be allowed to become inspirations for the people at large, for fear such commanders might pose threats to the civil government of the sovereign in peacetime.

Perhaps a more convincing reason for the emergence of the *compartmentalist* solution is that it grew out of the enormous sociopolitical changes under way in the Zhanguo period. Whereas in Chunqiu times and before, aristocrats' sons were trained in letters and administrative skills as well as military techniques, the complexity of government and the increased technology and frequency of war in the Warring States era had made specialization necessary.[59] Gradually this specialization bred alienation between realms that had once been unified. Also, as armies began to be populated overwhelmingly by commoner infantrymen in lieu of noble chariot-warriors, military service lost some of the high status it once enjoyed, while the serviceman (*shi* 士) class, which increasingly populated civil offices, rose to prominence.[60]

Thus, it may be that changing routes of social mobility helped to deemphasize the importance of the former ideology of *wen*/*wu* reciprocality and balance and to spawn a pacifist theory that devalued *wu*. Ruists, Daoists, and eclectics who, for the most part, had established themselves as men of letters or had little or no contact with military operations, began to discredit the view of *wen*/*wu* mutuality long valued in the Sinitic realm.[61] With time, this opposition was successful in transforming the older beliefs about martiality into an exclusionism, which was characteristic of the scholarly attitude toward war during much of Chinese history after the early Han dynasty.[62]

Syncretism

A third major solution to the problem of martiality and civility that emerged in the Zhanguo period attempted to refocus the *wen*/*wu* debate on the need for balance and reciprocality between martiality and civility and to integrate these elements more closely in their application. For evidence of this *syncretist* view, and its differences with *militarism* and *compartmentalism*, we turn first to passages in the *Huangdi sijing*.

> To participate with Heaven and Earth in movement and quiescence is called civility; to execute . . . [missing text] when the time is proper is called martiality. . . . With civility there is enlightenment; with martiality there is strength. . . . With enlightenment one can attain Heaven; with strength one can act with awesomeness. Participating with Heaven and Earth, according with the minds of the people, civility and martiality stand together. . . . To accord with Heavenly timing and attack what Heaven would destroy is called martiality. If martiality is full and civility follows close behind, then you will have complete accomplishment. One who uses two parts civility and one part martiality is a true king.[63]

> To begin with civility and end with martiality is the way of Heaven and Earth. That there are regularities to the four seasons is due to the ordering principle of Heaven and Earth, and that there are periodicities for the sun, moon, and constellations is due to the constant order of Heaven and Earth. That in three seasons there is completion and achievement and in one season there is punishment and killing is the way of Heaven and Earth. . . . First established, then disposed, first born, then killed, the four seasons are successively foremost, and at the end they return to the beginning. This is the ordering principle of human affairs.[64]

> In war, martiality is analogous to a [mature] plant, while civility is analogous to a seed; martiality is outer, while civility is inner. One who can comprehend these two [components] knows [the bases of] victory and defeat. Civility is that whereby one can discern benefit and loss, and distinguish peace and danger; martiality is that whereby one can provoke the strong and combative, and forcefully [execute] an attack or defense.[65]

Evident throughout these passages is the kind of reciprocality between *wen* and *wu* that was noted earlier in quotations from the *Zuozhuan*.

Martiality is not just complementary to civility or a disdained or overpraised component in political behavior, but an organic, natural constituent of the Way. *Wen/wu* is a continuum wherein the elements interpenetrate, constituting a unity. Therefore, instead of either concentrating on the value of *wu* as opposed to *wen*, or segregating *wu* from *wen*, the *syncretist view* refashions the ancient idea of balance between martiality and civility to create a new solution of the *wen/wu* problem that integrates the two elements into a single whole.

To understand *syncretism* more fully, one can consult the *Yi Zhoushu* 逸周書, which appears to have had its genesis in the pre-Han period or the early part of the Western Han.[66] This work takes as one of its objectives the construction of a vision of *wen/wu* that is an evolution of the older paradigms of Western Zhou and before. In a detailed listing of the features of martiality, the *Yi Zhoushu*, makes the following points that illustrate this evolution:

> To attack the disruptive, the morally ill, and the contagiously wanton—these are the axioms of martiality. To assist the worthy, arrest the factious, encourage the conscientious, obstruct the indolent, harass the fearful, and tempt the avaricious—these are the applications of martiality.
>
> . . . To pardon the adversary's common people, aid them in time of catastrophe, provide for their sustenance, and assist in their material well-being—these are the divisive [tactics] of martiality. . . . That having overcome an opponent one raises his banner as a sign [of authority], commands his subordinates to prohibit the ravaging [of the population], ventures no oppressive treatment, causes noble titles and government positions to be undiminished and fields and homesteads to be unscathed, [so that] all are at peace with their families and the people are willingly submissive—this is pacification in martiality. That the major clans all submit; that wars are ended and virtue is exalted; that one levels his barricades and stores away his instruments of war; and that the world submits in awe and the kingdom is consolidated—this is stabilization in martiality.[67]

As in the *Zuozhuan*, *wu* is considered in the *Yi Zhoushu* as essential to state success and stability and as a correlate to *wen*. Now, however, one sees more continuum than reciprocality between the two factors. *Wen* and *wu* are now mutually dependent parts of a single Way that can be applied flexibly and proportionately to control conflict. Proponents of *syncretism* contended that martiality is best applied in tandem with civility and worst applied as *militarism*. Using this formula, one avoids the situation in which the functions of *wen* and *wu* are segregated, as in *compartmentalism*, causing irresolution of conflict and long-term instability. As the *Yi Zhoushu* states:

> Awesome and majestic is great martiality, for the world, in awe of military power, is pacified. Martiality produced in Heaven [means] arms and weapons readied to aid the righteous and correct the wayward. . . . Even as you maneuver [your troops against the enemy], you must be respectful [of the common people]. This is called enlightened martiality. . . . After overcoming your enemy in battle and gaining their submission, cause the people all to be properly treated and extirpate their weapons and armor. This is called great pacification.[68]

There are strategic and ethical implications in these lines that will be explored further in later chapters as we examine other texts of the Zhanguo and Western Han eras. But already one can see how the *syncretist* view advanced beyond the older reciprocality solution of the Western Zhou to create a more unified approach to the *wen/wu* problem, altering the older paradigm in response to new circumstances.

Conclusion

In this chapter we have examined the evolution of thought from earliest times in China through the Zhanguo era regarding the proper roles of martiality and civility to achieve state stability and prosperity. What started as a problem about general relationships and maintaining balance between these two human elements and the natural cycles of Heaven and Earth evolved in Western Zhou times toward a more nuanced reciprocality designed to preserve harmony in a more extended realm. With the changing demographic conditions of Zhanguo and an increasingly perilous political scene, demand increased for new solutions to the *wen/wu* problem, which in turn led to the formulation of three major alternatives for the attention of state leaders—*militarism*, *compartmentalism*, and *syncretism*. Together these alternatives formed the main framework for early Chinese military thinking in the Warring States era and beyond.

Chapters 2, 3, and 4 will continue to examine these three solutions as they were presented by expositors using three distinct applications or perspectives—*metaphysical*, *pragmatic*, and *ethical*. Each of these discussions will show how these three applications/perspectives were variously combined by a wide spectrum of thinkers with the three major *wen/wu* solutions already identified to form a frame of reference for military thought in early China through Zhanguo times and into Western Han.[69]

Chapter 2

The Metaphysics of Generalship

Having discussed the issue of martiality vis-à-vis civility and the major alternative solutions developed in regard to this issue in pre-Han times, the next task is to examine the nature and function of the military general employing one of the three principal applications or perspectives used by Zhanguo writers to address the *wen*/*wu* problem, namely, the *metaphysical* perspective.

The General as Sage

Many of the qualifications for ideal Chinese generalship as seen in the Zhanguo era differed little from those listed in Western works on warfare, whether ancient or modern. Integrity, a sense of justice, decisiveness, prudence, courage, and intelligence, among other attributes, are common to both the Chinese and European traditions. However, the early Chinese military treatises and other works of the Zhanguo period established a more rarefied model for the military commander than any in Western literature. In spite of the diversification of solutions for the *wen/wu* problem that appeared in Chunqiu and Zhanguo times, the archetype general was still seen to possess many of the characteristics of former sage-rulers as described in song and legend. The quintessential military leader was not merely a physically strong and courageous man; he was also distinguished by a supernatural capacity to fathom an enemy's circumstances and foresee the outcome of a confrontation. The ideal general, in other words, had a sagely or *metaphysical* wisdom that one would normally associate with Daoist or Ruist paragons of *wen*.

The origins of a sage-general's military prescience varied. Some were said to gain their powers through the contemplation of esoteric texts. As an example, the *Zhanguoce* 戰國策, a compilation of Zhanguo anecdotes by the Western Han scholar-official Liu Xiang 劉向 (79–8 BCE), includes a story about how the Zhanguo freelance strategist Su Qin 蘇秦 (fl. 312–286 BCE), having failed to persuade the king of Qin to take the initiative in battle, returned home to take solace in personal study.

> That night he brought forth his books to the number of some two score boxes and found within them *Tai Gong's Secret Talisman* (*Tai Gong yin fu* 太公陰符).[1] Bowed over it, he recited the schemes therein, thumbed and pored to fit and fathom it. If ever he dozed while at study, he drew forth a gimlet and stabbed his thigh until the blood ran off at his heel and asked, "Where stands the man who persuades a ruler and will not put forth whatever wealth he has for honor and ministry?"

The *Zhanguoce* anecdote goes on to say that, due to his indefatigable study, Su Qin became a source of strategic wisdom of wide renown.

> And in those times the vastness of the empire, the multitude of its people, the authority of the powers and princes and the skill of its advisers were all devoted to the plans of Su Qin. Not a dipper of grain was wasted and not a weapon was raised. Not a soldier fought, not a bowstring parted, not a dart was broken; and the lords cherished one another. Closer were they than are brother to brother.[2]

Although Su Qin was a strategist and not a field general, his study of what appears to be a secret text on the use of military potency demonstrates the aura of mysticism surrounding the role of an ideal military leader. Moreover, Su Qin was not alone in gaining spiritual assistance in strategizing from mystical sources. Probably the most famous case is that of Zhang Liang 張良 (d. 187 BCE), noted military planner and general for the Han dynasty founder Liu Bang 劉邦 (Han Gaozu 高祖; r. 202–195 BCE), who according to legend was initiated into military lore through a chance encounter with a mysterious old man and a talismanic text on strategy.

According to the story as it is recorded in the *Shiji*, Zhang was once strolling idly along an embankment in Xiapi 下邳 when an old man wearing a coarse gown appeared before him.[3] As he approached Zhang, the old man deliberately dropped his shoe down the embankment. Turning to Zhang Liang, he said, "Fetch me my shoe, young man!" Taken aback by this impertinent command, Zhang was about to hit the old man but then decided to swallow his resentment and climb down to get the shoe and replace it on the old man's foot. Laughing, the old man left Zhang, but then returned a short time later to say, "You could be taught, young man." He then bid Zhang to meet him at the same place at dawn in five days' time. Zhang Liang returned to the embankment at the appointed time, but he found the old man had already arrived before him. "When you have an appointment with an old man, how is it that you come late?" the old man asked angrily. "Go away, and meet me at dawn five days from now, only come earlier!" When another five days had passed Zhang arrived at the embankment before dawn, only to find that the old man had again preceded him to the site. The old man repeated his call for Zhang to meet him once more five days hence. The next time Zhang arrived at the site before the night was half gone. When the old man subsequently arrived to look for Zhang, he said, "This is the way it should be!" He then produced a book and told Zhang: "If you read this you may become the teacher of kings, and ten years from now your fortune will rise. I will see you again after thirteen years, for there will be a yellow stone (*huang shi* 黃石) at the foot of Mount Gucheng 穀城山 in Jibei 濟北, and that will be me." Subsequently Zhang examined the book that the old man had given him and found it to be *Tai Gong's Military Methods* (*Tai Gong bingfa* 太公兵法).[4] After constantly reading the tome and fervently absorbing its content, he eventually became an aide to the Lord of Pei 沛公, the future first emperor of the Han dynasty. Thirteen years after seeing the old man, Zhang was accompanying the duke through Jibei when he saw a yellow stone at the foot of Mount Gucheng. Taking away the stone, Zhang treated it with the utmost reverence. When Zhang died the stone was placed with him in his grave mound, and in the sixth and twelfth months, when his descendants ascended the grave mound to pay their respects, they worshipped it.[5]

What we glean from these two tales is evidence of a longstanding Chinese tradition in which a man of tested potential, whether of martial or civil background, receives philosophical truth from a mystical master in a magical way. Moreover, it is no coincidence that Tai Gong of Qi (Qi Tai Gong 齊太公) was the putative author of both of the military manuals in the above two stories, for in similar legends it is the Grand Duke himself who is the esoteric master to a man of exceptional promise. The *Liutao*, for example, describes Tai Gong's role in indoctrinating King Wen of Zhou in the philosophical principles of war and peace, using the persona of a cosmic fisherman.[6]

According to the *Liutao* account, King Wen, in preparation for a hunting expedition (a trope for a military venture), consults a scribe (*shi* 史)—i.e., a recorder and sometime performer of divinations and ancestral rites—about the possible outcome of the expedition.

> As King Wen was about to start a hunting expedition, Scribe Bian 史编 cast divining stalks and said: "Do your hunting south of the Wei 渭 River. You will catch great bounty there. Not a dragon or a tiger or a bear, but rather the omen [says you] will secure a lord, that Heaven has granted you a preceptor by whom you will be assisted to a glory approaching that of the Three Kings (*san wang* 三王)."[7]
>
> King Wen then fasted for three days, after which he drove out his horse-chariots to hunt south of the Wei River. At last he saw Tai Gong, who was sitting in the reeds, fishing. King Wen asked him in a courteous way, "Do you enjoy fishing?"
>
> Tai Gong said: "A true gentleman (*junzi* 君子) enjoys securing his ultimate aims. A mean man enjoys completing his [immediate affairs]. My fishing is very similar."
>
> King Wen said, "What do you mean it is similar?"
>
> Tai Gong replied: "Fishing has three types of power (*quan* 權): the power gained by [giving] rewards, by [threatening] death, and by giving office. By fishing, one seeks to obtain [these three powers]. Their predispositions (*qing* 情) are profound to hear about and readily apparent [in the outcomes]."[8]
>
> King Wen said, "I would like to hear about their predispositions."
>
> Tai Gong replied: "When the spring is deep, water will flow; and when water flows, fish will be generated. [This is such] a predisposition. When the roots are deep, a tree will grow, and when a tree grows, fruit will be generated. [This is such] a predisposition. When a true gentleman's predispositions are unified, his feelings will be in accord, and when his feelings are in accord, [good] deeds will be generated. [This is such] a predisposition. Correspondences in language are [only] glosses of such predispositions. One may speak of the fullest actualization of such predispositions [only] in the ultimate completion of the deed."[9]

Tai Gong then goes on to elaborate on the theme of predispositions to illustrate how King Wen can create a harmonious realm and a unified society. It is key, according to Tai Gong's advice, for the ruler to be a man of humaneness (*ren* 仁), righteousness (*yi* 義), and virtue (*de*) and that he act in accord with the periodicities of Heaven and Earth, for then the world will gravitate to him and the state will be united. The story ends with King Wen deciding to take Tai Gong's advice and to accept the mandate of Heaven to proceed with the formation of a new dynasty.

One significant point to make about this Tai Gong story is that, despite its appearance in a military treatise, the passage addresses themes of leadership that are as much civil as martial in nature. While Tai Gong, as we have seen, was associated with secret military texts, he was also viewed, as this fictional encounter with King Wen demonstrated, to be equally capable of advocating for civil approaches to government leadership. Thus, the *Liutao* legend illustrates through Tai Gong the *syncretist* approach to the *wen/wu* problem, in which martiality and civility are integrated along a single continuum, each element mutually supporting the other.

A complementary point to be made about this *Liutao* story is that the martial-civil nature of the Tai Gong persona is not just a literary contrivance. We know of at least a few peripatetic generals of the Zhanguo era who, like their scholar-official counterparts, roamed from state to state to offer their services to individual state rulers as interstate conflict waxed and waned. Wu Qi, Fan Li 范蠡, Sun Bin, Yue Yi 樂毅, and Yue Yi's general-son Xian 閒 all led itinerant existences, providing expert advice on warfare wherever they would be heard.[10] Moreover, these martial counselors, like their civil counterparts, adopted an independent attitude toward their patrons. Not wishing to be simply hired consultants, they preferred the privileges of a sage, who, in their eyes, should be given free rein to carry out the political or military programs of their design without ruler interference. As a result, some generals were shown great deference by their ruler employers. Wang Jian 王翦 (d. after 221 BCE), for example, when proved correct about the necessary forces for battling Chu, was much praised by the king of Qin—the future Qin Shi huangdi 秦始皇帝.[11] On the other hand, some generals, such as Bai Qi 白起 (d. 257 BCE), were subject to dismissal or worse for errors in strategic judgment.[12]

On the whole, then, the purveyors of martial wisdom in Zhanguo times tended to see themselves on a par with their counterparts in the civil realm. Both types touted their intellectual wares as individual expositors, risking that military or political success would vindicate their assumed sagacity. This parity between exponents of *wen* and *wu* in actual historical circumstances suggests that the content of their counsels may also have certain fundamental resemblances. The remainder of this chapter will attempt to demonstrate this similarity by discussing how certain *metaphysical* ideas of civil philosophers were applied to the *wen/wu* problem by martial thinkers.

Psychical Power

The primary assumption of the *metaphysical* perspective is that military methods are not, ultimately, applications of materiel and manpower, but the interplay of abstruse mental powers and objective circumstances. The *Heguanzi* 鶡冠子, a Zhanguo-era work generally associated with Huang-Lao thought, stresses the notion that the sage-general is a participant in universal processes.[13] The work suggests that when such a military leader yields to the Way of things as detected by his psychical power (*shen* 神), he can be successful in war.[14]

> Formerly, those skilled in war took up arms and followed each other [to battle]. They formed according to the Five Phases (*wuxing* 五行), fought according to the Five Tones (*wuyin* 五音), directed themselves to the pinnacle of Heaven, and coexisted with the spirits.[15] Every class [of reality] was generated and consummated, [and yet] they never exhausted the unity of things. They took the enlightened as models and trod the path of subtlety. Their regularity went beyond [mere] advance and retreat; they participated with Heaven and Earth. . . . They cruised along the current, and soared along the path; soaringly they gave [battle] and seized [victory]; unflinchingly they [conducted] a solid defense. Like exhaling and inhaling, stopping and starting, they changed with proper timing.[16]

To some this view may indicate a sublimation of individual psychical power in the absolute. But examining the *Heguanzi* as a whole, one sees that the transcendental quality of the above description is only partially applicable. Seeming to secrete himself in the Way, the sage-general actually creates situations that will accord with the Way. The *Heguanzi*, like nearly every early work that speaks of military leadership, allows for the general's manipulative genius and, to some extent, his independence from exterior absolute powers. "Heaven cannot enthrall man, nor can man enthrall Heaven. By according with the way things are there will be fulfillment and attainment."[17] Or as stated in the Zhanguo military treatise, the *Weiliaozi*: "A general is not regulated by Heaven above, or by Earth below, or by man in between."[18]

The sage-general can perceive the predispositions of events, and further he can act in accordance with these predispositions (*qing*) for his own ends. At the same time, he is restricted by the Way, for he cannot stray from the dynamics of Heaven and Earth without losing at once his capacity for creativity and his opportunities for victory. He is, in short, an active participant in the microcosm of universal forces known as war, and he directs events according to abstruse universal principles pertaining to Heaven and man alike. According to the *Weiliaozi*:

> One who is versed in military arts seems more mysterious than Earth, more abstruse than Heaven. He appears from the Void.[19]
>
> A general is an officer of ordering principle (*liguan* 理官), a master of the ten thousand things, who shows no partiality for any man. And because he is without partiality for any man, he regulates and directs the ten thousand things as they appear to him.[20]

As in the realm of political thought and individual self-cultivation, so in military thought there was an attempt to find the fundament of martial activity in the workings of the cosmos—to view war, and conflict in general, as the functioning of *metaphysical* entities along natural principles.[21]

As has already been implied, in the evolving Zhanguo philosophy of war the contestants in a battle were not merely bone-and-flesh officers and soldiers with metal weapons and leather armor. They were also, in the sage-general's eyes, universal realities contending and yielding in a manner evocative of the *Zhouyi* 周易 (*Changes*) hexagrams. With that as a starting point, there developed an entire lexicon of analysis, a whole mode of theorizing, based on philosophical principles common to the realm of *wen* but applied to the particular problem of conflict.

The first of these principles revolves around the concept of vital energy (*qi*). The *Heguanzi* tells us:

> With unity comes vital energy; with vital energy come motives (*yi* 意); with motives come purposes (*tu* 圖); with purposes come definitions (*ming* 名); with definitions come forms (*xing* 形); with forms come things (*shi* 事); with things come limitations (*yue* 約). As limitations are regularized, time (*shi* 時) is created; as time is established, discrete objects (*wu* 物) are created. Hence, where vital energy mutually applies there is time; where limitations mutually apply there are periodicities; where periodicities mutually apply there are completed actions (*gong* 功); where completed actions mutually apply there are attainments and failures; where attainments and failures mutually apply there is victory and defeat. There is nothing that does not derive from vital energy and is not permeated by the Way, limited in things, normalized in time, separated by definitions, or fulfilled in institutions (*fa* 法).[22]

> Vital energy is generated by psychical power and the Way is completed by psychical power.[23]

In this context one may define vital energy as that massless continuum of proto-reality that emerges uncreated from Unity and constitutes the potential for all differentiation and coordinate activity. This purposeless vital energy, however, requires psychical power to be "metabolized" into palpable or impalpable reality.[24] Then, and only then, according to the *Heguanzi*, does vital energy have definition, form, thing-ness, and limitation. Finally, with regularized limitation—that is, time—comes discreteness and space-time relation. The chain reasoning continues until, at its terminus, one finds conflict and resolution. Thus warfare, as viewed in the *Heguanzi* and all of the other early treatises that consider the problem, is originally derived from vital energy, that is, metabolized vital energy. This metabolism, in turn, occurs in the functioning of psychical power—that psychic property of Heaven-Earth-man whose human embodiment guides the procreation of reality. One can say, therefore, that martial activity, being integral to reality and vice versa, is constituted by psychically metabolized vital energy in its constantly changing forms, where psychical power is the dynamic, but unseen, catalyst in the ever-varying reactions of martial chemistry.

In the common view of Zhanguo works on military matters, psychical power allows for change in vital energy, but only in consonance with the Way of Heaven-Earth-man. Also, because each space-time entity is purposeful and relational and is endowed with psychical power, each may act as a processor of vital energy. However, being relational, such entities differ in the extent of their psychical powers. Moreover, while man has the greatest psychical power among the earth's species, a few men—ideal men—have psychical power far beyond others. To use the metabolic analogy here, these outstanding men can process vital energy with greater fluency and at a greater rate, meaning they can absorb proto-reality and metabolized reality and then re-digest this vital energy into new space-time entities with infinite relational translations. The nature of these psychical applications entails that such outstanding men have foreknowledge of entities and thus are able to far exceed the lesser metabolic capacities of others. The *Sunzi bingfa* highlights the preeminence of a sage-general possessing such superior psychical power in the following way:

> Now, the reason the enlightened prince and the wise general conquer the enemy whenever they move, and their achievements surpass those of ordinary men, is foreknowledge. What is called foreknowledge cannot be elicited from spirits, or from gods, or by analogy with past events, or from calculations. It must be obtained from men who know the enemy situation.[25]

Thus psychical power and enlightenment are the primary factors in any battle. From the Zhanguo theorists' point of view, success in combat is not the summation of the efforts of his officers and men, but a general's *tour de force*. He controls through his psychical power all facets of the conflict and is totally responsible for the outcome. To that extent, he represents the nexus between Heaven and Earth and is the spirit-like conductor of martial reality. Through him alone can the fortunes of war be known and exploited, for martial activity is centered entirely upon his acumen for metabolizing vital energy.[26]

Still, the sage-general is not solipsistic. He does not, after all, create vital energy; the objective circumstances are just as important in his overcoming the enemy as his capacity to metabolize those circumstances. Time and again the general is urged in the military treatises to determine his enemy's dispositions (*xing* 形) and circumstantial power (*shi* 勢), and at the same time to conceal his own dispositions and circumstantial power.[27] On this point the *Sunzi bingfa* has the following remark:

> If I am able to determine the enemy's dispositions while at the same time I conceal my own, then I can concentrate and he must divide. And if I concentrate while he divides, I can use my entire strength to attack a fraction of his. There I will be numerically superior. Then, if I am able to use many to strike few at the selected point, those I deal with will be in dire straits. . . . Thus I say that victory can be created. Even if the enemy is numerous, I can prevent him from engaging. Therefore, determine the enemy's plans and you will know which strategy will be successful and which will not; agitate him and ascertain the pattern of his movement. Determine his dispositions and so ascertain the field of battle. Probe him and learn where his strength is abundant and where deficient. The ultimate in disposing one's troops is to be without ascertainable shape. Then the most penetrating spies cannot pry in nor can the wise lay plans against you. It is according to the shapes that I lay the plans for victory, but the multitude does not comprehend this. Although everyone can see the outward aspects, none understands the way in which I have created victory. Therefore, when I have won a victory, I do not repeat my tactics, but respond to circumstances in an infinite variety of ways.[28]

The "Shu yan" 樞言 chapter of the *Guanzi* 管子, a work of mixed origins but containing material from the pre-Han period, adds to this discussion:

> Their weapons may be ready, but [the enemy] will be defenseless, because your passage [through their territory] will not be known [until too late]. Their instructions may be practiced, but [their effectiveness] will not be manifested, because your onslaught will be unanticipated. Since your passage [through their territory] will not be known, no one will be able to stop you. Since your onslaught is unanticipated, no one will be able to meet it. Since no one will be able to meet it, you will be completely victorious without any harm to yourself. Since no one will be able to stop you, you will certainly be victorious and unrivaled [in battle].[29]

If the general can discern the vital energy that constitutes the dispositions and relative power of contending forces, then he has in his psychical power the important element for success in battle. But even knowledge of dispositions and circumstantial power will not suffice. Conflict entails dynamism—vital energy in-process—and therefore the temporal factor ranks as just as essential for good generalship as the spatial. The very anticipatory powers of the psychical general are grounded in change, and this integration of space-time characterizes the objective vital energy of a general's concern. One of the *Heguanzi* passages quoted earlier speaks of "forms" and "things" preceding "time." But to the intuitive mind these consequences of the emergence of vital energy are at once everywhere. Psychical power, as the mediating agent between Heaven and Earth, on the one hand, and vital energy, on the other, likewise functions in this space-time integration. Operating in such a way, the sage-general perceives succession and return; the vicissitudes of war appear in consonance with Heavenly timing (*tianshi* 天時) and the Five Phases, particularly the mutual overcoming (*xiang ke* 相克) of phenomena correlated variously with the five elements of wood, earth, water, fire, and metal. The sage-general metabolizes the vital energy of dispositions and of circumstantial power as "shape in flux"—circumstances in omni-temporality—and though Heavenly timing may be constant and Earthly advantage (*dili* 地利) infinite, he intuits the limitlessness of the permutations and the uniqueness of each permutation in space-time. The *Sun Bin bingfa* gives a fuller description:

> It is the ordering principle (*li* 理) of Heaven and Earth that, like the sun and moon, when something reaches an ultimate point, it then retreats, and when something becomes full, it wanes; or, like the four seasons, there is successive rise and decline; or, like the Five Phases, there is overcoming and loss; or, like the myriad things, there is birth and death; or, like the myriad species of life, there are those who can [survive] and those who cannot; or, like circumstances of power, there are surpluses and deficiencies. Thus a multitude which has a clear shape can always be named, and a multitude that can be named can always be overcome. Therefore, a sage uses the mode of victory peculiar to each of the myriad things in order to overcome them, and his victories are inexhaustible. A military leader uses dispositions to overcome [his adversaries]. With known dispositions one cannot but be victorious, and yet one never knows the [precise] disposition with which to achieve victory. The variations in the dispositions for victory are coextensive with Heaven and Earth; they are limitless. Though one may use the [seemingly endless]

> bamboo of Chu and Yue to write out the possible dispositions for victory, there would not be enough.[30]

The sage-general can act to provide himself with critical flexibility and the ability to maneuver at will. As the *Sun Bin bingfa* puts it, "Those said to be skilled in warfare cause the power situation to be suitable and the terrain to be favorable."[31] But always the sage-general is effectual only by abiding with correct timing and powers outside himself. As addressed in the *Sunzi bingfa*:

> If I know that my troops are capable of striking the enemy, but do not know that the enemy is invulnerable to attack, my chance of victory is but half. If I know that the enemy is vulnerable to attack, but do not know my troops are incapable of striking him, my chance of victory is but half. If I know that the enemy can be attacked and that my troops are capable of attacking him, but do not realize that because of the conformation of the ground I should not attack, my chance of victory is but half. Therefore, when those experienced in war move, they make no mistakes; when they act, their resources are limitless. And therefore I say, "Know the enemy, know yourself, and your victory will never be endangered. Know the ground, know the weather [lit., 'know Heaven, know Earth'], and your victory will be total."[32]

Again, it is important to stress that the success of the sage-general lies in his superior anticipatory powers and not in the total inability of lesser military leaders to determine the key permutations—a task they could accomplish given sufficient time. The military treatises, in particular, do not preclude all but the innately gifted from the status of sage-general. Rather, they give descriptions of the ideal leader to which anyone can aspire. Having cultivated himself in the principles of war, a man of martiality can become an enlightened commander who is able to maintain his own dispositions and circumstantial power in obscurity and appear to others as possessing supernatural powers.

But what is his procedure for determining dispositions and circumstantial power? One nonmilitary treatise provides compelling counsel in this regard: the *Guiguzi* 鬼谷子, a text apparently of Zhanguo origin, which offered advice to itinerant scholar-officials of the Zhanguo era on how to persuade their political masters.[33] Throughout the *Guiguzi* is wisdom that is as valid for military generals in the planning of successful battles as it is for civil persuaders in winning debates at court. In the "Reflecting and Responding" ("Fan ying" 反應) chapter of the *Guiguzi*, for example, we read:

> When another man speaks in images and metaphors, use these to observe his disposition. Images symbolize his deeds, while metaphors exemplify his phrases. Use the formless to probe what he voices. If one's fishing words (*diao yu* 釣語) fit another's deeds, then one can grasp another's situation. It is like casting a net to catch wild animals. The more you cast, the more you will be able to align with what you are after. If your way of proceeding fits with another man's deeds, then he will naturally emerge. Such is the net that one uses to fish for another man. By persistently holding on to the net you can drive him in.[34]

For the sage-general, such advice suggests how to observe and keep in contact with an enemy in order to learn about the enemy without becoming decisively engaged or allowing his own situation to be known. With such a means the enemy is provoked into showing its dispositions, and yet one's own dispositions remain secret. Only by discovering the adversary's predispositions (*qing*) can the general discern his enemy's outward dispositions (*xing*). However, one's methods for doing so should be indirect and obscure. By being flexible and circuitous, a general can not only secure the enemy's predispositions, he can hide his own. In the analogous words of the *Guiguzi*:

> Before perceiving another man's disposition, circle about and guide him along, and after perceiving the man's disposition, square off and fix on him. Advancing and retreating, turning left and right, you can take command of him. . . . If first you thoroughly establish your own situation in order to control another, then you can create stratagems in which your dispositions have no form and no one can see an entrance. This is called Heavenly psychical power (*shen*).[35]

Finally, the *Guiguzi* provides a method for taking control of an interlocutor that also works for a sage-general. By first "praising" (*fei* 飛) one's opposite number, one can use "pincers" (*qian* 箝) to bind the interlocutor to one's will.

> When using this [the praises and pincers] method with men, you should measure the man's knowledge and talents, weigh his resources and strength, assess his vital energy (*qi*) and circumstantial power (*shi*), and become his pivot (*shu* 樞) and trigger (*ji* 機). First you should use praise by welcoming whatever the man has to say and following him wherever he may wish to go, and then use pincers to bring him into harmony with you and make him manifest his intentions. This is how praise and pincers are combined.[36]

Thus, just like the skillful civil official in the realm of oral persuasion, the sage-general on the battlefield requires a battery of sophistical methods to deceive his opponent and so take command of the situation before him.[37] The practice of deception on the battlefield, as well as the Ruists' objections to such behavior, will be addressed further later in this study. Here the discussion will focus on defining the methodological principles underlying both devious and straightforward military behavior, including those already mentioned in connection with the determination of dispositions and circumstantial power.

Metaphysical Dynamics

Having comprehended the vital energy constituting an enemy's dispositions and circumstantial power by means of harmony and resonances, or by devious means, the sage-general applies his own dispositions and circumstantial power to that of his opponent in such a way that there is complementarity rather than resonance. That is, he matches strong soldiers with weak ones, fresh troops with fatigued ones, concentrated forces with scattered ones. As described in the *Sun Bin bingfa*:

> Those concentrated overcome those dispersed; those full overcome those empty; those who [penetrate by] narrow path overcome those who [penetrate by] broad path; those who are quick overcome those who are slow; those who are many overcome those who are few; those at ease overcome those fatigued. If the enemy possesses any of the above characteristics, then treat him accordingly. That is, since these characteristics can be altered to their counterparts, engage him in the guise of the appropriate

> counterpart. Do not counter concentration with concentration, or dispersion with dispersion. . . . Concentration and dispersion are counterparts . . . [so that] if the enemy is concentrated, then you may counter him with dispersed forces.[38]

To a large degree, battle tactics are viewed as a pairing of opposites, or a simultaneous application of complementarities. Such is the case even when the attacking force is ostensibly lacking in strength. That is, one may use dispersed troops against a concentrated force, or a fatigued unit against a fresh force, so long as one retains the initiative and/or the morale and esprit de corps of one's own force. The *Shangjunshu* provides the following advice in this regard:

> In defending walled cities, the best way is to fight the fresh strength of the invaders with the strength of the worn-out men. It is assaults upon walled cities that wear out the strength of men. As long as the walled cities have not all been razed, the invaders have no means of penetrating the country. Thus it is said that the strength of worn-out men should fight the fresh strength of the invading force. But when the walled cities have all been razed and the foreign army thus finds the means of penetrating, then certainly it will be exhausted, and the people within the country will be rested. Fighting with rested strength against those of exhausted strength is said to be fighting with the strength of fresh men against the worn-out strength of invading forces.[39]

And this paradox is affirmed in the *Daodejing*: "The submissive and weak will overcome the hard and strong."[40]

Besides this general use of complementarities, there are two pairs of terms—regular (*zheng* 正) and irregular (*qi* 奇), and empty (*xu* 虛) and full (*shi* 實)—which are worth separate discussions.

Regular and irregular refer to the two principal modes of offensive-defensive deployment: the regular mode pertains to an element that initially meets an opponent directly. Such a force does not conduct what in the modern West are known as frontal attacks or penetrations in that mode. Rather, it conducts a holding or fixing action for irregular forces.[41] The irregular mode pertains to those troops that cause the opponent to defend on one or both of their flanks, or to the rear. They may be independent harassing troops—snipers, combat patrols, and the like—or they may constitute the main attack in a single or double envelopment or turning movement, in coordination with a regular support attack. Alternatively, they may be reserve forces in a defensive situation—that is, the chief counterattack elements in a mobile defense.[42] The tasks of two irregular or two regular forces may therefore differ, depending on specific missions and on the friendly and enemy situations. But the type of deployment will remain constant for each. Consequently, in the course of an attack, the actions of the enemy or objective circumstances may necessitate switching the roles of regular and irregular forces. Just as the permutations of dispositions and circumstantial power may be limitless, so the deployment of irregular and regular forces may vary infinitely with the vicissitudes of battle. The *Sunzi bingfa* informs us:

> That the army is certain to sustain the enemy's attack without suffering defeat is due to operations of irregular and regular forces. . . . Generally, in battle, use the regular force to engage and the irregular to win. Now the resources of those skilled in the use of irregular forces are as infinite as Heaven and Earth, as inexhaustible as the flow of the great rivers. This is because they end and recommence, cyclically as the movements of the sun and moon; they die away and are reborn, recurrently as the passing seasons. The musical notes are only five in number, but their melodies are so numerous that one cannot hear them all. The primary colors are only five in number, but their combinations are so many that one cannot visualize them all. The flavors are only five in number, but their blends are so various that one cannot taste them all. In battle there are only regular and irregular forces, but their combinations are limitless; none can comprehend them all. For these two forces are mutually reproductive; their interaction as endless as a ring. Who can determine where it ends?[43]

In the initial battle order, regular forces, because they are visible to the enemy in advance of the attack, are perforce unconcealed; the attacker must expose this fraction of his ostensible dispositions and circumstantial power to enemy regular forces. Irregular forces, on the other hand, must have no perceivable disposition if the attacker wishes his diversionary attack to be successful. All depends on applying universal principles of overcoming, while simultaneously keeping the adversary ignorant of one's applications. In the words of the *Sun Bin bingfa*:

> The use of one [unconcealed] disposition in response to another is regular deployment; to be without [apparent] disposition, and yet control the dispositions [of one's adversary], is irregular deployment. That irregular and regular deployments are inexhaustible means they have their allotted purposes. They are allotted by means of irregular reckoning (*qishu* 奇數) and are directed by means of the Five Phases. . . . If the allotments are determined, then there are [visible] dispositions; if the dispositions are determined, then they may be named [and therefore defended against].[44]

At the direction of the commander, irregular and regular forces may displace one another as the situation dictates. And yet, the alternation of roles cannot be predicted in advance of the engagement. The *Liutao* recounts the following story in this regard:

> King Wu asked Tai Gong, "What is the way of making an attack?"
>
> Tai Gong said: "The power situation is in accordance with the movements of the enemy; changes [in relative power] appear in between the two [facing] battle orders; irregular and regular deployments issue from inexhaustible sources. Therefore one cannot tell the outcome of events nor speak of the employment of troops. Moreover, when a mission has been completed, its recapitulation is not worth hearing; and in the employment of troops, the formations are not worth seeing. War is a matter of rapid movements to and fro, and one in which you may concentrate [your forces] and yet not control [the engagement]. One listens and then consults, observes and then plans, obtains intelligence and then harasses [the enemy], distinguishes [strengths and weaknesses] and then threatens [the adversary]; victory lies in having no [apparent] dispositions.[45]

The terms "regular" and "irregular" refer not only to the purposes and positioning of troops, but also to their roles relative to the tactics of the opponent. As the *Sun Bin bingfa* enjoins:

> A [tactic] similar [to that of your opponent] will not be enough to overcome him. Therefore one takes a dissimilar [tactic] as the irregular counterpart. Accordingly, standing fast is the irregular counterpart of movement; being at ease is the irregular counterpart of being fatigued; and likewise for satiety and hunger, order and chaos, and many and few. Those [first] deployed constitute the regular forces; those still not deployed are the irregular forces. When the irregular forces are deployed without effective resistance, you will be victorious.[46]

Finally, it is important to see that on the strategic level, away from the battlefield, regular and irregular have certain precise intentions. The *Daodejing* instructs us, "Use what is regular to rule a state and use what is irregular to wage a war," implying that regular actions are associated with the manifestation of *wen*, while irregular actions are a matter of latent *wu*.[47] From this larger perspective, regular actions pertain to those long-range preparations for conflict that impinge on the economic strength and morale of the general population. To that extent, regular actions are civil, constructive, directed toward the enhancement of virtue. As the modern scholar Peter Boodberg (1903–1972) once put it, regular actions, from a panoramic viewpoint, are a combination of "strategical offensive and tactical defensive."[48] Irregular actions, on the other hand, pertain in this wider perspective to the decisive military actions taken to maintain political homeostasis. As on the tactical level, these strategic, irregular actions are taken sparingly and in a complementary way to the strengths of the adversary's state.[49]

The second pair of complementarities to discuss here is that of empty and full. Here the term "empty" refers to those vulnerable portions of an army's battle order where security or support forces have not been committed. These are the crevices in an opponent's defenses that allow the penetration of full forces—that is, fully supported forces lacking any kind of disadvantage due to terrain, weather, manpower, weaponry, or leadership. The ability to deploy full against empty is, as before, dependent on apprehending the enemy's dispositions while masking one's own—that is, not allowing what is empty in the enemy's dispositions to become full and what is full in one's own dispositions to become empty. According to the *Sunzi bingfa*:

> To be certain to take what you attack is to attack a place the enemy does not protect. To be certain to hold what you defend is to defend a place the enemy does not attack. Therefore,

> against those skilled in attack an enemy does not know where to defend; against experts in defense the enemy does not know where to attack. Subtle and insubstantial, the expert leaves no trace; divinely mysterious, he is inaudible. Thus he is master of his enemy's fate.[50]

The *Sunzi bingfa* also points out particular tactics for applying the principles of empty and full:

> During the early morning spirits are keen, during the day they flag, and in the evening thoughts turn toward home. And therefore those skilled in war avoid the enemy when his spirit is keen and attack him when it is sluggish and his soldiers homesick. This is control of [human] vital energy. In good order they await a disorderly enemy; in serenity, a clamorous one. This is control of mind (*xin* 心). Close to the field of battle, they await an enemy coming from afar; at rest, an exhausted enemy; with well-fed troops, hungry ones. This is control of strength (*li* 力). They do not engage an enemy advancing with well-ordered banners or one whose formations are in impressive array. This is control of changing circumstances (*bian* 變).[51]

By using such tactical knowledge, matching full to empty, the sage-general is able to conduct successful operations with minimum effort. As noted in the "Zhifen" 制分 chapter of the *Guanzi*:

> If you attack a strong point, your [mission] will be tough [to complete], but if you take advantage of crevices [in his defenses], it will be [completed with] spirit-like ease. If you attack a strong point, then his crevices will [also] become strong points; but if you take advantage of his crevices, then his strong points will [also] become crevices. Butcher Tan 屠牛坦 carved nine oxen in a single morning and yet his knife was not dulled, for the blade moved along the [fleshy] interstices. Thus, if you do not follow the Heavenly Way, then even though [your adversary] may be exhausted, you cannot pursue him.[52]

Here the two sets of complementarities have converged into a single process: in the face of a full force one uses regular actions to fix and tire.

If one is successful, then the enemy's full force becomes empty, and this, in turn, allows for the rapid transformation of your regular forces into irregular forces, which can deliver the final blow.

Granted that such an integration of elements requires a profound knowledge of both pairs of complementarities and where they function suitably, there is yet another component of a sage-general's analysis that is the ultimate test of his psychical capacity. Besides being able to discern spatial dispositions and circumstantial power, he must be able to intuit the dynamics of deployment, the timing of his force commitments. The psychical power of the sage-general is demonstrated not merely in his ability to manipulate dispositions and circumstantial power and to metabolize vital energy at will, but in his capacity to manipulate vital energy in proper synchronicity. Vital energy being spatial-temporal in nature, martial activity must take into account the dynamics of dispositions and circumstantial as well as its instantaneous reality.

Vital to the general, then, is recognizing and taking advantage of transition points (*ji* 機) in dispositions and circumstantial power. The process of metabolizing vital energy is nonstop, with each quantum of vital energy minutely modifying an ongoing process of transformation. But during this process there will be certain instants when the distribution of vital energy in a microcosm will afford optimum opportunities for manipulation of dispositions and circumstantial power in one's favor. A passage from the *Zhouyi Xici zhuan* 繫辭傳 speaks to this point:

> The Master said, "To know the seeds (*ji* 幾[機]), that is divine indeed. In his association with those above him, the superior man does not flatter. In his association with those beneath him, he is not arrogant. He knows the seeds. The seeds are the first imperceptible beginnings of movement, the first traces of good fortune [or misfortune] that show themselves. The true gentleman perceives the seeds and immediately takes action. He does not wait even a whole day. In the [*Zhou*]*yi* it is said, 'Firm as a rock. Not a whole day. Perseverance brings good fortune.' Firm as a rock, what need is there of a whole day. The judgment can be known. The superior man knows what is hidden and what is evident. He knows weakness and he knows strength as well. Hence the myriads look up to him."[53]

Thus, transition points are inherent in the integrated space-time of dispositions and circumstantial power and must be acted upon to ensure success. A commander who fails to recognize transition points and exploit them risks eventual defeat. As stated in the *Sun Bin bingfa*: "In warfare, if you see a good [opportunity] and yet are remiss [in taking it]; if you come to a critical moment and yet are hesitant . . . then you have failed in the Way."[54] Having grasped the transition points in a martial confrontation, and having responded creatively to them, a commander shows that he has attuned himself to both Heavenly timing and Earthly advantage and can then be said to be close to the status of a sage.

The concept of transition points is expressed in various ways among the primary sources. The "You guan" 幼官 chapter of the *Guanzi*, for example, conveys the idea of a pivot of change in battle and its synchronicity with a time of greatest potency.[55] The *Sunzi bingfa*, on the other hand, uses the term in its literal sense as a crossbow trigger mechanism.

> When torrential water tosses boulders, it is because of its propensity; when the strike of a hawk breaks the body of its prey, it is because of timing. Thus the propensity of one skilled in war is overwhelming, and his attack precisely regulated. His potential is that of a fully drawn crossbow; his timing, the release of the trigger (*ji*).[56]

In both cases there is the concept of imminence within the larger, cyclic system of change. Indeed, the complementarities spoken of earlier as being parts of this system of change are effectuated on the basis of this concept of imminence. If irregular forces become regular forces and vice versa, the moment of reversal is the transition point, and likewise for an opponent's empty forces becoming full forces. Since regular and irregular and empty and full are integrated within a given microcosm, the transition point for one pair of complementarities may coincide with the transition point for the other pair. Further, these points, in reflection of existing dispositions and circumstantial power, do not occur as durational markers; duration is not important for transition points in the military context. Rather, they are unique space-time intersections, synchronicities, which, in the manner of the *Zhouyi*, cannot be re-enacted.

Our task of presenting the basic principles of the *metaphysical* perspective in early military thought is nearly complete, but one factor in the general's psychical domain remains to be described. This may be called human will or, as labeled in some early Chinese texts, "human vital energy" (*ren qi* 人氣). To some degree, this factor overlaps the vital energy constituting enemy morale, esprit de corps, and the predispositions of enemy leaders. As with such enemy conditions, human vital energy involves the use of psychological warfare as an adjunct to or substitute for a clash of arms. But here the focus is on one's own human resources. In *metaphysical* terms, the general must apply his psychical power to secure and develop the vital energy of his officers and men.[57] Attuning himself to Heavenly timing and affording himself of Earthly advantage, the sage-general can likewise cultivate human vital energy, thereby completing the perennial triad of Heaven-Earth-man. As explained in the *Sun Bin bingfa*:

> In mustering an army and rallying troops, the stress should be on accelerating vital energy. In advancing [into battle] and assembling the army [in combat formation], the stress should be on ordering arms and sharpening [the soldiers'] vital energy. In approaching the site of battle and coming near to the adversary, the stress should be on inspiring their vital energy. On the day of battle before the designated hour, the stress should be on emboldening their vital energy. When you are about to engage in battle, the stress should be on maintaining their vital energy.[58]

An enlightened commander must know the will of enemy and friendly forces alike and coordinate their respective translations of vital energy with existing dispositions and circumstantial power. By doing so, the sage-general can create his own dispositions and circumstantial power at the proper transition points—a process that involves the manipulation of the vital energy of both enemy and friendly troops as much as it entails the application of material potency. The *Sunzi bingfa* gives us illustrations:

> In the tumult and uproar the battle seems chaotic, but there is no disorder; the troops appear to be milling about in circles, but they cannot be defeated. Apparent confusion is a product of good order; apparent cowardice, of courage; apparent weakness, of strength. Order or disorder depends on organization; courage or cowardice on circumstances; strength or weakness on dispositions. Thus those skilled at making the enemy move do so by creating a situation to which he must conform; they entice him with something he is certain to take, and with lures of ostensible profit they await him in strength. Therefore a skilled commander seeks victory from the situation and does not demand it of his subordinates. He selects his men and they exploit the situation.

> He who relies on the situation uses his men in fighting as one rolls logs or stones. Now the nature of logs and stones is that on stable ground they are static; on unstable ground they move. If square, they stop; if round, they roll. Thus the potential of troops skillfully commanded in battle may be compared to that of round boulders which roll down from mountain heights.[59]

The triad of ancient Chinese thought has now been manifested in the microcosm of battle. Like those universals, the correlates of Heaven, Earth, and man—transition points, dispositions and circumstantial power, and the vital energy of soldiers, respectively—respond endlessly with each other. But as indicated before, this triad of correlates has no meaning for martial activity without the sage-general to create the psychical interstices and to coordinate the existing vital energy for ultimate re-establishment of homeostasis. As a complement and reflection of the sage-ruler—the representative of civility—the sage-general takes on a central role as the spirit-like mediator of *metaphysical* reality on the battlefield. As summed up in the *Heguanzi*:

> These two [principles of successive transformation of natural elements and accordance with the inherent nature of things] are reflected in command power and circumstantial power. When reflected in command power, the burgeoning of resources [human and material] is exceedingly rich; and when reflected in circumstantial power, one will be exceedingly victorious in war. For the burgeoning of resources there [must] be aggressiveness in the realm of Earth and yielding in the realm of Heaven, and for victory in war there [must] be yielding in the realm of the Way and harmony in the realm of man.[60]

The Ultimate Battle

With the above grounding in the characteristic vocabulary and methodology of *metaphysical* battle tactics, our earlier discussion of the basic purposes of martiality as seen in early China can be resumed. In Chapter 1 we saw that *wen*/*wu* theorists were, for the most part, imbued with the notion that *wu* as potency is the ideal, and that the sage-general wishes to limit his open display of force. In the *metaphysical* view of battle that assumption is expanded and given greater definition: the ultimate objective of the military commander is to render his opponent harmless by causing him to be incapable of using his strength effectively against a force that appears invisible (*wuxing*). Hence the saying, "Those who are skillful in manipulating armed forces are ones who cause the enemy to act as if they were grasping at empty air and striking at shadows."[61] Even though the creation of chaos in an adversary's ranks allows for pursuit and exploitation, total destruction of an enemy force is not the preferred outcome. Instead, the aim of warfare, which is embedded in the *metaphysical* perspective, is to neutralize the enemy, to render him incapable of further military activity. The *Weiliaozi* indicates the priorities among interlocking methods of war:

> In war there is victory by the Way (*dao*), victory by awesomeness (*wei* 威), and victory by strength (*li* 力). To analyze the military situation and estimate the enemy's [strengths]; to cause the enemy's vital energy to be lost and their army to scatter, so that despite the fullest [use of] punishments, it is unemployable—this is victory by the Way. To be decisive [in making] laws and regulations; to make clear rewards and punishments; to place conveniently at hand [military] tools and utensils; to make the people eager to fight—this is victory by awesomeness. To defeat an army and kill its general; to take advantage of breaks [in enemy lines]; to mount [the opponent's] corner gates and fire crossbows; to disperse [the opponent's] forces and seize his territory; to achieve success and then return [to home base]—this is victory by strength.[62]

Martial events consist of the confrontation of concentrations of vital energy in certain dispositions. Because *qi* cannot be obliterated but only dispersed, the sage-general's strategy is founded on the optimum method of dispersing the enemy's vital energy while avoiding the least dispersal of one's own vital energy.[63] This method is in turn based on employing mutually complementary subconcentrations of vital energy that cancel out the enemy's potential—hence the importance of employing regular/irregular and empty/full forces in a complementary manner. Further, one is cautioned not to use vital energy of a type similar to that of the enemy being confronted; for, if strong vital energy counters strong vital energy, stalemate or mutual dispersal results, and a minimum loss of friendly-force vital energy is never accomplished. The most opportune and advantageous juxtaposing of complementarities will, however, lead to the desired result with an economy of effort. The *Sunzi bingfa* offers an epitome of such a principle of restraint:

> Generally, in war the best policy is to take a state intact; to ruin it is inferior to this. To capture the enemy's army is better than to destroy it; to take intact a battalion, a company, or a five-man squad is better than to destroy them. To win one hundred victories in one hundred battles is not the acme of skill. To subdue the enemy without fighting is the acme of skill. Thus what is of supreme importance in war is to attack the enemy's strategy. Next best is to disrupt his alliances. The next best is to attack his army. The worst policy is to attack cities. Attack cities only when there is no alternative. . . . Thus those skilled in war subdue the enemy's army without battle. They capture his cities without assaulting them and overthrow his state without protracted operations. Your aim must be to take All-under-Heaven intact. Thus your troops are not worn out and your gains will be complete. This is the art of offensive strategy.[64]

Transition points, in this conception of the purposes of war, take on new significance. Instead of being merely a point of change in the flux of combat, a transition point becomes that temporal pivot when the dispersal of enemy vital energy is maximally possible. It is the time for optimum application of power, that is, an application that will resolve the conflict with least expenditure of resources by both confronting parties. The *Zhanguoce* gives graphic evidence of the effects such a determination of transition points can produce:

> "This is what I have heard is the secret of aggressive warfare: a million troops can be defeated at a state banquet, generals like [King] Helü 闔閭 [of Wu 吳] and Wu Qi can be captured by sitting in a room, and cities with thousand-foot walls can be captured between the wine and the spiced meats. A hundred-foot wheeled battering ram may be broken by a sleeping mat."[65]

Even at the verge of victory the successful general, according to the *metaphysical* perspective, checks his possible overuse of effort by yielding to the enemy, allowing a means to escape or a way to reconcile differences amicably. This principle is stated clearly in a stray fragment of the *Yi Zhoushu* and quoted in the *Zhanguoce*: "If you are on the point of defeating [an enemy] you must nevertheless assist him, and if you are about to overpower [an adversary] you must nevertheless give in to him."[66] In similar fashion, the *Sunzi bingfa* counsels: "To a surrounded enemy you must leave a way of escape. Do not press an enemy at bay."[67] By so yielding, there is no danger that vital energy will be concentrated against you again, or that new confrontations will be necessary.

Conclusion

Based on the above discussion, the philosophical principles of the sage-general and his activities, as posited by the *metaphysical* perspective on war, can be summarized as follows:

- The sage-general is an ideal man of martiality who by means of his psychical power perceives the vital energy that constitutes the dispositions and circumstantial power of a military microcosm and conducts the dynamics of vital energy concentrations in that microcosm.
- In the process of determining the dispositions and circumstantial power in a martial situation and effecting optimum changes in those dispositions and circumstantial power, the sage-general utilizes vital energy in certain complementary configurations—that is, regular and irregular, empty and full—in order to gain advantage over an adversary.
- Key to the functioning of psychical power is an awareness of the transition points that will afford optimum control of vital energy concentrations in the martial microcosm.
- Coequal with dispositions and circumstantial power, and with transition points, is the vital energy of participating troops, which, with the other two elements, constitutes a mutually binding combination, reflective of the omnipresent triad of Heaven-Earth-man. The sage-general manipulates these three elements with relative autonomy, but always in the role of mediator, acting in harmony with the Way by which this triad functions.

- Finally, because such manipulation is conducted in harmony with the Way, the ultimate objective of military activity, from the sage-general's point of view, is to neutralize inharmonious concentrations of vital energy in the most economical way, so that the total configuration of vital energy in a martial situation returns to homeostasis and civil order is regained.

A number of observations can be made about this summary of *metaphysical* concepts. First, one can discern among these principles a limited commitment to the existence of objective cosmic laws that minimize the effects of supernatural forces and maximize the potential of man to direct and accord with exterior events, in particular, martial events. Second, the *metaphysical* perspective was highly compatible with the *syncretist* solution to the *wen*/*wu* problem. The integration of martiality and civility in the *syncretist* solution can be deduced from the employment of *metaphysical* means, which were also civil methods, to achieve a desired dispersal of enemy vital energy in a military microcosm for the purposes of civil harmony.

That said, the *metaphysical* perspective was not an inherent feature of the *syncretist* solution. Rather, the *metaphysical* approach was a philosophical construct that served to support the viewpoint of those espousing a *syncretist* solution to the *wen*/*wu* debate in early China. In the next chapter, attention will shift to another element among the factors affecting this debate, the *pragmatic*.

Chapter 3

The Practical and Meta-Practical

As we have seen, a philosophy of war developed in Warring States times—perhaps for the first time in human history—in which the *metaphysical* aspect of martial conflict became an accepted and important element of generalship. This is not to imply, however, that military strategy was considered simply an intellectual exercise. On the contrary, throughout the Zhanguo period generals are enjoined in the military treatises and other texts to combine *metaphysical* insight with a practical knowledge of military organization, administration, training, war preparedness, and intelligence. Such counsel was impelled by the rapid changes in the ways battles were being fought in a period of continual interstate warfare.

Even as philosopher-strategists were setting a theoretical foundation for war, martial technology was advancing swiftly with the introduction of new combat arms such as cavalry and light infantry and the invention of such devices as "cloud ladders," battering rams, boring devices, and early warning wells for siegecraft. The increased employment of common infantry soldiers in relatively large armies during Zhanguo times required changes in training and methods of command and control. As new combat formations evolved to afford greater flexibility in the use of offense and defense, new techniques of discipline and communication for untried troops developed, all of which became an important part of military expertise. No longer could a general rely on military rites (*junli*), as was applied in Chunqiu and earlier times. Instead it was necessary to devise new legal standards—military law (*junfa* 軍法) and military orders (*junling* 軍令)—for ensuring discipline in the ranks.[1] In addition, as military expenditures mounted in the Zhanguo era, awareness increased among both generals and scholar-statesmen of the practical importance of economic preparedness and logistical estimates, even though the latter elements did not, so far as is known, advance to the same level of sophistication as the art of tactical planning. Finally, there was a sustained emphasis on intelligence collection and analysis, deception, and covert action to overpower one's foes.

This chapter will examine the evidence in the military treatises and contemporaneous texts for these various practical features of war-making, as well as techniques that went beyond the practical—that is, the meta-practical—that became enduring parts of Chinese military thought. Together these methods constituted the *pragmatic* application to the *wen/wu* problem in Zhanguo times and later.

Organizational Models

Many if not most of the elaborate structural hierarchies presented in the *Zhouli* 周禮, including those pertaining to military organization, may be creations of the early Han and do not accurately reflect Zhou dynasty practice.[2] Nevertheless, in surveying earlier texts, one finds that the correlation of military and agricultural divisions made in the *Zhouli* is congruent with that made in prior, clearly authentic descriptions, and there are even certain consistencies between this Han recounting and genuine pre-Han texts with regard to numbers of military units and their mutual proportions. First, as verified by passages in the *Shangshu*, the *Shi*, and the *Zuozhuan*, the Zhou royal army did indeed have an organizational base of six main divisions (*liu shi* 六師), as indicated in the *Zhouli*.[3] Second, major states, with temporary changes interceding, maintained, in reflection of the *Zhouli*, a standard tripartite division in their armed forces.[4] And third, there are internal ratios that fit the *Zhouli* ascriptions. Not only did pre-Qin states typically divide their land forces into three parts, they correlated the hierarchy of each part to a unit of agricultural population and, importantly, preserved five- and ten-to-one proportions in each hierarchy.[5]

It is plausible to say that the three-five arrangement that appears in these various texts suggests a continuing belief in the numerological or quasi-formulistic nature of the human order and of the martial realm in particular. Indeed, such numerological consonance in Chunqiu times was also a lesser feature of Zhanguo military organizational theory, and there was a close association between army structure and other fields influenced by three-five arrangements, namely, astronomy and music. However, it would be an exaggeration to conclude that these arithmetic proportions predetermined military organization in early China. During Chunqiu and Zhanguo times this ancient formulism was tempered by a certain degree of realism, as advances in tactical thinking and the decline of military rites encouraged innovations in the older system. Already in the *Zuozhuan* one finds previously unknown battle formations and ad hoc harassing forces within the framework of the three armies (*sanjun* 三軍).[6] In many cases, the term "three armies" referred not to a three-unit force, but to a single unit that could be reorganized as the situation demanded, or to military affairs in general.[7] As seen in the Jin forces during the Battle of Chengpu (632 BCE), or in the Chu army during the Battle of Bi (597 BCE), soldiers were given more specialized functions even within a combat arm.[8] Clearly during the latter part of the Chunqiu era, purely tactical considerations—albeit with continued regard for numerological constants—were beginning to encroach on older traditions as the basis for orders of battle.

Moreover, in Zhanguo times, when lines of nobility and family ceased to have any significant impact on the organization of armies, this earlier tendency toward a rationalization of orders of battle in accord with tactical considerations became the dominant mode, while numerological formulas retained only a conventional utility. Most informative among the military treatises in this regard is the *Weiliaozi*, which depicts an organization based on the Chunqiu tripartite arrangement but also gives a complete prescription of insignia and internal hierarchy that allows for diversified segmentation. In addition to a breakdown of units into groups of five, the *Weiliaozi* describes an armed force in formation as being further sorted into the traditional three columns, each column consisting of five subdivisions and each subdivision consisting of five ranks (see figure 3.1 on page 62).

Oriented toward the south, each column was assigned a unit color correlating to the compass point and season traditionally associated with that color; banners for the column were in the assigned color, as were the feathers of the member soldiers' headdresses. The five army subdivisions were also each divided into ranks with insignia whose colors succeeded each other in generating (*sheng* 生) progression, clockwise around the compass—starting with green (spring, east) and ending with black (north, winter). Additionally, each rank of subdivisions, running from left to right armies, had a separate placement for insignia.[9]

One can see at a glance the cosmological correlations in the battle order. And yet, it would be overstating the case to deduce that such ascriptions were made solely according to preset locations in a cosmic chart, such as the legendary "Luo River Document" (*Luoshu* 洛書) (Luoshu Square) or the "Yellow River Diagram" (*Hetu* 河圖). The arrangement is neither symmetrical nor cosmologically complete, nor does it resemble the

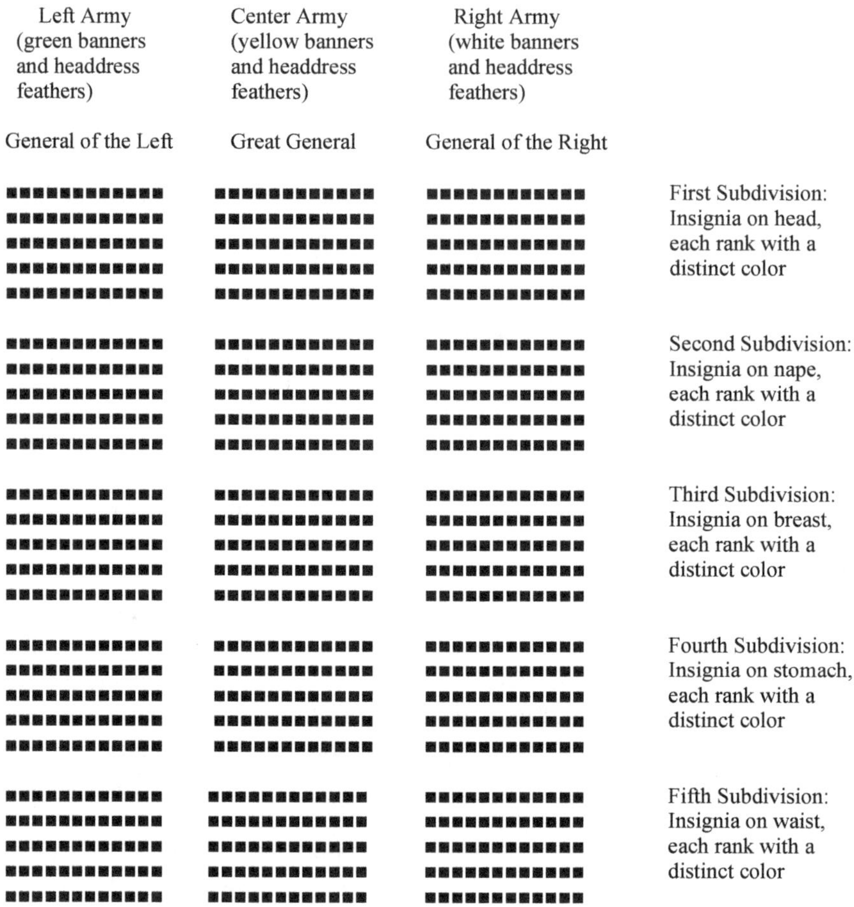

Source: *Weiliaozi*, "Jing zu ling" 經卒令

Figure 3.1. Static Battle Order, Armies in Column. The order of colors for each rank in each column is, from top to botton, green, red, yellow, white, and black.

idealized military charts that appear in later, especially post-Han, times. Rather, one may say that, although the compilers of the *Weiliaozi* may have been mindful of traditional military-agricultural organizational models and current cosmological theory, it was probably easiest, for reasons of mnemonic convenience and efficiency, to adopt a three-five arrangement in order to identify specific units and even individuals in an armed force.[10]

This noncosmological practicality in tactical organization can be further demonstrated by the flexibility of the armed hosts described in the *Weiliaozi*. On the march, the three columns of soldiers could become individual task forces with missions to make initial engagement or to follow up (*zhong* 踵), that is, exploit or pursue (see figure 3.2).

Alternatively, they could be re-combined into two entirely different fighting configurations: (1) a perimeter defense force in which contingent A

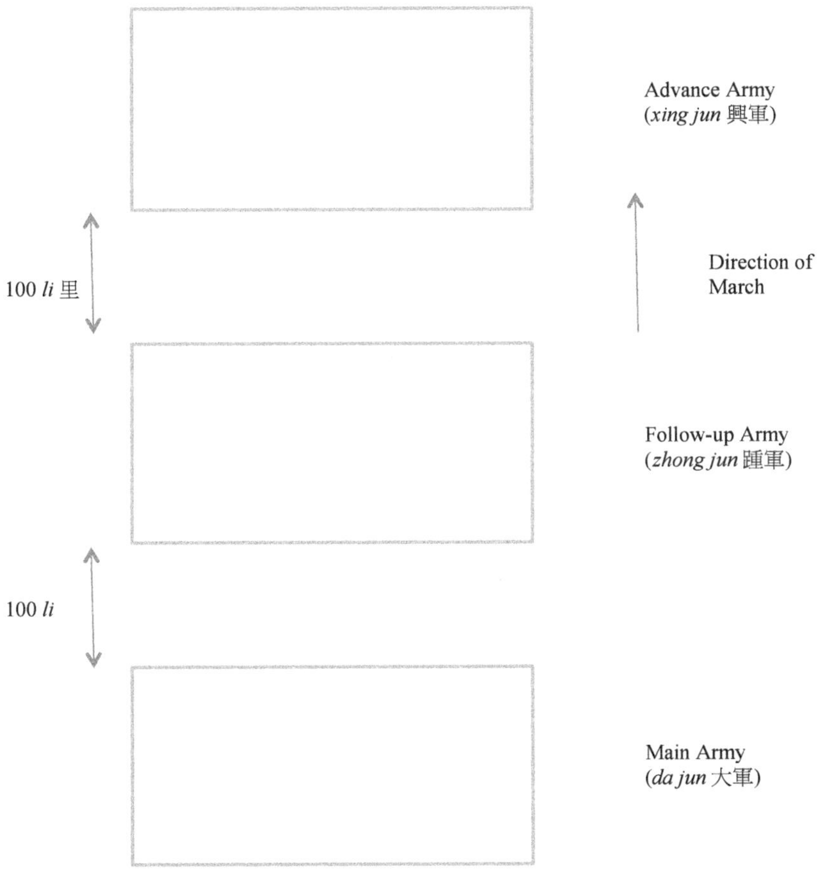

Source: *Weiliaozi*, "Zhong jun ling" 踵軍令

Figure 3.2. Army on the March.

was charged to face inward toward the center of the formation, in order, it was said, to prevent internal sabotage, while contingent B was commanded to face outward to protect the bivouac against external danger; and (2) an offensive unit consisting of standing formations (*lizhen* 立陣) and sitting formations (*zuozhen* 坐陣), the former wielding halberds and crossbows, ready to advance in attack, and the latter wielding swords and battleaxes, remaining in reserve as a holding force. Because these latter formations are described in a section of the *Weiliaozi* apart from that depicting the static formation of figure 3.1, it is difficult to tell whether these specialized configurations were to be incorporated into larger, five-rank subdivisions in the manner of an ancient Greek phalanx or a Roman legion, or whether such assignments pertained to an entirely separate tactical organization consisting of troops from various subdivisions. One is told only that the three columns of the static formation had different designations when the force was on the march, implying that their internal organization might also differ. The issue is not satisfactorily resolved.

While combining practicality and formulism, the *Weiliaozi* also stresses the necessity for organizational precision, and in doing so occasionally refers to *metaphysical* conceptions. In the "Fen sai ling" 分塞令 chapter a garrison organization is described that resembles the system for Roman legions developed a couple of centuries later. Each unit must be carefully distinguished from another and maintained separately; personnel within each unit may not enter another unit's territory without express permission. Sentinel posts (*fuzhu* 府柱) are situated 120 paces (*bu* 步) apart along main thoroughfares crisscrossing the garrison area, and only persons holding a general's or staff officer's tally were allowed to travel such thoroughfares. Further, soldiers on foraging duty had to be marched in formation along garrison roads. Last, personnel ledgers (*fu* 符) were maintained for each five-man squad (*wu* 伍) by the general's staff to prevent desertion and guarantee proper security.[11] Thus, in cantonment as well as in battle order, precise segregation of units and absolute control of individual soldiers was demanded.[12]

The conventionality of a three-five arrangement for military organization and the spirit of rational application in the *Weiliaozi* are also apparent in other Zhanguo military treatises, although the descriptions are sometimes obscure.

The *Wuzi* suggests a quadrilateral arrangement that might at first indicate certain mystical connections: "Over the left wing flies the banner of the Green Dragon (*qinglong* 青龍); over the right flies the banner of the

White Tiger (*baihu* 白虎); over the van flies the banner of the Vermilion Bird (*zhuque* 朱雀); and over the rear flies the banner of the Black Tortoise (*xuangui* 玄龜)."[13] But it is apparent from the *Wuzi* as a whole and from what is known of Wu Qi's background that such regalia were a means, then as now, to encourage esprit de corps, to provide a means of orientation for soldiers during combat, and to ensure easy control of troop populations.[14]

The *Sunzi bingfa* has long been noted for its realistic approach to war-making. But in the area of tactical organization the work's only unique contribution to battlefield maneuvers was the pincers (*shuairan* 率然) movement, also known in Western tactics as envelopment.

> Now, the troops of those adept in war are used like the pincers snake of Mount Chang 常 [i.e., Mount Heng 恆].[15] When struck on the head, its tail attacks; when struck on the tail, its head attacks; when struck in the center both head and tail attack.[16]

For its part, the *Sun Bin bingfa* describes an army organization that is generally nonformulaic in character, although the details are somewhat indefinite and traces of numerological influences remain. On the one hand, we are told that the so-called three armies actually constitute a single force divisible into three, four, or five battle teams as circumstances require.[17] However, the "Ba zhen" 八陣 chapter, more in accord with the traditional three-five pattern, outlines a tripartite arrangement similar to that in the *Weiliaozi*, consisting of a point force for initial penetration, a main body, and a reserve force. The *Sun Bin bingfa* further advocates two alternatives for the use of such forces: either the deployment of one-third of the unit and the retention of the other two-thirds as a base of support, or the deployment of two forces forward (left and right) and one force to the rear, as reserve. As for specialized formations, the "Guan yi" 官一 chapter is replete with obscure titles, but niggardly with information about their respective meanings. The "Shi zhen" 十陣 chapter, on the other hand, is more specific. In addition to detailed, though often impressionistic, descriptions (some lost) of each formation, the chapter begins with these short summaries:

> In general, there are ten formations: square (*fang* 方), round (*yuan* 圓), dispersed (*shu* 疏), dense (*shu* 數), awl (*zhui hang* 錐行), geese (*yan hang* 雁行), hook (*gou hang* 鉤行), dark wings (*xuanyi* 玄翼), fire (*huo* 火), and water (*shui* 水).[18] These all have their particular advantages. The square formation is for cutting

> through the enemy. The round formation is for concentrating the enemy. The dispersed formation is for . . . [undeciphered text].[19] The dense formation is for preventing enemy penetrations. The awl formation is for penetrating enemy lines. The geese formation is for closing with the enemy with bow and arrow. The hook formation is for making rapid changes in battle plans. The dark wings formation is for placing the enemy in doubt and encumbering the enemy's resoluteness. The fire formation is for seizing the enemy [by means of fire or extracting oneself from enemy attack by fire]. And the water formation is for disrupting the enemy [when attacking by water or defending against enemy attacks by water].[20]

The *Liutao*, while providing three *pragmatic* organizational patterns and other empirical models, differs from the other military treatises in glossing two of these descriptions with a *metaphysical* sense.[21] The first is a general distribution of personnel by apparent intention (disciples and sons hoping for revenge, degraded ministers desiring renewed merit, orphans from poor families seeking higher status), as well as by characteristics and abilities—a method that foreshadows the Han dynasty policy of dividing soldiers into branches according to past experience and special aptitudes.[22] The second pattern, an irregular (*qi*) technique called "birds and clouds" (*niaoyun* 鳥雲), apparently pertains to an alternating scattering of troops (like birds) and a gathering of troops (like clouds) for confrontations in woodlands and marshes.[23] And the third formation, "rushing formation" (*chongzhen* 衝陣), appears to represent probing forces of various arms, along with strike troops, cavalry, and crossbowmen, to deliver the *coup de grace* against a trapped enemy.[24] In contrast, the *Liutao* has passages describing battle formations in a less *pragmatic* fashion and with more *metaphysical* references.

> King Wu asked Tai Gong, "To conduct military operations, how does one constitute the Heavenly battle order, the Earthly battle order, and the human battle order?"
>
> Tai Gong replied, "When the sun and moon and the stars and Big Dipper are [distributed in ranks] left and right, to one's front and rear, this constitutes the Heavenly battle order. When hills and water sources are situated to one's advantage before and behind, to left and right, this constitutes the Earthly battle order.

> The employment of chariots and horses, civilian and military, constitutes the human battle order."[25]

One cannot infer from this *Liutao* passage a dominance of cosmological thinking in this or other Zhanguo military treaties. Despite the greater abstractness in the *Liutao* description, the goal of the writers of the military treatises was, on the whole, to define practicable means for deploying men in any combat situation that may arise. Nevertheless, the *Liutao* passage does point to a cardinal principle of Zhanguo military philosophy, namely, that a general exerts his *metaphysical* powers through objective, human agents, using *pragmatic* methods.

This combination of *pragmatic* and *metaphysical* can also be seen in the lengthy list of titles of staff personnel in the "Wang yi" 王翼 chapter of the *Liutao*, along with numbers of such staff and descriptions of their respective functions:

> *Fuxin* 腹心 (1)—(lit., "belly and heart") strategic planning supervisor and "guarantor of the lives of the people"
>
> *Moushi* 謀士 (5)—strategy planners, tacticians, and advisors on military justice, personnel appointments, and general affairs
>
> *Tianwen* 天文 (3)—astrologers, diviners, and "psychologists" who "know the mechanism of the going and coming of the enemy's mind/heart"
>
> *Dili* 地利 (3)—specialists in selecting sites with the best dispositions and circumstantial power
>
> *Bingfa* 兵法 (9)—tacticians concerned with actual battle preparations
>
> *Tongliang* 通糧 (4)—men in charge of assuring a constant supply of foodstuffs for the army's men and livestock
>
> *Fenwei* 奮威 (4)—men possessing supreme military skills, who can select soldiers of high-quality military talent and advise on the use of weapons and armor

Fuguqi 伏鼓旗 (3)—men in charge of drums and banners, who have sharp eyesight and hearing, carry forged tallies, can confuse the enemy with deceptive battle signals, and are skilled in evasion techniques and combat patrolling

Gugong 股肱 (4)—(lit., "legs and arms") men in charge of especially difficult physical assignments, such as the digging of moats and sluices and the building of walls and other earthworks

Tongcai 通材 (3)—men concerned with correcting errors throughout the command, arranging facilities for guests (*binke* 賓客), and advising on the resolution of problems in the ranks

Quanshi 權士 (3)—men in charge of espionage and subterfuge

Ermu 耳目 (7)—(lit., "ears and eyes") men in charge of intelligence training

Zhaoya 爪牙 (5)—(lit., "claws and teeth") men who are in charge of "displaying the martial prowess of the army and raising esprit de corps among the forces," and who can serve as point men against difficult objectives

Yuyi 羽翼 (4)—(lit., "wings") men in charge of psychological warfare—that is, broadcasting the army's renown far and wide in order to weaken enemy morale

Youshi 遊士 (8)—men in charge of intelligence agents, who can report changes in the enemy situation, attempt to influence enemy loyalties, observe enemy movements, and act as saboteurs and fifth-columnists

Shushi 術士 (2)—men in charge of ruses of a supernatural kind to confuse the enemy

Fangshi 方士 (2)—men in charge of medical activities, especially the concocting of medicines for stab wounds and "myriad diseases"

Fasuan 法算 (2)—men in charge of keeping accounts of expenses for construction, provisions, and general supplies[26]

This roster of seventy-two assistants—a number of quasi-magical significance "corresponding to the Way of Heaven"—is indicative of a *metaphysical-pragmatic* interrelationship.[27] On the one hand, a large percentage of the men in this list are concerned with matters closely associated with those of the sage-general described in Chapter 2, including the determination of enemy positions, the obfuscation of one's own status and intentions, and the choice of favorable battle terrain. On the other hand, a selection of mission-oriented staff positions with a specificity of job description reminds one of the administrative principles of Shen Buhai 申不害 (d. 337 BCE). Thus, there is a connection between the supranormal faculties of the sage-general and the real-world requirements for organizing soldiers, so that the latter carry out the commander's psychical wishes. Moreover, it is a symbiotic relationship, because sagely qualities, such as Tai Gong is quoted as giving at the beginning of the *Liutao*, depend on the harmonious performance of one's officers and men, and because *metaphysical* factors significantly influence objective techniques of leadership. Organization for combat is, therefore, the physical embodiment of a sage-general's extraordinary abilities, in which both practical and psychical resources are indispensable for the conduct of war.

Training and Administration

The military treatises of the Zhanguo period describe several other *pragmatic* control measures whereby a superior general could ensure the projection of his psychical power. The most widely recorded of these are drums and gongs (or bells), used principally for signaling advance and retreat, respectively, and employed occasionally in intricate rhythmic patterns for commanding certain battle movements.[28] Reed instruments and flutes are prescribed in the *Wuzi*, and it has already been shown how banners and flags had long been important means of communication, not only for soldiers in the using force, but also for the enemy as displays of the order and strength of its foe.[29]

Despite all these practical measures for controlling his army, a general in the Zhanguo period needed something more to assure responsiveness to his commands. In particular, he required a program of basic troop training that had not been necessary for previous generations of aristocratic warriors, who had been schooled from youth in the military arts. Among the Zhanguo military treatises, it is the *Weiliaozi* that best outlines a schedule of individual and unit instruction—a schedule that has great similarity with post-Napoleonic military instruction in the West. According to the *Weiliaozi*, indoctrination began in the five-man squad with a principal instructor teaching basic weapon techniques and squad battle drill, laying emphasis on building confidence in one's fellow squad members and obedience to one's superiors. Having mastered these small-unit tactics, the five-man squad was then integrated into successively larger units, each requiring more intricate movements and greater cooperation.[30] The *Weiliaozi* is silent on the precise instruction given intermediate-size units, but it does briefly describe certain training procedures at the highest, or army (*jun* 軍), level. Signaling with a standard combination of drums and gongs, masses of men were drilled in marching along a prescribed axis, first at a walk, then a trot, and finally a sprint, in order to duplicate the stages of a frontal assault. Predetermined distances (one hundred paces) between each change of gait were set, and the process could be repeated for as long as required to habituate soldiers to acting as a disciplined unit.[31] This, of course, constituted only one type of battle movement and, therefore, probably did not exhaust the kinds of training actually employed.

From these discussions one sees again that, as valuable as common soldiers must have been in executing the oracles of the sage-general, they were, from the viewpoint of the *metaphysical*, only inanimate vital energy. In a manner reminiscent of Shang Yang's dicta, the soldiers and even his staff existed only to be manipulated for the success of a campaign, albeit in a cynically benevolent way. In the *Sunzi bingfa* we see this combination of strategic inscrutability and objective indifference:

> It is the business of a general to be serene and inscrutable, impartial and self-controlled. He should be capable of keeping his officers and men in ignorance of his plans. He prohibits superstitious practices and so rids the army of doubts. Then until the moment of death there can be no troubles. He changes his methods and alters his plans so that people have no knowledge of what he is doing. He alters his campsites and marches by devious routes, and thus makes it impossible for others to anticipate his purpose. To assemble the army and throw it into a desperate position is the business of the general. He leads the army deep into hostile territory and there releases the trigger. He burns his boats and smashes his cooking pots; he urges the army on as if driving a flock of sheep, now in one direction, now in another, and none knows where he is going.[32]

Certainly treatment of troops was not always harsh. During the Zhanguo period, Wu Qi was praised as a general who showed consideration for the physical plight of the common soldier. Indeed, the admonition for the military leader to experience the same inconveniences and pain as his subordinates is standard in the military treatises, both in the Zhanguo period and afterward. Still, the ultimate purpose of such humaneness was not to construct a close-knit community for its own sake but to facilitate the accomplishment of the mission. In other words, the ideal general must be allowed, in *metaphysical* terms, to transform the vital energy of his troops in whatever fashion he wills in order to fulfill his martial responsibilities.

Military Law

To carry out these responsibilities, however, the sage-general requires another *pragmatic* tool. His psychical power must be aided by legal rubrics. Again, the *Weiliaozi* is unusual among the military treatises in devoting considerable space to the explication of military regulations and especially penal law. Consistent with the fragments available of Han law, the *Weiliaozi*'s military code shows little mercy for disobedient soldiers and officers.[33] The severity of the code can be seen in the following catalog: of the forty-eight offenses listed in the *Weiliaozi*, sixteen were punishable by death, one by either demotion or banishment to border duty for three years, and one by simple three-year banishment to border duty. Three offenses were apparently not punishable, and twenty-seven are either assigned no punishment in the text (thirteen) or the type of punishment is in doubt (fourteen). Comparing these latter offenses with ones for which punishments are assigned, death was very possibly the judgment in many cases. The severity of such judgments is further evidenced by the range of applicable offenses. Those punishable by death include such varying acts as "speaking loudly in the presence of the commander in chief," abandoning one's subordinates in combat, failing to report a capital crime, and failing to appear at an ordered time and place.[34] Great emphasis was placed on maintaining one's insignia and staying with one's squad in whatever circumstances, even upon the death of one's immediate commanders. Additionally, stress was placed on moving about the battlefield only upon signals to do so. Training being a matter of master-pupil transmission within a unit, failure of one member to perform according to orders meant heavy punishment for the instructor(s) in the unit. Furthermore, accomplices or abettors to one member's infraction were liable for the punishment received by the principal offender. Such collective responsibility was particularly great for the officer corps, since the harshness of the punishment increased with the rank of the offender. For company commanders and higher, one finds not only judgments of death for the principal, but also extermination of the offender's family adults, enslavement of his children, and occasionally confiscation of his property.[35]

Aside from this strict obedience to superiors, the single most important principle implied by this scattered list of penal statutes in the *Weiliaozi* is that of unit integrity and mutual cooperation. It is an axiom which, since Chunqiu times, was considered more important to success in battle than mere numbers of troops.[36] As previously shown, units had to be carefully distinguished by insignia so that only those of the same squad wore the same regalia in the same manner. By this careful regulation of attire and encouragement of unit consciousness, the general, provided he had the requisite personal qualities, was allowed, ideally, to exercise his psychical power unencumbered by subordinate autonomy, while retaining harmony in the ranks.

The "Zhan wei" 戰威 chapter of the *Weiliaozi* promotes the use of legalistic means to ensure unit integrity and discipline, linking these measures to awesomeness (*wei*) in the general and inspired harmony in the ranks. "To be decisive in making laws and regulations; to make clear rewards and punishments; to place conveniently at hand military tools and equipment; to make the people eager to fight—this is victory by awesomeness."[37] At the same time, care must be taken in ensure a willingness of common people to contribute to military success whenever called to do so.

> One must accord with the ways people live and thereby control them; one must accord with the ways people behave themselves and thereby make these ways manifest. [To assure] that they have the fruits of harvest; that they have the affections induced by food and drink; that towns and villages encourage one another [in resolving common problems]; that they help one another in times of death and mourning; that they all respond for military and corvée duties—this is the way to encourage the people. Cause the soldiers to be as relatives, the troops to be as friends.[38]

Once again a link is made in the military treatises between martial necessity and civil unity.

In the *Lüshi chunqiu* 呂氏春秋, a work compiled under the tutelage of Lü Buwei 呂不韋 (291–235 BCE) in about 239 BCE, Wu Qi is reported, as in the *Wuzi*, to have stressed the importance of unequivocal statutes to meld the loyalties of the people—to coalesce their vital energy into a malleable and motivated whole.[39]

> Wu Qi, while governing Xihe 西河, wished to illustrate his trustworthiness to the people.[40] Therefore for a night and a day a post was set up outside South Gate and an order given those living in the town: "Whoever by tomorrow is able to strike down the post outside South Gate will be appointed a senior official (*zhangdafu* 長大夫)." By late the next day no one had struck down the post, for the people said to each other, "This cannot be believed." But one man spoke up, "Merely to go and knock down the post will only mean no reward. What harm is there in that?" So he went and struck down the post, and [with it] came to visit Wu Qi. Seeing him arrive, Wu Qi came out and appointed him a senior official. . . . After this the people put trust in Wu Qi's rewards and punishments.[41]

Clearly, legal strictures were seen to have great usefulness for the sage-general in allowing him to cohere the vital energy of his subordinates in a harmonious way—a way most salutary for success on the battlefield. In the "Qi fa" 七法 and "Fa fa" 法法 chapters of the *Guanzi*, the priority of law administered by great men over lesser men in martial situations, whether they are soldiers in the ranks or the general populace, is affirmed:

> The lord discourses on the Way and follows ordering principle (*li* 理), and therefore his ministers submit to his instruction and the petty officials are dealt with strictly; no one dares to show partiality before him. . . . Thus soldiers in the ranks think lightly of death and rest in adversity to execute the lord's business. This [clarification of rewards and punishments] is the acme of martial principle.[42]

> When the ruler's orders are entirely executed and his prohibitions completely effective, he may draw in and employ them, and the people will not dare to divert their efforts. He may impress and go to battle with them, and the people will not dare to begrudge

> their lives. When they do not dare to divert their efforts, there will be achievement, and when they do not dare to begrudge their lives, there will be no enemy to match them.[43]

Thus we see in a variety of Zhanguo sources that, as with organizational methods, *pragmatic* legal strictures, unhesitatingly applied, support the *metaphysical* qualities of the sage-general. Concurrently, the complementarity between virtue and punishment seen in the ideology of the Western Zhou is sustained among the military treatises and other works from the Zhanguo era in a legalistic form, as rewards and penalties become essential for the maintenance of state power. The *Jingfa* asserts, for example:

> When a state loses its proper place, then the empire must perform a great correction, seizing [the usurpers] and giving them no [license]; the state will then not be lost. If you do not exhaust the ultimate [principles] of Heaven, then those who would corrupt [the realm] will prosper again. However, if your executions and interdictions are not meet, then you will suffer calamity. To interdict or attack those deserving punishment or death you must put their states to ruin, incorporating them without presuming [undue] power. This is called Heavenly achievement.[44]

Similarly, the *Simafa* argues that war, used as punishment, is the best option for achieving pacification during a time of continual conflict. "To go to war in order to stop war—even though it is also war, it is permissible."[45]

In general, then, we see overall agreement among a variety of Zhanguo texts that martiality, applied in *pragmatic* fashion in the form of punishments, can serve a useful purpose in a period of military strife. And yet, the expositors of the prevailing solutions to the *wen/wu* problem looked at military punishment in different ways. Advocates of the *militarist* approach, as represented in the *Shangjunshu*, averred that "punishment produces force, force produces strength, strength produces awesomeness, and awesomeness produces kindness; thus kindness has its origin in force."[46] On the other hand, the compilers of the military treatises and related writings of the era looked on martial law, especially military punishment, in a generally *syncretist* way, as a tactically legitimate means for effecting order in the ranks and a strategically proper tool for bringing a return to harmony. As for the defenders of the *compartmentalist* solution, they tended to see military punishment as moral retribution for transgressions against civil order and the Way of Heaven-Earth-man and sought to downplay the value of martial means, even when such means may be unavoidable, in order to reacquire equilibrium.[47]

War Preparedness

Another facet of the *pragmatic* application worth examining is that of war preparedness. With the stress that law was given in the Zhanguo military treatises, it is not surprising that other concerns—agriculture and defense measures—would also have a prominent role in early military writings. The beginning chapter of the *Simafa* indicates, for instance:

> Thus, although a state may be large, if [its ruler] is fond of war, it will surely fail. And although the world may be at peace, if [a ruler] forgets [the ways of] war, he will surely be in danger. After the world is set at peace, the king is greatly pleased, [but] there is spring and autumn hunting, and the lords of the realm conduct maneuvers in spring and training exercises in autumn in order not to forget [the ways of] war.[48]

For its part, the *Weiliaozi*, in some passages, sees the necessities of war preparedness and legalistic control through a *metaphysical* prism.

> Directing war seems to be more obscure than Earth, more abstruse than Heaven; it is engendered in the void. Thus, in revealing it, important things should not be slighted, nor insignificant things magnified. [The ruler] should be knowledgeable about prohibiting [perversity], overlooking [small excesses], developing [ways of livelihood], and blocking [attempts to overcorrect]. He should show affection for refugees, assign land to those without it. For if the land is extensive and assigned for tilling, then the state will be prosperous, and if the people are numerous and regulated, then the state will be in order. With prosperity and order the people will not be mobilized [for war], armor will not be exhibited [in battle], and yet his awesomeness will control the world. Hence it is said, "Victory in war occurs in court."[49]

The above suggests that preparedness is really a matter of *wen*, rather than *wu*, that it is the actions of a ruler in governing a state that determine the strategic dispositions and circumstantial power on which the martial specialist relies. But this stress on the civil is not uniformly advocated throughout the *Weiliaozi*, nor is it a characteristic of the other Zhanguo military treatises. Evidence for this can be gleaned elsewhere in the *Weiliaozi* where there is a juxtaposition of the need for precise laws and the need for economic strength in a way that is comparable to the *militarist* doctrine of the *Shangjunshu*:

> If [the people of] the world do not devote themselves to agriculture, there will be no means of obtaining food; if they do not devote themselves to war, there will be no means for obtaining high status. But if the people willfully dedicate themselves to agriculture and war, there will be no adversary throughout the world.[50]

This point of view is likewise reflected in some portions of the *Sun Bin bingfa*, where war preparedness is said to require ruthless manipulation of wealth in order to control both the people's livelihood and the supply of goods.

> Only enlightened sovereigns and sages know when the people have insufficient life spans but a surfeit of goods, or have insufficient goods but overly long life spans. Thus, they are able to retain [their allegiance]. . . . When goods are abundant, then life is easy, and because it is easy, [the people] do not respect their superiors. When goods are scarce, then [life is difficult, and because it is difficult,] the world esteems [their masters]. Accordingly, this way to accumulate goods for the people is what I mean by accumulating goods; it has long been [the basis for] war . . . [missing text].[51]

These passages suggest a martial approach that is close to *militarism*. It is one we also see advocated in the "Quan xiu" 權脩, "You guan," and "Li zheng jiu bai jie" 立政九敗解 chapters of the *Guanzi*. In the latter chapter, for example, we read:

> If the ruler wishes merely to put war-making aside, then ministers and guests [i.e., guest experts] will not venture to speak of

> weapons. Thus, internally he will not know whether the state is in order or in confusion, and externally he will not know whether the lords of the realm are strong or weak. Accordingly, fortress walls will collapse and no one will repair them; armor will deteriorate and weapons will decay, and no one will maintain them. Hence, defense preparations will disintegrate.[52]

As for the *Shangjunshu*, it is well known that Shang Yang seemed bent on inculcating a Spartan-like obsession with martiality in a state's population, but war had an additional connotation for the Qin state minister. War preparedness appears in the *Shangjunshu* as a kind of antibiotic for warding off civil disease.

> If a state, when poor, applies itself to war, the poison will originate on the enemy's side, and not having the six parasites, it will certainly be strong. If a state, when rich, does not apply itself to war, the poison is transferred to its own interior, and having the six kinds of parasites, it will certainly be weak. . . . The six parasites are: rites and music, odes and history, moral culture and virtue, filial piety and brotherly love, sincerity and faith, uprightness and integrity, humaneness and righteousness, criticism of the army and being ashamed of fighting.[53]

Taking all the evidence into consideration, one may conclude that the military treatises, while occasionally adopting a pro-martial attitude, demonstrate concern for war preparedness from both civil and martial standpoints in a generally *syncretist* way, while proponents of a *militarist* approach consider war preparedness a matter of placing martial means at the forefront in order to protect the integrity and health of the state.

It is worth pointing out here that the widespread interest in economic strength in the military treatises is not coupled with numerous instructions on logistics. The *Zuozhuan* indicates that supply trains (*zi* 輜 or *zhong* 重) were used in Chunqiu times and that supply routes (*liangdao* 糧道) were important military targets.[54] But in spite of the intensification of war during the Zhanguo period, relatively little attention is paid in the military treatises to logistics as an issue coequal with tactical planning and execution. The compilers of the *Liutao* suggest that, unless campaigns last for ten days or less, defeat is inevitable, but they offer no supply system to obviate that limitation.[55] Likewise, the *Weiliaozi*, though recognizing the need for a balance between strong inner defense stores and the capabilities of outer support forces for a campaign, and speaking of the necessity for controlling commerce in defense-connected goods so that armies may be properly provisioned, goes no further to analyze the specific requirements for moving supplies and equipment.[56] Only six positions for supply and accounting are included in the *Liutao*'s listing of seventy-two staff officers, whereas thirty officers have some connection with intelligence operations or training; twenty-two positions concern tactical plans and operations; four are in charge of engineer projects; three have inspector general duties; and two have medical functions. The *Sunzi bingfa* refers in its definition of five fundamental factors in the execution of war to the necessity for regulating supply routes and rapid resupply of principal materiel items, and elsewhere the treatise warns against protracted wars for the exhaustion of resources that may occur. However, nowhere does the *Sunzi bingfa* place logistics on a par with tactical maneuvers, and the other military treatises are similarly reticent on the issue.[57] As will be discussed in Chapter 4, the Mohists contributed guidance regarding logistical planning for siege defense. Indeed, the basic principles and techniques they established for such operations were applied throughout most of later Chinese history. Nevertheless, it is arguable that the problems of army support were not prime subjects of interest for military thinkers in pre-imperial China.

One could explain this paucity of interest by citing the relatively primitive transportation technology of the time; the traditional reliance on provisions obtained from the surrounding countryside en route to battle or after a victory, rather than from centralized depots; and the continued dependence on individual procurement and maintenance of weapons and equipment. One other possible answer is that logistical problems simply were not deemed significant enough by the writers of the military treatises. Whatever the reason, it is a striking feature of military manuals throughout Chinese history that, except for discussions of inherited siege defense methods, little attention is given to the topic of supply planning.[58]

Intelligence Measures

Another *pragmatic* factor of war of considerable import during the Zhanguo era was the application of wide-ranging intelligence measures, including intelligence collection and analysis, deception, and covert action. What is critical to understand at the outset about this feature of military thought in early China is that it embraces not only the kinds of intelligence activities familiar to us in the modern world—acquisition and manipulation of information on palpable human actions and the battle environment—but also traditional mantic practices. As was discussed in Chapter 1, warfare was initially viewed in the Sinitic realm as a way to maintain or regain human harmony with the cosmic forces of Heaven and Earth. Based on this creed, military rites (*junli*) were seen to be on par with other types of rites that equally revered the powers of ancestral spirits and the cyclic processes of Heaven and Earth. Accordingly, appeals for spiritual guidance and interpretations of astronomical and meteorological events were considered just as important for military strategy as for civil government, and just as important for military tactics as human observations of enemy activities and intentions. As a result, military intelligence measures in the Zhanguo period and earlier comprised not only analysis and utilization of directly observed data on weather, terrain, and enemy dispositions, but also divination and prognostication techniques based on longstanding beliefs about the interconnectedness of Heaven, Earth, and man. This characteristic of military thought in early China was to become an enduring part of military strategy throughout the imperial era.[59]

Collection and Analysis

The first evidence we have of the development of this kind of broad-based approach to military intelligence comes from the employment of oracle-bone divination in the Shang dynasty as a means for intelligence collection and analysis. One of the purposes of such divination was to obtain advice from natural powers and ancestral spirits about whether a proposed military expedition should be launched.[60] The procedure called for a diviner to set forth a pair of "charges" (*mingci* 命辭 being the modern phrase for this technique), which stated the proposition under consideration in both positive and negative terms. The diviner then heated hollows made in cattle scapulae and tortoise shells, which produced cracks that were then interpreted, typically by the sovereign, as to which was favored by the Heavenly powers. In his study of oracle-bone inscriptions in the 1970s, David N. Keightley prepared the following reconstruction and translation as an example of a military-related divination from the initial period of this Shang practice.

Negative charge

> [Preface:] Crack-making on *xinyou* 辛酉 day, Que 㱿 divined:
>
> [Charge:] This season, the king should not follow Wang Cheng 望乘 to attack the Xia Wei 下危, [for if he does, we] will not perhaps receive assistance in this case.

Positive charge

> [Preface:] Crack-making on *xinyou* day, Que divined:
>
> [Charge:] This season, the king should follow Wang Cheng to attack the Xia Wei [for if he does, we] will receive assistance in this case.[61]

A version of the Shang tradition of oracle-bone divination continued to be used for military purposes into the Zhou dynasty and beyond, but was supplemented with a different form of spiritual intelligence assessment, now found in the *Zhouyi*, which relied on the casting of milfoil stalks to determine whether a proposed action was auspicious (*ji* 吉) or inauspicious (*xiong* 凶). Like its Shang counterpart, milfoil divination was employed to acquire guidance for a great variety of state affairs during the Zhou times and afterward, to include the likelihood of success or failure in battle. Indeed, according to a count made by modern scholar Ralph D. Sawyer, divination of both types was conducted for roughly one-fourth of the approximately sixty important prognostications recorded in the *Zuozhuan* in advance of battles, excluding those made on nonmilitary issues but with martial implications.[62]

Another source of intelligence for military leaders consisted of meteorological events as signs of the possible outcomes of martial actions. Under the year 641 BCE in the *Zuozhuan*, for example, we find the following account, which combined tortoise shell divination with meteorological omens:

> The attack of Xing 邢 [by Wei 衛] was in return for the siege of Tupu 菟圃.[63] At this time there was a great drought in Wei, and the marquis [of Wei] divined by the tortoise shell whether he should sacrifice to the hills and rivers, and obtained an

> unfavorable reply. The officer Ning Zhuang 甯莊 [of Wei] said, "Formerly there was a scarcity in Zhou, but after the conquest of Yin [i.e., Shang] there ensued an abundant year. Now, Xing acts without any regard to principle, and there is no leader among the princes. May not Heaven be wishing to employ Wei to punish Xing?" The marquis followed his advice, and immediately after the army was in motion it rained.[64]

Similar evidence of intelligence-gathering from Heavenly sources can be found in astronomical analyses in later Chinese histories, which probably hark back to techniques used in Chunqiu times or before. The "Treatise on Heavenly Offices" ("Tianguan shu" 天官書) in the *Shiji* and the "Treatise on Astronomy" ("Tianwen zhi" 天文志) in the *Hanshu* both provide abundant examples of astronomical configurations which, by oral tradition and analogical thinking, came to mean the imminent outbreak of warfare. To cite only a few of these as examples: "If the Fire Planet [*yinghuo* 熒火—that is, Mars] crosses the *Jiao* 角 lunar mansion (*xiu* 宿), there will be war."[65] "If the Five Stars (*wuxing* 五星) enter the *Zhen* 軫 lunar mansion, there will be a great military uprising."[66] "If the *Fuer* 附耳 star enters the *Bei* 卑 lunar mansion, there will be a military uprising."[67]

Along with the traditions of divination, other branches of military intelligence collection and analysis founded on meta-practical lore developed in the Zhanguo period and became even more important in Western Han and later times. One of these was the assessment of accumulations or auras of vital energy over a battlefield—a practice known as "looking for vital energy" (*wang qi* 望氣) or "watching for vital energy" (*hou qi* 侯氣). The "Bing zheng" 兵徵 chapter of the *Liutao*, for example, speaks of how the different behaviors of supposedly visible vital energy over enemy fortress cities could help one know the potential results of military engagements against such cities.

> When attacking or laying siege to a city, if the color of the vital energy surrounding the city is deadly grey, the city may be slaughtered. If the vital energy emanating from a city drifts north, the city may be subdued. If the vital energy emanating from a city drifts west, the city will surely surrender. If the vital energy emanating from a city drifts south, the city cannot be taken. If the vital energy emanating from a city drifts east, the city may not be attacked. If the vital energy emanating from

> a city drifts back into the city, the host of the city has already fled. If the vital energy emanating from a city covers one's own army, one's troops will surely become ill. If the vital energy emanating from a city drifts high up without stopping, one's army will have to be engaged a long time.[68]

A passage from the "Treatise on Heavenly Offices" in the *Shiji* also gives examples of this lore, which probably date to pre-Han times.

> The vital energy indicating infantry forces is white; that for earthly achievements is yellow. The vital energy indicating chariot forces ascends and descends moving about and then congealing. The vital energy indicating cavalry forces is low and widespread, while that for infantry forces is concentrated. When the front is low but the rear is high, forces are urgently moving; when the front is square and high while the rear is angular and low, the forces are withdrawing. If the vital energy is tranquil, their movement is leisurely; if the front is high and the rear is low, they will turn back without halting. When two constellations of vital energy encounter each other, the forces [indicated by the] lower one will conquer those signified by the higher, and those indicated by the angular will conquer those symbolized by the square.[69]

A silk manuscript found in tomb no. 3 at Mawangdui in 1973, which scholars have entitled "Assorted Astronomical and Meteorological Prognostications" (*Tianwen qi xiang za zhan* 天文氣象雜占), provides a look into another body of meta-practical lore with military applications that dates very probably from Zhanguo times and before. Besides addressing star, comet, and vital energy prognostication, the manuscript contains a series of depictions of clouds in the shapes of five four-legged animals, with the following explanatory text:

> [Dog (?):] If this appears over a city wall, the city will not be taken.
>
> [Pig:] If this appears over the army, the general will die.
>
> [Horse:] If this appears over the army, there will be victory.

> [Ox:] If this appears over the army, there will be defeat.
>
> [Deer:] If this appears over the army, it will take [or be taken].[70]

The traditions associated with such military-related cloud prognostication lore in the *Tianwen qi xiang za zhan* are further documented at some length in both the "Treatise on Heavenly Offices" in the *Shiji* and the "Treatise on Astronomy" in the *Hanshu*.[71]

Also of note during Zhanguo and earlier eras was a longstanding practice of using certain musical resonances to guide a commander in the use of troops against military targets. In the "Five Tones" ("Wu yin" 五音) chapter of the *Liutao*, for example, we find a description of the intelligence that can be acquired through the detection of musical sounds in the vicinity of enemy dispositions.[72]

> There are twelve pitch pipes (*lü* 律) of which the chief pitches are the five tones: *gong* 宮, *shang* 商, *jue* 角, *zhi* 徵, and *yu* 羽. These are the standard tones, which have not changed for myriad generations. The spiritual factors (*shen* 神) of the Five Phases [constitute] the constancy of the Way. [With them] one can know the enemy. Metal, wood, water, fire, and earth, each has its overcoming function which can be used in the attack. In antiquity, during the age of the Three Sovereigns (*san huang* 三皇), conditions of vacuity were used to control strength.[73] There were not yet any written characters, so in all cases [the sequence of] the Five Phases was followed. The way of the Five Phases [represents] the naturalness of Heaven and Earth. The divisions of the sexagenary cycle [symbolize] the subtle powers of the spirits. . . .
>
> The technique is to send out a light cavalryman to the enemy defense lines at midnight when the weather is clear, free of clouds and storms. When he is 900 paces (*bu*) away [from the defense lines], he places a pitch pipe close against his ear and alerts the enemy with a loud cry. There will be a sound [from the enemy] which will resonate very softly in the pitch pipe. If a *jue* tone resonates in the pipe, it corresponds to the White Tiger (*baihu*); if it is a *zhi* tone, it corresponds to the Black Martiality (*xuanwu* 玄武) [or the Black Tortoise (*xuangui* 玄龜)]; if it is a

> *shang* tone, it corresponds to the Vermilion Bird (*zhuque*); and if it is a *yu* tone, it corresponds to the hook formation (*gou zhen* 勾陣). When five pitch pipes give no resonating tone, it is the *gong* tone, which corresponds to Green Dragon (*qinglong*). These are the signs (*fu* 符) pertaining to the Five Phases, and they are evidence of assistance in victory as well as opportunities for either success or defeat.[74]

Yet another source of intelligence information and analysis for the conduct of war in the pre-Han period was based on a body of Yin-Yang lore about how the natural cycles of the world, from dark (*yin*) to light (*yang*) and again to dark, in all their manifestations can affect human destiny. This lore was sometimes combined with concurrent theories about the cycle of the Five Phases and the determination of how this cycle impacts on human activity. There are several titles given in the "Bing yinyang" 兵陰陽 section of the *Hanshu* "Treatise on Literature" that suggest such lore was being applied to the art of war in the pre-Han era, although we have few actual examples to consult.[75] Because of various archeological discoveries in the late twentieth century, however, this lacuna has been partially filled.

One such text is the *Didian* 地典, which was unearthed at Yinqueshan, Shandong Province, in 1972. This text, whose title refers to an ostensible assistant ("regulator of the earth") to the legendary Huangdi, was buried in the early Han period but may represent views also circulating in the pre-Han period.[76] While the work as we now have it is highly fragmentary, a reconstruction and English translation by Robin D.S. Yates in the early 1990s revealed a text that has connections with Huang-Lao thought and, among other things, provides advice to military commanders about how to use the Yin-Yang characteristics of terrain and the most cyclically appropriate times of the year to best military advantage.

> Have your back to a town and fight, you will capture the men in charge of their brigades. If you have a town on your left and [use] the fire formation, the enemy will run and flee away. If you fight with water on the right, this is called "following . . ." and it is a Grand General that you will capture. . . . This is the season when we carefully use heavy [soldiers]. For this reason, you use heavy soldiers first and [use] light [soldiers] afterwards, and [as a result] for every one gain, you will triple the success.

> You may attack and besiege armies: the armies will be captured, but you will not capture [any] towns—there will be pestilence [if you do].[77]

Another Yin-Yang text with military intelligence applications is the *Gai Lu* 蓋廬 (referring to King He Lu 闔廬 or He Lü 闔閭 of the state of Wu [r. 514–496 BCE]), a version of which was uncovered at Zhangjiashan, Hubei Province, in 1983. Like the *Didian*, the unearthed *Gai Lu* text dates to the early Han period; however, as Olivia Milburn has concluded, there is good reason to believe the *Gai Lu* (*He Lu/He Lü*) was already old in the Western Han dynasty.[78] This work is significant here because it contains military intelligence guidance that draws on both Five Phases and Yin-Yang ideas, as well as the military implications of observed auras of vital energy and astronomical events.

> Gai Lu [i.e., He Lu/He Lü] said: "As for the way of warfare, how do I accord with it? How do I contravene it? How do I advance it? How do I pull back from it?"
>
> Shen Xu 申胥 [i.e., Wu Zixu 伍子胥, chief minister in Wu] said: "It is the way of warfare that when doing battle in winter you should attack from the heights, when doing battle in summer you should attack from low ground, and in this way you will be victorious. The seasons say: when the barley is yellow you can do battle, when the leaves turn in autumn you can do battle, when snow falls in winter you can do battle. When virtue (*de*) rests in the phases of Earth or Wood, or when it is in Metal, you can do battle. With the sun behind you during the day and the moon behind you during the night, you can do battle. This is called utilizing the eight propitious moments of Heaven. When Jupiter is on the left and when the Five Phases are on the right, you can do battle. When the Vermilion Bird (*zhuque*) is in front, when the Heavenly Drum (*tian gu* 天鼓) is at your back, you can do battle. When the Green Dragon (*qinglong*) is on the left, and when the White Tiger (*baihu*) is on the right, you can do battle.
>
> . . . Do not attack [an army] with a flourishing aura (*qi*). . . . When Venus passes the moon, when Mars passes the moon, you can do battle. When there is a solar or a lunar eclipse, you can do battle. This is called following up the four

> disasters of heaven. If you do battle accordingly you are sure to be victorious."[79]

A third set of excavated documents having military intelligence applications are the *Xingde* 刑德 texts (A, B, and C) found in tomb no. 3 at Mawangdui, Hunan Province, in the early 1970s. These texts, whose content is based on a long history of concept development dating back to early Sinitic times, contains a complex analysis of the cycles associated with punishment (*xing*) and virtue (*de*), ideas that we have already addressed in considering the *metaphysical* approach to the *wen*/*wu* problem in Chapter 2. In these documents, the emphasis is on gauging through divination and other omen interpretation the appropriate spiritual timing for applying punishment and virtue to optimum martial effect.[80]

While we have spent time discussing intelligence measures based on spiritual and other meta-practical techniques, we should not forget that direct observations and assessments by human participants in warfare were also considered critical to military success. Indeed, there is a large body of evidence from pre-Han times of systematic analysis of observable, human actions that were sources of actionable intelligence on the battlefield. According to an account in the "Shenda" 慎大 chapter of the *Lüshi chunqiu*, the success of the Shang conquest of the Xia was due in part to the intelligence information provided by Yi Yin 伊尹, an official in the court of King Tang 湯王 of Shang, who was putatively sent secretly by the Shang king to the court of King Jie of Xia to obtain information about the latter's rule.[81] This story also appears in the "Using Spies" ("Yong jian" 用間) chapter of the *Sunzi bingfa*, along with the assertion that the Zhou conquest of Shang was partly due to the intelligence provided by Lü Shang 呂尚 (Tai Gong of Qi) when the latter defected to King Wen after having served in the court of King Zhou of Shang.[82]

For the Chunqiu period, the utility of human intelligence collection and analysis for battle planning is amply illustrated in the *Zuozhuan*. The earliest example can be found in a passage dated to the summer of 706 BCE, when the marquis of Qi and the earl of Zheng went to pay court in the small state of Ji 紀. According to the account, Qi and Zheng wanted to attack Ji, but "people in Ji knew [of their intent]" (*Ji ren zhi zhi* 紀人知之), suggesting that the Ji regime had collected intelligence in advance.[83] In a more explicitly stated instance, the *Zuozhuan* records that in advance of an engagement between armies of Jin and Qin in 645 BCE, the marquis of Jin dispatched one Han Jian 韓簡 to make observations of the Qin army. Han later returned to report that "their army is smaller than ours, but their men of fighting spirit (*dou shi* 鬪士) are double ours." When the marquis asked why this was so, Han pointed out that previously the marquis had thrice received Qin's benefits and yet had not returned the favor. As a result, resentment of Jin had built up in Qin. "Now when we are about to attack Jin, we are out of spirit and they are all ardor." In the end the marquis of Jin rejected this analysis, led his army against the Qin army, and was defeated.[84] As a third example from the *Zuozhuan*, we find under the year 630 BCE the first known reference to a reconnaissance force, which Jin forces used to make an incursion into Zheng "in order to see whether Zheng might or might not be attacked" (*yi guan qi ke gong yu fou* 以觀其可攻與否).[85]

A final instance from the Chunqiu period worth more extended description is the Battle of Yanling in 575 BCE, during which multiple forms of intelligence-gathering, based on both human activities and Heavenly signs, were employed. The action began when forces from the state of Jin moved against Zheng after the latter had switched its allegiance to Chu, and Chu forces, allied with troops from Man 蠻 tribes, marched to Zheng's aid. In the account of the battle in the *Zuozhuan* (Cheng 16), we are told that in advance of the engagement, Yao Gouer 姚句耳, a high official in Zheng who had been dispatched to Chu to seek the latter's assistance against Jin, reported his observations of the approaching Chu army to the Zheng court:

> Chu's forces are advancing rapidly but in passing through constricted terrain are not well ordered. When an army moves quickly it has lost its resolve; when disordered, strength of formation is sacrificed. When their resolve is lost and formations sacrificed, how will the engage in battle? I fear that they cannot be employed.

When the two armies finally confronted each other at Yanling on the last day of a lunar month—deemed an inauspicious day—Luan Shu 欒書, commander of Jin's center army, made the following intelligence assessment of the forces led by Chu, based on information on conditions in the Chu army ranks. "Chu's army is skittish, so if we solidify our fortifications and wait them out, within three days they will certainly withdraw. If we then suddenly attack their retreating forces, victory will be inevitable." Xi Zhi 郤至, a Jin official and military strategist, had a different intelligence analysis, based on apparently separately acquired intelligence.

> Chu has six gaps that cannot be left unexploited. Its two ministers detest each other; the king's troops are fatigued; Zheng's formations are not well ordered; the Man tribal regiments cannot be deployed; and in deploying for combat, Chu has not avoided the most inauspicious lunar day. When in formation they are noisy when uniting for deployment increasingly clamorous, every man looking behind him, no one having the will to fight. Since their veterans are not necessarily outstanding and they have offended the prohibitions of Heaven, we shall certainly conquer them.

As for the commanders of the Chu forces, they were also assembling intelligence information to determine their chances of beating their Jin counterparts. When the king of Chu ascended a mobile observation tower (lit., "bird's nest vehicle" [*chao che* 巢車]) to look out at Jin's armies, Bo Zhouli 伯州犁, a grand counselor (*dazai* 大宰) and defector from Jin, stood behind the king to provide a running commentary on what was happening in the Jin camp. Although Bo Zhouli confessed he could not foretell the outcome of the coming battle, his informed observations of activities in the Jin ranks evidently helped the Chu forces in making tactical judgments.

Meanwhile, back on the Jin side, the marquis of Jin performed a divination by milfoil to ascertain the prospects for the impending engagement. The scribe (*shi* 史) interpreted the results as auspicious. "You have encountered the hexagram *fu* 復 [i.e., "return"], whose implications are that a southern state will shrink, there will be a shot, and the king of the state will be hit in the eye." As a complement to this analysis, Lü Qi 呂錡 [i.e., Wei Qi 魏錡], a general in the Jin forces, had a dream before the battle in which he shot at the moon during the battle and hit it, but after withdrawing from the scene he became mired in mud. When a dream interpreter was summoned to explain the vision, Lü was advised: "The sun represents the royal surname of Ji 姬 [also the surname of the Jin ruling house], while those of different surnames [such as Chu] are the moon. That is certainly the king of Chu. You will shoot and hit him, but in withdrawing you will be mired down in mud and also die." We are later told in the *Zuozhuan* that the dream omen and the milfoil divination interpretation proved accurate. In the end, the Jin forces were victorious in their battle with the Chu alliance, retaining their dominance, at least for a time, among the Zhou states.

When we reach the Zhanguo period, the acceleration in warfare increased the need for effective employment of intelligence measures. We have already seen in the *Liutao* that four categories of men specializing in intelligence training, information collection, deception, psychological warfare, and sabotage were seen to be needed to prosecute effective military action. In addition, the *Sunzi bingfa* provides a list of five different kinds of spies (*jian* 間) that should be at a general's disposal for carrying out intelligence collection, as well as offensive counterintelligence operations. These include local agents (*xiang jian* 鄉間), who are secretly recruited from an enemy's country; inside agents (*nei jian* 內間), who are covertly hired agents from within an enemy's officialdom; turned agents (*fan jian* 反間), who are enemy spies secretly turned back to infiltrate their former masters, either with or without the spies' knowledge; dead agents (*si jian* 死間), who are purposely given fabricated information to deceive an enemy and then may be killed by the enemy when the information is discovered to be false; and live agents (*sheng jian* 生間), who collect information from an enemy and return safely to report their findings.[86]

Even as pro-active intelligence collection is stressed in the relevant sources, also important in the Zhanguo military treatises is advice about utilizing defensive counterintelligence and security measures to protect one's forces against infiltration by enemy spies and leaks of military information. Besides the general imposition of strict military regulations, stringent communication procedures must be enforced to prevent an enemy force from learning one's dispositions and intentions. The "Secret Tallies" ("Yin fu" 陰符) chapter of the *Liutao*, for example, gives Tai Gong's ostensible advice to King Wu of Zhou about the use of eight different tallies for transmitting certain battle plans or conditions from a distance. Each of the tallies bears no inscription but has a prescribed length that equates to a specific, preset battle action or situation.[87] Further, Tai Gong putatively counsels King Wu in the "Secret Letters" ("Yin shu" 陰書) chapter of the *Liutao* that if a more complex message needs to be sent to higher authority from a distance, one should divide the message into three parts, each unintelligible in isolation from the others, and send the three parts via three different messengers, thereby preserving the secrecy of the entire message.[88]

Regarding the collection and analysis of field intelligence for military planning in the Zhanguo period, the military treatises provide lengthy compilations of human intelligence indicators that were probably based on many years of inherited battlefield experience. The "Xing jun" 行軍 chapter of the *Sunzi bingfa*, for example, has several pieces of guidance regarding the meanings of various enemy activities. To cite only a few:

> When the trees are seen to move the enemy is advancing.
>
> When many obstacles have been placed in the undergrowth, it is for the purpose of deception.
>
> When birds rise in flight, it is a sign that the enemy is lying in ambush; when wild animals are startled and flee, the enemy is trying to take you unaware.
>
> Dust spurting upward in high straight columns indicates the approach of chariots. When it hangs low and is widespread, infantry is approaching. When dust rises in scattered areas, the enemy is bringing in firewood, and when there are numerous small patches which seem to come and go, the enemy is encamping the army.[89]

Similarly, the "Liao di" 料敵 chapter of the *Wuzi* lists eight conditions in which a general may defeat an enemy force without performing divination, as well as six circumstances in which a commander should not attack an enemy force, even without performing divination.[90] Also, the "Jiang shi" 將失 chapter of the *Sun Bin bingfa* lists thirty-two situations in which the commander of an enemy force can be defeated. To list but a few of these:

> If he constantly wrangles over right and wrong and in planning affairs is argumentative and disputatious, he can be defeated.
>
> If the sun is setting and the road is long while the masses are dispirited, he can be defeated.
>
> If in engaging in battle, he is concerned about the front, and the rear is therefore empty; or he is concerned about the rear, and the front is therefore empty; or he is concerned about the left, and the right is therefore empty; or he is concerned about the right, and the left is therefore empty, then by being filled with worry to engage in battle, he can be defeated.[91]

To recapitulate, the theory and practice of military intelligence collection and analysis in early China involved the acquisition and interpretation of information from all three dimensions of the Sinitic cosmos, namely, Heaven,

Earth, and man. By relying on this all-source approach, and making use of his psychical and command powers, a sage-general could manipulate the knowledge—that is, the vital energy—he had acquired, while also employing both defensive and offensive counterintelligence measures to thwart and pervert reciprocal information-gathering efforts by the enemy.

Deception and Covert Action

When it comes to deception and covert action measures in war during Zhanguo times, the available sources provide abundant evidence. Such devices as bribes, assassins, and sex had long been practiced during Zhou times and before as means for achieving certain state or personal goals, and military forms of these clandestine activities carried over to the prosecution of war, as shown in our consideration of the deceptive methods advocated in the *Guiguzi* and the military treatises in Chapter 2. To illustrate this trend in the Zhanguo period, we turn to one of the most famous military engagements of the era: the defense waged in 279 BCE by Tian Dan 田單 (fl. third century BCE), commander of forces in Jimo 即墨, in the state of Qi, against a siege by forces of the northern state of Yan 燕, Qi's chief rival during the early third century BCE.

As background to this event, forces from Yan under the command of Yue Yi, and in league with armies from other states, attacked Qi in 285 BCE, following the latter's costly attack on the state of Song to its south. In 284 BCE, Qi's forces were defeated by Yue Yi, and King Min 湣 of Qi was forced to flee the state. Yue Yi then pursued Qi's remaining forces to the Qi capital of Linzi 臨淄, where he plundered the city's treasures and destroyed its palaces and ancestral temples. The rest of the state of Qi was eventually subjugated by Yan, with the exception of two walled cities, Ju 莒 and Jimo, which still held out against the Yan incursion. Three years passed, and still the two cities did not submit. In the meantime King Zhao 昭 of Yan died and was succeeded by his son, King Hui 惠. Tian Dan thereafter sent a turned agent (*fan jian*) to the court of the new king charged with exploiting a rift that had developed between King Hui and Yue Yi in order to spread a rumor that Yue was intending to defect from Yan and establish himself as king in Qi. Believing the false accusation, King Hui replaced Yue Yi as general in chief in Qi with a new commander, Qi Jie 騎劫, who was a less capable, overly self-confident general whom Tian Dan thought he could defeat.

After this successful maneuver, Tian Dan proceeded to give the new Yan general the impression that Jimo was about to surrender, while at the same time taking steps to inflame the anger of Jimo's residents against a possible Yan occupation of the city. As told in Tian Dan's biography ("Tian Dan liezhuan" 田單列傳) in the *Shiji*, these steps were designed and executed with deliberate ruthlessness.

> Subsequently, [Tian Dan] publicly announced: "The only thing I fear is that Yan's army might cut off the noses of our countrymen who have fallen captive and then parade them in front of us. If they then engaged us in battle, Jimo would be defeated." Yan's soldiers heard about this and acted accordingly. When the city's inhabitants saw all the prisoners who had surrendered from Qi with their noses cut off, they were completely enraged and mounted a solid defense fearing only that they might be captured. . . .
>
> Tian Dan also let loose turned agents who said: "The only thing that Yan's soldiers fear is that you will excavate the graves outside the city and disgrace our ancestors. This would turn our hearts cold." Yan's army thoroughly excavated the mounds and graves and burned the dead. Witnessing it from atop the city walls, the people of Jimo all cried and wept, and wanted to rush forth to engage in battle. Thus their anger increased tenfold. . . .
>
> Tian Dan also gathered up the people's gold, accumulating a thousand ounces, and had Jimo's rich families send it out to Yan's generals, saying, "When Jimo surrenders, we hope that you will not plunder the homes of our clans or make prisoners of our wives and concubines, but let us be in peace." Yan's generals were overjoyed and agreed to it. From this Yan's army was increasingly lax.[92]

After employing these devious means both to degrade the martial will of his Yan foe and ignite the fighting spirit of the people of Jimo, Tian Dan then used a unique form of attack to break out of the siege. Herding up more than one thousand cattle from within the city, he had the beasts decorated with red silken cloth and five-colored dragon markings (*wu cai long wen* 五彩龍文), attached naked blades to their horns, and bound reeds soaked in fat to their tails. Then, one night, he set the cattle's prepared tails afire and released the beasts through prepared holes in the city walls toward the Yan encampments, followed by a force of five thousand soldiers. When their rears grew hot, the cattle became enraged and raced into the midst of the Yan army. Thrown into confusion by the panicked cattle with their blazing tails, the Yan troops were unprepared to fight back against the subsequent onslaught from Tian Dan's forces, whose attack was supported by a fearsome clamor from the beating of bronze implements by the citizens of Jimo. The Yan commander, Qi Jie, was killed in the melee, and Tian Dan later followed up on his victory at Jimo to recapture all the Qi cities earlier taken by Yan, thereby reestablishing Qi in its former territory.[93]

Views of Military Thinkers

Having briefly examined the main features of military intelligence measures used in the pre-imperial era, what can be said about their significance for military thought in early China? More precisely, how did Zhanguo military thinkers fit these various practical and meta-practical intelligence measures into their views about the underlying principles of war? The answers to these questions are varied, depending on the sources, but in general we can say two things. First, Zhanguo military thinkers believed intelligence measures afforded the *metaphysical* sage-general a *pragmatic* means to detect and manipulate the vital energy of the dispositions and circumstantial power of his adversary while preventing the detection and manipulation of his own army's vital energy. Second, the kind of deception and covert action seen in the siege of Jimo offered a way for a sage-general to more efficiently achieve civil peace—that is, to resolve the *wen/wu* problem at least in particular situations. After the Western Zhou, as war became increasingly de-ritualized, new methods were required to temper the severity of conflict and thus take on the role that military rites once played. Devious intelligence measures became one of those means. Various Zhanguo objectors to war, many of whom will be discussed in the next chapter, expressed their distaste for the incivility that had become a regular feature of Warring States battles. But, ironically, they were essentially decrying what could be considered civil measures that involved no confrontation of troops and, in the end, reduced the harshness of armed conflict. In effect, deception measures, even if taken as acts of war, mitigated the harmful effects of war and thus ultimately constituted a positive factor in an otherwise socially destructive activity. Thus it was that the *Liutao* described these deception measures as "civil attack" (*wen fa* 文伐)."[94]

This is not to say that Zhanguo theorists were united in their opinions about the usefulness of all types of intelligence methods being used during the period. Some considered devious methods alone to be insufficient to win victory. The *Weiliaozi*, in particular, makes it plain that "crooked victories" (*qu sheng* 曲勝), achieved only through deception, are imperfect models for the general. Instead, a general must cultivate a more comprehensive command power (*quan*) that allows him to assess accurately the strengths and weaknesses of a given military situation before taking martial action. With such command power he can manipulate a situation at will and so achieve "complete victories" (*quan sheng* 全勝).[95]

The Zhanguo military treatises were also not unanimous on the question of using omens and prognostication to chart military plans. In spite of the above quotations from the "Bing zheng" and "Wu yin" chapters of the *Liutao*, opinion in the military treatises of the Warring States period regarding such methods ranges from outright disdain to only partial acceptance. At one extreme, the *Weiliaozi* is decidedly opposed to astronomical and other kinds of prognostications.

> King Hui 惠王 of Liang 梁 asked Weiliaozi: "Huangdi could use punishments and virtue to win a hundred victories. Is that possible?"
>
> Weiliaozi replied: "He used punishments to attack and virtue to defend, and not what are called celestial influences, calendrical reckoning, Yin-Yang analysis, or [superstitions about] one's orientation. Huangdi [was concerned] only with human actions. Now, what if there were fortress walls that could be attacked neither from east and west nor from north and south? How could one, by according with proper timing, not surmount [the walls] from any of the four directions? On the contrary, it could not be taken, because the walls were high, the moats deep, the [enemy's] weapons prepared, their goods and provisions in great abundance, and their soldiers unified into a plan of battle. If the walls had been low, the moats shallow, and the defenses weak, [the fortress] would have been taken. From this we see that celestial influences and calendrical reckoning are inferior to human action."[96]

With regard to the question of applying cosmologies, such as Yin-Yang divination and Five Phases theory, to military tactics, the military treatises likewise provide little evidence of acceptance. The *Sunzi bingfa* uses the terms *yin* and *yang*, either singly or in conjunction, but without any suggestion that divination based on Yin-Yang principles has a practical application to military decision making.[97] Also, the "Xu shi" 虛實 chapter of the *Sunzi bingfa* refers to Five Phases theory but does not provide any examples of its practical application to battle tactics: "Thus, the Five Phases have no constant overcomings, and the four seasons have no constant positions."[98] Likewise, the *Wuzi* has only one passage—the one cited earlier concerning battle formations—indicating any interest in the applications of Yin-Yang and Five Phases theories to military strategy.[99] The *Simafa* manifests some affirmation of the importance of the Five Phases in the "Tianzi zhi yi" 天子之義 chapter: "The black of Xia [showed] the direction pertaining to man; the white of Yin [i.e., Shang, showed] the righteousness pertaining to Heaven; and the yellow of Zhou [showed] the Way pertaining to Earth." However, no direct impact of these correlatives for battlefield maneuvers is evident.[100] The *Sun Bin bingfa* contains more mentions of Five Phases theory than its counterpart military treatises, but the references are still few and, in some cases, anomalous. In the "Qi zheng" 奇正 chapter at the end of the work, the Five Phases are cited as constituting a model of war in which natural and successive overcomings are said to be a basis for martial activity. The work also includes a passage that seems to derive from Five Phases theory, but this passage postulates only four phases, in contradiction to traditional beliefs: "The overcomings of the five soils are: green overcomes yellow; yellow overcomes black; black overcomes white; and white overcomes green."[101]

Thus, where Yin-Yang and Five Phases ideas appear in the military treatises of the Zhanguo period, they are generally the naturalistic conceptions that had been slowly developing since Chunqiu times and earlier. There is little evidence of influences from the synthesis of these two streams of thought that Zou Yan 鄒衍 (305–ca. 240 BCE) was developing in the pre-Qin era. On the other hand, as we have suggested, military prognostication lore in general prospered during the Han dynasty and became a permanent feature of Chinese military thought in the imperial era.[102]

To sum up, Zhanguo military thinkers lay great stress on intelligence measures in general as a crucial tool of war, since they represented a useful means for ensuring a successful outcome to military confrontations that also facilitated the achievement of ultimate civil stability. At the same time, many of these thinkers were skeptical of some of the divination and other philosophical constructs being used to collect and analyze intelligence information for military purposes. To that extent, debate continued on how to employ military intelligence measures to resolve the *wen*/*wu* problem.

Conclusion

In examining various *pragmatic* applications in Zhanguo military thought, an attempt has been made in this chapter to analyze the connections between the practical and meta-practical in military lore and the *metaphysical* perspective presented in Chapter 2, as well as the *militarist* and *syncretist* solutions to the *wen/wu* problem discussed in Chapter 1. Along the way we have noted the confluences that existed between these elements and their manifestations during the Zhanguo period in organizational methods, administrative techniques, legal strictures, war preparedness, and intelligence measures. In general, we see a combination of real-world military techniques and abstract philosophical theories that is rare in the whole history of military thought.

Our job for the Zhanguo period is not done, however. What we now must examine is the *ethical* perspective, which in a time of brutal warfare such as the Zhanguo period began to grow in importance as writers started to lodge systematic moral arguments against the dire consequences of conducting war to preserve civil order. The next chapter will be devoted to examining these various criticisms of martiality and their meaning for the *compartmentalist* and other solutions being argued in the ongoing *wen/wu* debate.

Chapter 4

The Moral Dimension of War

As earlier outlined, the *compartmentalist* solution to the perennial *wen/wu* problem in Chinese history was founded on the theory that martiality posed such a dangerous threat to the human order that its use, even though sometimes necessary, should be strictly separated from the administration of civil government. The *compartmentalist* approach based its plausibility on a number of different ingredients, including *metaphysical* arguments. Its emphasis, however, was on applying *ethical* criteria to the problem of aggression. That is, the stress was on defining certain moral principles of behavior that should condition and channel the use of martial force so that it would not impinge on the maintenance of a civil society. Over time, this *compartmentalist* formulation, combined with the *ethical* perspective, significantly influenced perceptions of how to conduct martial activity. Indeed, this moralistic interpretation, though only one of other competing viewpoints on *wen/wu* in the pre-Qin period, became so prominent after Western Han that it became an orthodox solution for succeeding regimes.

Because the Ruists were the chief objectors to war in the pre-Qin period and later, they will be the principal subject of this chapter. However, along with them were other contributors, such as those masters who we have come to know as Laozi 老子, Yanzi 晏子, Mozi 墨子, and Songzi 宋子, as well as some of the compilers of the Zhanguo military treatises. Together they helped to form a *compartmentalist-ethical* view of *wen/wu* that exerted a lasting impact in Chinese history.

Laozi

We begin with the putative founder of philosophical Daoism, Laozi.[1] In a number of places in the *Daodejing*, attributed to Laozi, appear warnings of the dangers inherent in military action, particularly the probability of economic loss and government demoralization. And in every such passage the work argues in favor of avoiding warfare if at all possible, for otherwise one may be beset with militaristic delusions. War, after all, is an occasion of mourning, not a time for victory shouts.

> One who assists the ruler of men by means of the Way does not intimidate the empire by a show of arms. This is something which is liable to rebound. Where troops have encamped, there will brambles grow; in the wake of a mighty army bad harvests follow without fail. One who is good aims only at bringing his campaign to a conclusion and dares not thereby intimidate. Bring it to a conclusion, but do not boast; bring it to a conclusion, but do not be arrogant; bring it to a conclusion, but only when there is no choice; bring it to a conclusion, but do not intimidate.[2]

The best method of waging battle, according to the *Daodejing*, is by non-contention.

> One who excels as a warrior does not appear formidable; one who excels in fighting is never roused in anger; one who excels in defeating his enemy does not join issue; one who excels in employing others humbles himself before them. This is known as the virtue of non-contention; this is known as making use of the efforts of others; this is known as matching the sublimity of Heaven.[3]

Through non-contention one evades disaster and conflict disappears.

> I have heard it said that one who excels in safeguarding his own life does not meet with rhinoceros or tiger when traveling on land nor is he touched by weapons when charging into an army. There is nowhere for the tiger to place its claws; there is nowhere for the weapon to lodge its blade. Why is this so? Because for him there is no realm of death.[4]

In sum, one cannot call the compilers of the *Daodejing* strict adherents of *compartmentalism*, for they would not even permit the development of *wen* in their ideal, primitive society. Nonetheless, they were committed to the avoidance of *wu*, and they lent support to the notion that martial activity should be placed outside the realm of human social choice.[5]

Kongzi

Kongzi 孔子 (Confucius) (551–479 BCE), who has often been perceived as the arch-advocate of civility, actually took a more conciliatory or realistic view of martial activity. As he is quoted in the *Lunyu* 論語, a collection of sayings attributed to Kongzi and his disciples, war is so dangerous to society that it deserves one's close scrutiny.[6]

> The things in reference to which the Master exercised the greatest caution were fasting, war, and sickness.[7]
>
> Zilu 子路 [a disciple of Kongzi] said: "If you had the conduct of the armies of a great state, whom would you have to act with you?"
>
> The Master [Kongzi] said: "I would not have him to act with me who would attack a tiger unarmed or cross a river without a boat, dying without any regret. My associate must be the man who proceeds to action full of solicitude, who is fond of adjusting his plans and then carrying them into execution."[8]
>
> The Master said, "Let a good man teach the people seven years and they may then likewise be employed in war."[9]
>
> The Master said, "To lead an uninstructed people to war is to throw them away."[10]

In furtherance of his call for great caution in matters of war, Kongzi conjured up the ceremonial nature of *wu* in Western Zhou times and, to some extent, in his own day, and viewed the judicious conduct of war alongside rites and music (*liyue* 禮樂)—the two most cherished features of his ideal state.

> Kongzi said, "When good government prevails in the realm, ceremonies, music, and punitive military expeditions proceed from the king. When bad government prevails in the realm, ceremonies, music, and punitive military expeditions proceed from the lords of the realm. When these things proceed from the lords of the realm, as a rule the cases will be few in which they do not lose their power in ten generations. When they

> proceed from the senior officers [of the lords of the realm, as a rule] the cases will be few in which they do not lose their power in five generations. When the associated officials of the senior officers hold in their grasp the orders of the state, [as a rule] the cases will be few in which they do not lose their power in three generations."[11]

At the same time, Kongzi is said to have confessed that he knew little of the ways of war: "Lord Ling 靈公 of Wei 魏 asked Kongzi about tactics. Kongzi replied, 'I have heard all about sacrificial vessels, but I have not learned military matters.' "[12]

There is also in the *Lunyu* a suggestion about the inner will of the common soldier in battle, borne of a trust in the goodness of his leaders that later Ruists were to hail as the chief motive of military success. Here, the moral intent of man is applied to military situations, and it is the importance of this moral commitment that is underscored in the famous *Lunyu* passage on priorities in state defenses.

> Zigong 子貢 [a disciple of Kongzi] asked about government. The Master [Kongzi] said, "[The requisites of government are] that there be sufficiency of food, sufficiency of military equipment, and confidence of the people in their ruler."
>
> Zigong said, "If it cannot be helped, and one of these must be dispensed with, which of the three should be foregone first?"
>
> "Military equipment," said the Master.
>
> Zigong [again] asked, "If it cannot be helped, and one of the remaining two must be dispensed with, which of them should be foregone?"
>
> The Master answered: "Part with the food. From of old, death has been the lot of all men, but if the people have no faith [in their rulers], there is no standing [for the state]."[13]

Yanzi

While Kongzi set what became the foundation for *ethical* arguments regarding martiality and civility, the *Lunyu* offers us little in elaboration of his views. For a more expansive treatment we must turn to other commentators. One such commentator, who lived in Kongzi's own time, was Yanzi 晏子 (d. 500

BCE; born Yan Ying 晏嬰), a long-serving senior minister of the state of Qi during the sixth century BCE. In the *Yanzi chunqiu* 晏子春秋, a work consisting of anecdotes about Yanzi collected during the pre-Han and early Han periods, we find Yanzi objecting to excessive martiality and advocating righteousness (*yi*) in the prosecution of war as well as the cultivation of harmonious allegiance to a state ruler among the common people.[14] Yanzi's general philosophy toward the use of martial force is epitomized in an anecdote in which Yanzi counseled Lord Jing 景公 of Qi (r. 548–490 BCE) about the wisdom of a contemplated attack on Lu.

> Having raised an army to attack Lu, Lord Jing asked Yanzi about this plan. Yanzi replied: "This is not acceptable. The lord of Lu is fond of righteousness and the people of Lu support him. Those rulers who are fond of righteousness will enjoy peace, and those who are supported by their people will enjoy harmony. The rule of Bo Qin 伯禽 [designated lord of Lu during the initial years of the Western Zhou] survives there. Thus, an attack is not acceptable. To attack a state where righteousness prevails is not auspicious, and to endanger a state where peace prevails will surely lead to disaster. Moreover, I have heard that an attacking ruler must have sufficient virtue to bring peace to his own state and sufficient uprightness to bring harmony to his own people. Only after his own state is secure and his own people are in harmony may he raise an army to wage war on an evil regime. Today, Your Lordship craves drink and harbors evil ways. Thus, you do not have the virtue to make the state secure. You impose onerous taxes and are intent on the execution of your edicts. Thus, you do not have what it takes to bring harmony to the people. Without the virtue to make the state secure, the state will be in danger, and without the good government to bring harmony to the people, the state will be in disorder. To want to attack a secure and harmonious state without first averting danger and disorder in one's own state is not acceptable. It would be better to cultivate good government in one's own state and wait for the downfall of the lord of another state. When the lord of another state has departed from good government, causing resentment among those below him—only then may you attack. Hence, where righteousness prevails, benefits are many and opponents are few; and where benefits are many, the people are happy."[15]

Rather than pointing out the dangers of attacking an enemy with superior force, Yanzi spoke of avoiding military action against the righteous. It is government policies, he asserted, not combat orders that are of critical importance in military encounters. While the method of attacking with correlative forces is still valid, Yanzi has recast this method in *ethical* terms. His message is that war may be initiated against another state only when the attacking state is united and strong, and only in a sincere effort to reestablish political-social integration in an otherwise divided country.[16]

Another anecdote from the *Yanzi chunqiu* shows Yanzi's frequent borrowing of putative Shang or Western Zhou normative values to substantiate his Chunqiu-era view of the proper use of martiality. In the story, Lord Jing of Qi is preparing to attack the state of Song to the south. As the lord's army crosses Mount Tai 泰, a spiritual mountain situated in the southern part of Qi, the lord has a dream in which two men stand before him in such a rage that the lord grows afraid. When the lord awakens, he calls for a dream interpreter, who says that the lord's dream is a sign the lord has failed to perform the proper rites of sacrifice to the spirit of Mount Tai. Later, however, Yanzi arrives before the lord and rebuts this interpretation, saying that the two men in Lord Jing's dream are actually King Tang of Shang and Yi Yin, whose descendants were allowed by the Zhou founders to establish themselves in Song. As Yanzi goes on to explain:

> "Tang, Tai Jia 太甲, Wu Ding 武丁, and Zu Yi 祖乙 were all accomplished lords of the kingdom, and it would not have been right for them to have no descendants. Today such descendants are only in Song, and yet you have come to attack Song. As a result, Tang and Yi Yin are angry. I advise that you disperse the army and allow Song to remain at peace."[17]
>
> Lord Jing did not accept Yanzi's advice and moved on to attack Song.
>
> Yanzi said: "Attacking a blameless state and thereby angering its spirits, choosing not to alter one's conduct in an effort to maintain good relations, and advancing one's troops only to invite disaster—these are things I do not know about. If Your Lordship's army advances, then it will surely meet disaster."[18]

Yanzi's words are vindicated when Lord Jing's troops suffer losses of generals and equipment even before he engaged Song forces and he had to disperse his army and withdraw to the Qi capital.

In this *Yanzi chunqiu* anecdote Yanzi appears to invoke archaic notions of military rites to support his argument against using military force to attack a virtuous state. As we previously indicated, the inheritance of Western Zhou rules for military conduct had its effects on later tactics and strategy, but the evolution of these ritual standards along with their spiritual antecedents into an *ethical* policy for war during later times, when the practice of older military rites was becoming obsolete, was due in part to thinkers like Yanzi who sought to preserve those ancient norms in order to curb martial excesses.

Mengzi

As the intensity of war in Zhanguo times grew, some thinkers of the period began paying more attention to developing a moral philosophy to obviate violence. As a result, the roles of righteousness and harmonious government with respect to martial activity became more defined. One example of this effort can be seen in the views of Mengzi 孟子 (Mencius) (fl. late fourth century BCE; born Meng Ke 孟軻), who gave a more complex philosophical explication of the *ethical* perspective on war than what appears in the *Yanzi chunqiu*. Beyond rejection of unwarranted military activity on moral grounds, Mengzi sometimes expressed a negativism that rivaled that found in the *Daodejing*: "There are men who say, 'I am skillful at marshaling troops, I am skillful at conducting a battle!' They are great criminals."[19] In the "Li Lou shang" 離婁 上 chapter of the *Mengzi*, he was even more vehement.

> "Kongzi rejected those who enriched rulers not given to the practice of humane government. How much more would he reject those who do their best to wage war on their behalf. In wars to gain land, the dead fill the plains; in wars to gain cities, the dead fill the cities. This is known as showing the land the way to devour human flesh. Death is too light a punishment for such men. Hence those skilled in war should suffer the most severe punishments; those who secure alliances with other lords come next, and then come those who open up wasteland and increase the yield of the soil."[20]

But this opposition to *militarism*, rather than being based on the primitivism of the *Daodejing*, is founded on the supreme importance of moral will in government and war, particularly the former. In Mengzi's view, the ruler, not the general, should be the focus of military affairs, for it is the practice of moral principles by the ruler, not the general, which prevents martial confrontations. "If the ruler of a state loves humaneness, he will have no enemy in the kingdom."[21] Further, a moral ruler will not subject his people to unnecessary violence. "If it were merely taking the place from the one state to give it to the other, a humane man would not do it. How much less he will do so when the end is to be sought by the slaughter of men!"[22] Thus, it is through moral will that war is prevented, and it is by moral will that success in war, if waged, is achieved.

> When one by force subdues men, they do not submit to him in heart. [They submit because] their strength is not adequate [to resist]. When one subdues men by virtue, in their hearts' core they are pleased, and sincerely submit, as was the case with the seventy disciples in their submission to Kongzi.[23]

For Mengzi, it was not, as in the military treatises, the sage-general who effects an overcoming of the enemy. It is the ruler in his personal example, together with the cumulative will of his subjects, who decides issues of state such as war.

> The people of Qi attacked Yan and conquered it. King Xuan 宣王 [of Qi (r. 319–301 BCE)] said: "Some tell me not to take possession of it for myself, and some tell me to take possession of it. For a kingdom of ten thousand chariots to attack another of ten thousand chariots and complete the conquest of it in fifty days is an achievement beyond [mere] human strength. If I do not take possession of it, calamities from Heaven will surely come upon me. What do you say to my taking possession of it?"
>
> Mengzi replied: "If the people of Yan will be pleased with your taking possession of it, then do so. Among the ancients there was [one] who acted on this principle, namely, King Wu [of Zhou]. If the people of Yan will not be pleased with your taking possession of it, then do not do so. Among the ancients there was [one] who acted on this principle, namely, King Wen [of Zhou]."[24]

Mengzi's comparison with the Zhou founders was not simply rhetorical; his reference was made in full recognition of the inner power that masses of people have in deciding the outcomes of political-military campaigns. Later in the *Mengzi*, we find the following citation of the legend of the reception given to King Wu of Zhou by the population in eastern China.

> There being some who would not become the subjects [of Zhou, King Wu] proceeded to punish them on the east. He gave tranquility to their people, who [welcomed him] with baskets full of their black and yellow silks, [saying,] "From henceforth we shall serve the sovereign of [our dynasty of] Zhou, that we may be made happy by him." So they joined themselves, as subjects, to the great city of Zhou. Thus, the men of station [of Shang] took baskets full of black and yellow [silks] to meet the men of station of [Zhou], and the lower classes of the one met those of the other with baskets of rice and vessels of congee. [King Wu] saved the people from the midst of fire and water, seizing only their oppressors [and destroying them].[25]

Finally, three times in the *Mengzi* the legend of the sage-king Tang subduing his non-Sinitic neighbors is told to demonstrate how a ruler by right action in one arena can excite plaudits in another through moral induction.[26]

But what constitutes this popular will, and what are the specific contradictions or contradistinctions between Mengzi's *ethical* view and the *metaphysical* perspective? For an answer one may turn to the declaration at the beginning of the "Gongsun Chou xia" 公孫丑下 chapter of the *Mengzi*:

> Mengzi said, "Heavenly timing is not equal to Earthly advantage, and Earthly advantage is not equal to human harmony. [Imagine a city] with an inner wall of three *li* 里 in circumference and an outer wall of seven *li*. [The enemy] may surround and attack it, but they are not able to take it. Now to surround and attack it they must have Heavenly timing, and in such a case their not taking it is because Heavenly timing is not equal to Earthly advantage. [Imagine a city whose] walls are distinguished for their height and whose moats are distinguished for their depth, where the arms [of its defenders], offensive and defensive, are distinguished for their strength and sharpness, and the stores of rice and other grain are very large. [Yet it is obliged to] be given up and abandoned. This is because Earthly advantage is not equal to human harmony (*renhe* 人和). In accordance with these principles it is said, 'People are bounded in not by

> the limits of dikes and borders; a state is secured not by the strengths of mountains and rivers; the kingdom is overawed not by the sharpness [and strength] of arms.' He who finds the proper course has many to assist him. He who loses the proper course has few to assist him. When this—being assisted by few—reaches its extreme point, his own relations revolt from [the lord]. When being assisted by many reaches its highest point, the whole kingdom becomes obedient to [the ruler]. When one to whom the whole kingdom is prepared to be obedient attacks those from whom their own relations revolt, [what must be the result?] Therefore, the true ruler will prefer not to fight; but if he does fight, he will surely overcome."[27]

Whereas the sage-general of the military treatises, in accordance with the *metaphysical* view, considers Heavenly timing, Earthly advantage, and human harmony to be of equal importance, Mengzi in his battle estimates established a tripartite hierarchy, with the greatest value placed on an integration of human society. Without harmony among your followers to provide the support you need in combat you will not survive as ruler/general. From the *metaphysical* perspective, the concepts of turning points, dispositions, and circumstantial power are not as decisive for Mengzi as human vital energy. This is because for Mengzi, and most other thinkers who ascribed to a *compartmentalist* solution to the *wen/wu* problem, *ethical* commitments simply did not apply to nonhuman factors. Since their major concern was the effects of war on the human participants, it is human vital energy and the relationship of human vital energy to the ruler/general that is the critical determinant in the outcomes of martial events.

One of the most important expositions by Mengzi regarding the preeminence of human vital energy lies in the "Gongsun Chou shang" 公孫丑上 chapter of the *Mengzi*, in which Mengzi is quoted as outlining key conceptual relationships in a fashion that is useful in interpreting his views on *wen/wu*. The relevant section begins with a question about the unperturbed mind (*budong xin* 不動心) and how to attain it:

> [Gongsun Chou] asked, "Is there any way to an unperturbed mind?"
>
> [Mengzi replied:] "Yes. Beigong You 北宮黝 [a man of renowned bravery] had this way of nourishing his courage: He did not flinch from any strokes at his body. He did not turn

> his eyes aside from any threats at them. He considered that the slightest push from anyone was the same as if he were beaten [before the crowds] in the marketplace, and that what he would not receive from [a common man] in his loose, large garments of hair neither should he receive from a lord of ten thousand chariots. He viewed stabbing a lord of ten thousand chariots in the same way as stabbing a fellow dressed in cloth of hair. He feared not any of all the lords. A bad word addressed to him he always returned. Meng Shishe 孟施舍 [another man of renowned bravery] had this way of nourishing his courage: He said, 'Look upon not conquering and conquering in the same way. To measure the enemy and their advance and to calculate the chances of victory and then engage—this is to stand in awe of the opposing force. How can I make certain of conquering? I can only rise superior to all fear.' Meng Shishe resembled [Kongzi's disciple] Zengzi 曾子, while Beigong You resembled [Kongzi's disciple] Zixia 子夏. I do not know which of these men was superior in courage, but Meng Shishe attended to what was of greater importance. Formerly, Zengzi said to [Kongzi's disciple] Zixiang 子襄, 'Do you love courage? I heard an account of great courage from the Master [Kongzi]. [He said:] "If, on self-examination, I find that I am not upright, shall I not be in fear even of a poor man in his loose garments of hair-cloth? If, on self-examination, I find that I am upright, I will go forward against thousands and tens of thousands."' [Yet,] what Meng Shishe maintained, by being [concerned only with] his vital energy, was after all inferior to what Zengzi maintained, which was of the most importance."[28]

In the comparison of two exemplars of courage, Mengzi, in the end, seems to have given preference to a mode of behavior that goes beyond the mere control of vital energy and the absence of fear. He appears to laud the perfection of a moral vital energy, a kind of energy transformed by the normative mind, like that of Kongzi's disciple Zengzi, who exhibited a greater courage, a greater inner strength against outer resistance.[29] In his comparison of men of courage Mengzi implied that success in military combat is not a result of vital energy alone, or even, as in the *metaphysical* perspective, the optimum distribution and application of vital energy. Rather, it is the cultivation of an inner moral vital energy, which fortifies the individual, and presumably an entire military force, in waging battle. In other words, an "unperturbed mind," which reflects the presence of this moral vital energy, is a trait that both civil sage and sage-general can achieve.

The importance of the inward-looking nature of this self-preparation against aggression emerges from the following lines of a succeeding passage in the "Gongsun Chou shang" chapter of the *Mengzi* on the "unperturbed mind," in which Mengzi critiques a theory of moral training ascribed to the Zhanguo-era philosopher Gaozi 告子 (ca. 420–350 BCE; born Gao Buhai 告不害):

> [Gongsun Chou] inquired, "May I venture to ask an explanation from you, Master, of how you maintain an unperturbed mind, and how Gaozi does the same?"
>
> [Mengzi replied:] "Gaozi says, 'What cannot be attained in doctrinal words (*yan* 言) is not to be sought in the mind (*xin* 心), and what produces dissatisfaction in the mind is not to be helped by vital energy.' It is correct to say that when one cannot attain what one wants in the mind, one should not seek for satisfaction in vital energy, but it is not correct to say that when one cannot attain what one wants in doctrinal words, one should not seek satisfaction in the mind. The will (*zhi* 志) is the master of vital energy, while vital energy pervades and animates the body. The will is foremost and vital energy is subordinate to it. Therefore [I] say, 'Maintain firm the will and do not abuse vital energy.' "

Gaozi appears here to have endorsed the notion of a determinate doctrine (*yan*) outside of the normative mind, which supersedes in importance a person's individual capacity for moral reflection. Mengzi rejected this notion, opting instead for innate human aptitudes for moral development. In Mengzi's view, the will (*zhi*), or normative mind, is the source of true doctrine, since it is the will that transforms vital energy into normative reality. Consequently, one should firmly maintain the will, and at the same time not allow human vital energy to lose its capacity for actualizing the normative essence of the will.

What can be said, then, of the association between the will and human vital energy espoused by Mengzi as compared to the association between psychical power and vital energy in the *metaphysical* perspective? Gongsun Chou's further queries in the *Mengzi* assist in answering this question.

> [Gongsun Chou observed:] "You say that 'the will is foremost and vital energy is subordinate,' and that one should 'maintain firm the will, and not abuse vital energy.' What do you mean?"
>
> [Mengzi] replied: "When it is the will alone which is active, it moves vital energy. When it is vital energy alone which is active, it moves the will. Now, in the case of a man falling or running, that is [due to] vital energy, and yet it moves the mind."
>
> "I venture to ask," [said Gongsun Chou,] "wherein you, Master, surpass [Gaozi]."
>
> [Mengzi] replied: "I understand words. I am skillful in nourishing my vast, flowing vital energy (*haoran zhi qi* 浩然之氣)."
>
> [Gongsun Chou said], "I venture to ask what you mean by your vast, flowing vital energy?"
>
> "It is difficult to describe," [replied Mengzi]. "Vital energy is exceedingly great and exceedingly strong. Being nourished by rectitude (*zhi* 直) and sustaining no injury, it fills up all between Heaven and Earth. Vital energy is matched with righteousness and the Way. Without it, man is in a state of starvation. It is produced by the accumulation of righteous deeds; it is not obtained by incidental acts of righteousness. If in acting one is dissatisfied in the mind, then vital energy is starving."

In this passage, Mengzi seems to posit that vital energy and human nature (*xing* 性) are equivalent, and that from this equivalence one can draw connections between human nature and the normative mind—a mind that assigns moral values to human activities. For Mengzi, the vital energy that fills an individual responds completely to the innate inclinations or movements of the individual's will, and thus the results of these movements are the normative outcomes of human activities. It is one's will that ultimately determines outer events, acting through one's inner vital energy.[30]

This conception differs from the *metaphysical* perspective's relationship between psychical power and vital energy as evidenced in the military treatises. In the *metaphysical* perspective on the *wen*/*wu* problem psychical power is a morally neutral entity that metabolizes vital energy in ways consistent with an objective cosmic order. Furthermore, vital energy in the *metaphysical* perspective is not solely human, but applies as well to nonhuman entities. When psychical power is most developed in a sage-general, vital energy, wherever it may reside, is most easily metabolized.

Human events do not require the intermediate action of will upon the vital energy of that individual for those events to exist. Instead, psychical power functions directly with respect to all types of vital energy. The sage-general in the *metaphysical* perspective is as much concerned with personal cultivation of his abilities to function with psychical power as Mengzi was concerned with cultivating a normative mind. However, while the sage-general, from the *metaphysical* perspective, acts on vital energy as an objective, nonmoral reality, Mengzi, from the *ethical* perspective, seeks the cultivation of vital energy as part of a subjective, moral endowment.

It is this fundamental cleavage in the philosophical interpretation of vital energy and its guiding force that makes for the difference between Mengzi's view of action in the face of conflict and the *metaphysical* perspective on the *wen/wu* problem. For Mengzi, it is not concentrations of vital energy metabolized by a man of *wu* that determine one's decisions in martial situations. Rather, it is the concentrations of normative vital energy, transformed by a man of *wen*, that affect the outcomes of such situations.

Mengzi's interpretation may also be explained in an historical way. Although moral values associated with civil virtue were applied to warfare as far back as the Shang period, such a valuation was not predominant. As suggested in Chapter 1, the prevailing view in Western Zhou times was one of balance and reciprocality between martiality and civility and between virtue and punishments in resolving conflict. By Zhanguo times, however, philosophers such as Mengzi were reacting strongly to the growing strife and political cynicism of the time by devising arguments to invalidate that view. Such thinkers no longer accepted the justifications for *wen/wu* parity but judged that civil restraints, in the form of normative rules, were imperative to offset the surfeit of martiality in the Zhanguo environment. The Ruists were particularly active in this intellectual reaction, because as champions of what they believed to be early Zhou political values, they wished to reinvigorate the norms that were said to apply to martial activities in legendary times and reverse the trend toward an overwhelming martial state of affairs in the present. Mengzi and his followers participated in this revaluation by creating a wholly new pro-civil argument that relegated martiality to an inferior status.

One final ingredient in Mengzi's thinking about vital energy is worth mentioning here. In the latter part of the "Gongsun Chou shang" chapter of the *Mengzi*, the master is quoted as talking about the relationship between righteousness and vital energy as being an inner process, in which righteousness, along with the Way, must nourish (*yang* 養) vital energy, so that it never fails to actuate the normative mind. It is difficult to discern in the *Mengzi* what the precise relationships are between righteousness and will, or righteousness and vital energy. However, based on other passages in the work, righteousness appears to be a mode of guiding force that the will exerts on vital energy, which in turn becomes actualized in outward behavior.[31] By nourishing vital energy through this application of the will, it is possible to take possession of the world of men and, in the process, avoid conflict. It is even plausible to say that this implied connection by Mengzi between an application of the will and military behavior led to strong support for the notion of righteous war (*yibing* 義兵), a term that was first broached in the Zhanguo period and was the subject of much discussion in the early Han period.[32]

Xunzi

Moving on to Xunzi 荀子 (fl. late fourth century to mid–third century BCE; born Xun Kuang 荀况; also known as Xun Qing 荀卿 and Sun Qingzi 孫卿子), one also finds a normative approach to vital energy, as opposed to the amoral treatment of vital energy in the *metaphysical* perspective. In the case of Xunzi, however, the contrasts between these two views of martiality and civility are more definitive than with Mengzi. While there are varying opinions about the authenticity and origins of various chapters in the *Xunzi* 荀子, the "Yi bing" 議兵 chapter of the work, which appears to originate with Xunzi's followers, probably provides an accurate account of the master's views on the *wen*/*wu* problem.[33]

The chapter begins with a debate between Xunzi (Sun Qingzi) and the "Lord of Linwu" 臨武君 (lit., "lord of approaching warfare"). The latter speaks, rather inaccurately, on behalf of the amoral thought of the military treatises (especially the *Sunzi bingfa*), citing the need to observe Heavenly timing, Earthly advantage, and enemy dispositions and circumstantial power, and to use deception and stealth to achieve success. According to the "Lord of Linwu," there is no need to win the support of the people when these factors have been taken into account. Clearly, by having his debating adversary deny the need for human vital energy and lay emphasis on deception and tactical analysis, Xunzi either purposely misrepresented the mixed philosophy of the military treatises or misunderstood it. Whatever the case, the "Lord of Linwu" is only a temporary foil for Xunzi, who launches into a long exposition on the relationship between normative principles and military affairs, with only occasional interruptions from interlocutors who pose new questions in service to Xunzi's polemic.

Throughout the discussion Xunzi presents himself as someone committed to the effectiveness of humaneness, righteousness, and especially propriety (*li* 禮) in preventing and quelling conflict. This means that wily traps and ruses will not ultimately overwhelm a state and win the loyalty of its people. Only the manifestation of virtue by the ruler, with no regard for similar qualities in his generals, will soothe aggressive instincts. In answer to the "Lord of Linwu's" advocacy of deception and the employment of circumstances, Xunzi replies:

> You speak of the value of plots and advantageous circumstances, of moving by sudden attack and stealth—but these are matters appropriate only to one of the lords of the realm. Against the soldiers of a humane man deceptions are of no use. They are effective only against a ruler who is rash and arrogant, whose people are worn out, and they are effective only against a state in which the ruler and his subjects, superiors and inferiors are torn apart and at odds. Therefore a tyrant like Jie [last king of the Xia dynasty] may practice deception upon another Jie, and depending upon how cleverly he proceeds he may happily achieve a certain success. But for a Jie to try to practice deception against a sage-king like Yao 堯 would be like trying to break a rock by throwing eggs at it, or trying to stir boiling water with your bare finger. He will be like a man consumed by fire or drowned in water.[34]

Xunzi here seems to suggest that the cultivation by the ruler of his moral vital energy will, when manifested through his subordinates, ensure the decisive concentrations needed to defeat his adversaries with little or no confrontation. Hence, the principle of economy of force and restraint in applying penal law to recalcitrant violators of morality is one point of agreement between Xunzi and the theorists he otherwise scorned.[35]

Xunzi also showed a familiarity with the common axioms of the military arts, especially those expressed in the *Sunzi bingfa*. Asked how to become a good general, Xunzi responds with numbered categories whose contents are surely not his invention.[36] Also, later in the "Yi bing" chapter

Xunzi sermonizes in terms that are as likely to appear in the military treatises as in Ruist tracts.

> Plan before any undertaking and carry it out with circumspection; be as careful about the end as about the beginning and the end and the beginning will be alike. This is most auspicious policy. The success of all undertakings rests upon circumspection; their failure derives from negligence. . . . When planning prevails over personal desires, the result will be progress; when personal desires prevail over planning, the result will be disaster. Fight as though you were already in battle; regard any success you achieve as merely lucky.[37]

In addition, Xunzi's acquaintance with contemporary military thought may be seen in passages in which Xunzi called a man who follows the above principles of leadership "a true general of the realm" (*tianxia zhi jiang* 天下之將) and, in accord with the *metaphysical* perspective, one who "partakes of godlike intelligence" (*shenming* 神明).[38]

That said, Xunzi's principal interest in describing the traits of good military leadership was not simply to praise these virtues but to demonstrate their proper relationship to state power and normative values.[39] In Xunxi's view, the prosecution of good government (i.e., of civility) was primary and the execution of good military strategy was a secondary matter (*mo shi* 末事).[40]

> [King Xiaocheng 孝成王 of Zhao 趙 and the "Lord of Linwu" inquire,] "And may we ask what ways and what modes of action the true king should follow in employing his soldiers?"
>
> Sun Qingzi [i.e., Xunzi] said: "Such detailed matters are of minor importance to your Majesty, and may be left to the generals. What I would like to speak about, however, are the signs which indicate whether the king and the other lords of the realm are strong or weak, whether they are destined to survive or to perish, and the circumstances which ensure safety or invite danger."[41]

The implication of this passage is that Xunzi did not recognize the ideal of a sage-general. For him, military men fulfill a subordinate function in the prevention of conflict and the maintenance of stability. The great generals of the past and present are at worst gang leaders and at best lesser students of propriety and righteousness.

> Thus, for examples, Tian Dan of Qi, Zhuang Qiao 莊蹻 of Chu, Wei Yang [i.e., Shang Yang] of Qin, and Miao Ji 繆蟣 [i.e., Yue Yi] of Yan were all men who were popularly said to have been skilled in the use of soldiers.[42] Yet, though these men achieved varying degrees of cleverness and might, they all followed essentially the same methods, and none of them ever got so far as to bring true harmony and unity to their armies. They all relied upon sudden seizures, deceptions, stratagems, and swift overthrows, and for this reason their armies were no different from robber bands. Lord Huan of Qi, Lord Wen 文公 of Jin, King Zhuang 莊王 of Chu, King Helü of Wu, and King Goujian 勾踐王 of Yue 越 were all able to attain harmony and unity in their armies, and it may therefore be said that they at least entered the realm of the true Way. And yet they never grasped the essentials of the matter. So they were able to become hegemons (*ba*) but not to become true kings (*wang*). These are the signs of strength and weakness.[43]

Consequently, for Xunzi, only models of *wen*, expositors of virtuous government, can be said to possess the knowledge to deal with military affairs in a comprehensive way. Men of *wu* are only conscious of the microcosm in which they operate; they rely simply on immediate rewards and punishments to attain short-term objectives. Thus the state of Qin, by relying on militaristic and legalistic theories of human behavior, had gained rapid success but would ultimately fail to survive. In an almost prophetic interchange between Li Si 李斯 and Xunzi, Li Si is made to defend Qin's policy against Ruist virtue.

> Li Si said to Sun Qingzi [i.e., Xunzi]: "For four generations now Qin has won victories. Its armies are the strongest in the world and its authority sways the other feudal lords. It did not attain this by means of humaneness and righteousness, but by taking advantage of its opportunities, that is all."
>
> Sun Qingzi replied: "This is not something that you would understand. When you talk about opportunities, you are speaking of opportunities that are in fact inopportune. When I speak of

> humaneness and righteousness, I mean opportunities that are in fact great opportunities. This humaneness and righteousness which I speak of are the means whereby government is ordered properly, and when government is properly ordered, then the people will draw close to their superiors, delight in their rulers, and think it a light matter to die for them. Therefore I have said that matters pertaining to the army and the leadership of the generals are of minor importance."[44]

The essential superiority of civil over martial therefore lies in the farseeing policy of government, and the sustainment of peace depends on normative principles applied to human vital energy. And yet, having recognized this verity and noting how it is perceived by the rulers of Qin and other past ephemeral regimes, Xunzi seemed to discount the limitations of Ruist virtues—humaneness, righteousness, and propriety—in dealing with potential or actual conflict. On the one hand, his arguments for the effectiveness of propriety are persuasive.[45] On the other hand, Xunzi relied heavily on the applicability of propriety to unforeseen military crises that could not have been prevented within the parameters of human virtue. Despite his expressed familiarity with the postulates of military thought, Xunzi seemed to dismiss the necessity for methods that could be applied both intellectually and practically to such crises. Instead, he tried to *compartmentalize* military affairs and to dilute their importance in line with the *ethical* perspective. By doing so, martiality became but a function of civility, in Xunzi's mind. For him, civility, in the forms of propriety and good government (*zheng* 政 [正]), will provide the means for achieving state security. With such means, he said, "If you defend, you will be secure; if you conduct punitive expeditions, you will be strong."[46] But at the same time, Xunzi did not recognize the necessity for the martial element to conduct those defenses and punitive expeditions, or to make the initial conquests. In short, he refused to accept parity between *wen* and *wu*.

Mozi

In treating Mozi (fl. late fifth century BCE; also known as Mo Di 墨翟), one is faced with anomalous philosophical positions with respect to martiality and civility. The received text of the *Mozi* 墨子, except for the military chapters, both decries the civil accomplishments that the Ruists praised and stresses the importance of righteousness and virtuous government, albeit based on the utilitarian principle of fulfilling the elementary needs of the greatest number of people. On the one hand, Mozi was an expert in defensive tactics; on the other hand, he was averse to offensive combat. When he espoused a civil regard for humanity, he at the same time preferred a quasi-legalistic social organization in which its constituents become, as modern scholar Vitaly A. Rubin (1923–1981) put it, participants in a "utopia of universal conformism" and members of a "militarized" society.[47] Below we will attempt to sort out these apparently contradictory stances in Mozi's attitude toward *wen/wu* and locate the nexus of their mutual consistency.

At the outset we can say that Mozi was probably influenced substantially by the notions of humaneness and righteousness that were also prized by Kongzi.[48] The terms appear often in the *Mozi* and are interpreted in ways comparable to how Kongzi approached these ideas. A passage from the "Lu wen" 魯問 chapter of the *Mozi*, for instance, demonstrates his affirmation of the Ruist concept of righteousness.[49] The passage begins with a description of chronic war on the Yangzi River between the forces of Chu and Yue, and of how a military expert, Gongshuzi 公輸子 (also known as Lu Ban 魯班 or Gongshu Pan 公輸盤) from Lu, came south and aided Chu with the manufacture of standardized grappling hooks and rams, with which Chu naval forces could more effectively manipulate the warships of the Yue to Chu's advantage in battle. The story then continues:

> Gongshuzi was proud of his cleverness and asked Mozi: "There are grappling hooks and rams in my warships. I wonder if your righteousness also has such hooks and rams?"
>
> Mozi replied: "The hooks and rams in my righteousness are more excellent than those in your warships. In my scheme, I pull with love and push with respect. If you do not pull with love, there will be no affection; if you do not push with respect, there will be rapid desecration. And if there is desecration and no love and affection, then there will be rapid disintegration. Therefore, mutual love and mutual respect actually mean mutual benefit. Now, you pull others up to stop their retreat, but they would also pull you up to stop your retreat. You would push others back to stop their advance, but they would also push you back to stop your advance. This mutual pulling and pushing is actually mutual injury. Therefore, the hooks and rams in my righteousness are more excellent than the hooks and rams in your warships."[50]

Similarly, the first part of the "Fei gong" 非攻 chapter of the *Mozi* stresses the importance of righteousness in military affairs as well as in civil situations.

> If someone kills one man, he is condemned as unrighteous and must pay for his crime with his own life. According to this reasoning, if someone kills ten men, then he is ten times as unrighteous and should pay for his crime with ten lives, or if he kills a hundred men, he is a hundred times as unrighteous and should pay for his crime with a hundred lives. Now, all the gentlemen in the world know enough to condemn such crimes and brand them as unrighteous. And yet when it comes to the even greater unrighteousness of offensive warfare against other states, they do not know enough to condemn it. On the contrary, they praise it and call it righteous. Truly they do not know what unrighteousness is. So they make a record of their wars to be handed down to posterity. If they knew that such wars were unrighteous, then what reason should they have for making a record of their unrighteous deeds to be handed down to posterity?[51]

In both of the above passages there is the implication that morality, for Mozi, was absolute and definable according to clear-cut rules of utility. In accordance with a faith in archaic, all-powerful gods, Mozi abjured offensive warfare, because it so often fails to meet Heaven-decreed standards of human conduct, which are simultaneously standards of social efficiency. Mozi later argues that offensive warfare destroys the benefits of civil society. He, like Mengzi and Xunzi, saw an imbalance in his Zhanguo world between martial and civil and sought a theoretical solution to correct this imbalance. Unlike his Ruist counterparts, however, Mozi did not rely exclusively on moral transformation. Paradoxically, he based his schema for restraining overweening martial tendencies principally on martiality itself, with borrowings from Ruist moralism.

As is well known, Mozi assembled a sect of committed disciples who pledged rigid obedience to his teachings and personal loyalty to him as the "great one" (*juzi* 鉅子).[52] Under him these pupils not only studied the master's dogma, but apparently trained in military defense techniques, which, also in accordance with sect doctrine, they offered to beleaguered states wherever the master ordered. This organization, to a great degree, represented Mozi's model of the utopian society, and its army-like structure reflected Mozi's penchant for martial affairs. Each member was a craftsman as well as a student—a specialist in a network of goal-oriented individuals whose convictions were those of the "great one" and him alone. Indoctrination and discipline were paramount, and rewards and punishments were crucial to the sect's efficient operation. In essence, Mozi and his acolytes constituted a kind of military unit, with absolute standards of right and wrong, unquestioning allegiance to superiors, technical proficiency in practical skills, a loose attachment to or detachment from familial bonds, and a belief among its members that they were devoting themselves to the well-being of ordinary people.

In parallel fashion, Mozi's vision of the ideal society was notably martial in tone. According to Mozi's utopian vision: ministers would have few remonstrating duties, but would follow orders and perform technical, routine tasks; emphasis would be on adhering to uniform operating procedures for social and ethical behavior, as well as on the powers of rewards and punishments to compel compliance with these procedures; familial ties would be unimportant, since one would be an interchangeable part of a machine-like organization, focused on assigned goals; an individual would be loyal to a single leader, and yet one's affections would be to the organization as a whole rather than to any particular individual in the group; and, finally, the emphasis would be on practicality, persistence, and resilience in adverse circumstances that would inspire a willingness to forgo extravagance and cultural amenities.

It should be said that despite the overall military nature of Mozi's ideology, Mozi felt a need to comfort the masses. In Mozi's view, through sincere beneficence the negative consequences of offensive warfare can be partly averted. In the "Lu wen" 魯問 chapter of *Mozi* one reads:

> The lord of Lu said to Mozi: "I fear that Qi will attack us. Can this be prevented?"
>
> Mozi replied, "Yes. In ancient times, the sage kings of the Three Ages, Yu, Tang, Wen, and Wu, were lords of small territories. Because they spoke loyally and acted righteously they gained the world. The oppressive kings of the Three Ages (*san dai* 三代), Jie, Zhou, You, and Li, caused resentment and oppression, and so they lost the world. I am hoping that you will honor Heaven and serve the gods, and at the same time love and benefit the people. Prepare plenty of furs and money and be humble in your proclamations and orders; rapidly extend courtesies to neighboring lords and hasten your state to take action [so that] Qi may be relieved of its troubles. Aside from this, nothing indeed can be done."[53]

This being said, it was Mozi's general belief that the principles of a military cadre could be expanded to society at large. In effect, Mozi apparently hoped to create a model military society that would serve to end offensive warfare by creating and maintaining a pervasive consciousness of strategic defensive in all facets of political life. It was not surprising that, of all the Ruist principles accepted by Mozi, he selected righteousness (*yi*), interpreted as duty, as a key ingredient in his thought, for that sense of obligation is integral to a military organization and was ingrained in Mozi's indoctrinated minions. By feeling a sense of duty not only to the task at hand but to the group of which one is a part—the whole of society, in Mozi's utopia—an individual can provide benefit to all and be strengthened in equal measure. Consequently, Mozi propounded a kind of socialist consciousness that affirmed universal love (*jian'ai* 兼爱) as a means of long-term protection against the possibilities of offensive warfare.[54]

Only one case is recorded in the *Mozi* in which the "great one" apparently accepted offensive warfare by one state on another state, and that was in answer to Heaven's decree that the offending state was undutiful and therefore could be punished, in the same way as sage-kings of the past overthrew unrighteous regimes.

> Now, those rulers who delight in offensive warfare attempt to put a pleasing façade upon their doctrines and criticize Mozi, saying, "Do you claim that offensive warfare is an unrighteous and unprofitable thing? In ancient times Yu launched an expedition against the ruler of the Miao, Tang attacked Jie, and King Wu attacked Zhou, and yet all three are regarded as sage-kings. Why is this?"
>
> Mozi said, "You have failed to examine the terminology which I employ and do not understand the reasoning behind it. What these men did was not to 'attack' but to 'punish.' "[55]

Without using the phrase "righteous war" (*yibing*), Mozi, like Mengzi, advocated the timely use of martial righteousness to dispel immoral threats to harmony. But even such action was classified in Mohist, and not Ruist, fashion as strategic defensive in the name of Heaven.

Two important similarities can be discerned between the strategic and tactical defensive measures practiced by the Mohist sect and the ideas of the military treatises. First, there is the ubiquitous idea of potency and economy of force. The Mohists warned their hearers to maintain strength with utilitarian policies; to develop a uniform belief system among a practically skillful people; to ensure loyalty to superiors, using rewards and punishments when necessary; and to develop among a state's inhabitants a feeling of regard for the state as a whole. In other words, there are many *pragmatic* elements to the Mohists' approach. Second, the "great one" in the Mohist sect, in much the same way as the sage-general in the military treatises, acts in mysterious fashion as supreme decision-maker, all-knowing but aloof. In other words, Mozi's leadership has a *metaphysical* flavor, which we have already seen in the military treatises.

In sum, Mozi attempted to reduce the omnipresent threat of conflict in Zhanguo times by designing a utilitarian, socialistic philosophy as the ideology of a highly motivated and doctrinally committed group of paramilitary followers. His partial success in spreading such an ideology was due in no small measure to the active nature of his organization and to Mozi's own leadership abilities. After Mozi's death, however, no one of a comparably high caliber of leadership appears to have replaced him. Neither did his ideology fulfill the theoretical demands of the drive for unification among the various states, as compared to those espousing *militarism* or even *compartmentalism*. Whatever the reasons for the demise of the Mohist group, including the rigors of Mozi's training program and the apparent decline in the ideological and charismatic leadership that such military orders require, an important cause may have been the Mohist ideology itself. Mozi was such a strong believer in a martial organization for society that he failed to absorb into his military outlook the civil concepts necessary to sustain adherence from both personal followers and a larger community.[56]

Songzi

One additional objector to Zhanguo martial excesses should be brought forward for comparison in order to fill out the panoply of theorists who are known to have resisted the *syncretist* and *militarist* solutions to the *wen/wu* problem—namely, the thinker Songzi (fl. ca. 300 BCE; born Song Xing 宋鈃; also known as Song Keng 宋牼 and Song Rong 宋榮). Songzi is known to have been among the philosophical masters living together in the neighborhood of Ji Gate 稷門 in the Qi capital of Linzi during the fourth and third centuries BCE—an assemblage that came to be called the "Jixia Academy" (*Jixia xuegong* 稷下學宮). Unfortunately, what is known of Songzi's ideas is only secondhand, derived from a handful of reports.[57]

Nevertheless, three main themes can be abstracted from surviving quotations and descriptions.

First, Songzi appears to have been an advocate of correct names (*zheng ming* 正名)—the analysis of the properties of things and the ascription of names that properly represent those properties. Like his contemporary, Gongsun Long 公孫龍 (ca. 325–ca.250 BCE), Songzi asserted that one can have a true perception of the reality of things only by assuring oneself that each object of an intention is placed in correct relation to other objects, that is, bears the correct nomenclature.

Second, Songzi advocated the notion of "limiting desirous feelings" (*gua yu* 寡欲), probably in reaction to the ideas of Tuo Xiao 它囂 and Wei Mou 魏牟, two other philosophers among the Jixia masters, and perhaps also to what Songzi considered to be misinterpretations of the ideas of egoistic purity and harmonious desires espoused by another contemporary, Yang Zhu 楊朱.[58] Countering these thinkers, Songzi taught the dictum, "Consider fewness and shallowness of emotions and desires as essential."[59] As modern scholar Jin Shoushen pointed out, Yang Zhu and Songzi, though starting with different premises, actually reached the same end point, namely, the idea of the preservation of self.[60] Both believed that by their respective approaches one could realize the essence of man. Songzi thought that simplicity—a delimiting of obfuscating and infecting desires (*qing* 情)—will allow for the preservation of true reality, while Yang Zhu believed that by expressing one's desires freely but in a harmonious fashion one can come to understand the true reality in the self and the basic significance of human aspirations. Applying the *metaphysical* perspective to this point, one might say that both Songzi and Yang Zhu were considering the meanings of vital energy and how its concentrations and dispersals relate to an actuality within each human being.

Third, Songzi demonstrated a commitment to pacifism, which he linked to the delimiting of desires. As Songzi's view is described in the *Xunzi*:

> To show clearly that to meet with insult is no disgrace will prevent people from fighting. Men all consider it a disgrace to meet with insult, hence they fight. When they know that it is no disgrace to be insulted, they will not fight.[61]

The *Zhuangzi* 莊子, a Zhanguo work of Daoist affiliation ascribed to Zhuang Zhou 莊周 (ca. 369–286 BCE), refers to Songzi's attitude toward human desires in the following comment:

> Not to be entangled with popular fashions; not to make a pretentious display of things; not to be reckless toward other men or antagonistic to the public; to desire the peace of the world in order to preserve the life of the people; to seek no more than is sufficient for nourishing oneself and others, thus revealing their hearts: these are some of the aspects of the way of ancient times. Song Keng and Yin Wen 尹文 heard of these and were delighted with them.[62]
>
> . . . They dealt with the ten thousand things by first making distinctions and limitations. They talked about what the mind allows and called it the actions of the mind. By warmth of affection they sought the harmony of joy in order to harmonize the world. They wished to establish these as their principles. They endured insult without feeling it a disgrace, so as to save the people from fighting. They checked aggression and proposed disarmament in order to save their generation from war. . . . "To check aggression and propose disarmament" were their external achievements; "to desire few things" was their inner cultivation.[63]

Thus, Songzi sought the basis for human aggressive tendencies in the mind itself, in the way people actuate their predispositions. Because the objective world tends to obscure the purity of those predispositions, it is best to restrain the expression of desires and to realize that man actually desires a modicum of physical satisfaction. Songzi established the verity of such a policy by means of correct names. The *Xunzi* describes Songzi's approach as follows:

> Songzi says, "Men's passions desire but little, but everyone supposes that his own passions desire much, which is an error." Hence he leads his disciples, splitting hairs in his discussions, making clear his examples and terms, so as to make men understand that their passions desire but little.[64]

By arguing for the preservation of the purity of mind that controls the actuation of desires, Songzi could not only prove rationally the value of limiting desires, but also establish a psycho-philosophical basis for his pacifism. In Songzi's view, war is essentially a result of a surfeit of desires; it is the outcome of a mind unable to control the desires that constitute the source of war. When a man can view insults as the expressions of uncontrolled minds, then he will not be insulted, and his own mind will not allow similar hostile expression.

As a final point, it is worth noting that Songzi's focus was not exclusively on the individual mind and its preservation. Unlike Yang Zhu, Songzi concentrated on the common weal—the expansion of his ideal individual to the whole of society.

Examining these various aspects of Songzi's thought, some commentators have assumed that Mozi was a singular influence on Songzi. One piece of evidence in support of this connection can be found in the "Fei shier zi" 非十二子 chapter of the *Xunzi*, which groups Songzi and Mozi.[65] Also, the "Gaozi xia" 告子下 chapter of the *Mengzi* suggests a transmission of ideas between Songzi and Mozi.[66] While the evidence of influence by Mozi is not solid, the modern Chinese scholar Feng Youlan (Fung Yu-lan) (1895–1990) was probably right in saying that Songzi "combined the ideas of Mozi, and also of Yang Zhu, and gave them a psychological basis."[67] Thus, Songzi may have established a mental foundation for pacifism that took into account the kind of utilitarian and moralistic reasons against offensive warfare forwarded by Mozi.

What is significant about Songzi for the present discussion of military thought in early China is that Songzi's pacifism, as it is currently known, was not convincing as a means for mitigating Zhanguo conflict. To posit that one's mind may control desires and preserve the natural fewness of desires in man, and to deduce from this that such control should become a model for state rulers and ministers in ending warfare, was unrealistic in the context of increasingly violent Zhanguo politics. While Songzi offered an interesting theory for the existence of martiality and its tendency to dominate society, his civil answer to martial excess did not provide an effective solution to the *wen/wu* problem.

Military Thinkers

From the above discussion of various pre-Qin objectors to war one can see how ideas against excessive martiality were more systematically articulated in Zhanguo times, as compared to the purely physical and emotional complaints of the *Shi* odes. Perhaps in response to these objectors and to the *militarist* position, the military treatises of the Zhanguo period show certain concerns about martial activity, especially when they speak of the long-term impact of interstate conflict. These works exemplify not only the *metaphysical* and *pragmatic* applications presented in Chapters 2 and 3, but also some *ethical* notions in reflection of attitudes toward martiality in Zhanguo times.

It is important to recognize that parts of the military treatises of the Zhanguo period, despite their focus on prosecuting war, use some of the same language employed by the objectors to support varying views regarding the *wen/wu* problem. While not emphasizing a moral imperative in war, a number of the military treatises make occasional use of the same *ethical* positions of the Ruists for a different objective—not to obstruct the use of war, but to ensure its successful conclusion.

The *Wuzi*, for example, refers to a moral order closely resembling Xunzi's ideal:

> Now, what is called the Way is the return to fundamental principles; righteousness is that by which affairs are advanced and merit established; planning is that by which harm is avoided and advantage gained; essentials (*yao* 要) are that which safeguard one's work and protect his achievements. If conduct is not in accord with the Way and action is not in accord with righteousness, then even though one's position is important and honorable, misfortune will overtake him. And therefore surely the sage controls the people with the highest principles and governs them with righteousness. He stimulates them with ritual and soothes them with humane treatment. When these four virtues are practiced the people flourish; when they are neglected the people decline. Therefore when Tang the Victorious (Cheng Tang 成唐) attacked Jie, the people of Xia rejoiced; when King Wu of Zhou attacked King Zhou [of Shang], the people of Yin [i.e., Shang] did not oppose him. They acted in accord with the will of Heaven and that of man, and thus were able to achieve these things.[68]

The *Wuzi* also lists an *ethical* gradation of military motives that takes into account the moral stances of the objectors to war:

> There are . . . five categories of war: first, righteous war; second, aggressive war; third, enraged war; fourth, wanton war; and fifth, insurgent war. Wars to suppress violence and quell disorder are

> righteous. Those which depend on force are aggressive. When troops are raised because rulers are actuated by anger, this is enraged war. Those in which all propriety is discarded because of greed are wanton wars. Those who, when the state is in disorder and the people exhausted, stir up trouble and agitate the multitude cause insurgent wars. There is a suitable method for dealing with each: a righteous war must be forestalled by proper government; an aggressive war by humbling oneself; an enraged war by reason; a wanton war by deception and treachery; and an insurgent war by authority.[69]

In the *Sun Bin bingfa* as well one can find instances of a denial of *militarism* and an affirmation of an *ethical* ideal.

> A general cannot fail to be righteous. If he is not righteous, then he cannot be strict, and if he is not strict, he cannot be awe-inspiring, and if he is not awe-inspiring, then his troops will not fight to the death. Therefore righteousness is the "head" of war. A general cannot fail to be humane. If he is not humane, then the army will not be victorious, and if the army is not victorious, then the army will achieve nothing. Therefore humaneness is the "abdomen" of war. The general cannot fail to have virtue. If he has no virtue, then he will have no strength, and if he has no strength, then he will not secure the benefits of the armed forces. Therefore virtue constitutes the "hands" of war. A general cannot fail to be trustworthy. If he is not trustworthy, then his orders will not be executed; if his orders are not executed, then his army will not be all-encompassing; and if his army is not all-encompassing, then he will have no success. Therefore trustworthiness constitutes the "feet" of war. A general cannot fail to have knowledge of how to overcome. . . . Therefore decisiveness is the "tail" of war.[70]

The *Simafa*, while showing the impact of Legalist rationality, demonstrates an *ethical* reverence for the people in affairs of state, especially war.

> If a general lays too much stress on awesomeness, then the people will be overburdened; if there is too little stress, then the

> people will not be victorious. If a superior causes his people not to obtain due righteousness, the prominent families not to be in proper order [of status], the techniques [of government] not to be effectively used, the lowly not to be properly employed, so that the authorities oppress them, this is called too much awesomeness. With too much awesomeness the people are overburdened. If a superior does not honor virtue but appoints the deceptive and perverse, does not honor the Way but appoints only the brave and brawny, does not value those who follow orders but rather those who violate orders, does not value those who act morally but rather those who act cruelly so that they insult the authorities, this is called too little awesomeness. With too little awesomeness the people will not be victorious.[71]

The *Liutao* shows similar parallels with Ruist views:

> Be respectful to the people, and bring their affections into accord. For if you are respectful to the people, then there will be harmony; and if you bring their affections into accord, then there will be happiness. These are called markings of humaneness and righteousness.[72]

For its part, the *Sunzi bingfa* impresses one as perhaps more callous than the other military treatises in its attitude toward treating soldiers. One might therefore expect less evidence of an *ethical* viewpoint in its passages. Yet there are places, especially in the "Wu wen" 吳問 chapter discovered among the Yinqueshan fragments, that demonstrate a reasoned affection for the masses. The passage begins with the king of Wu asking Sunzi about the order in which the six major clans of the state of Jin—known collectively as the "six senior ministers" (*liu qing* 六卿)—will fail. Sunzi answers that the Fan 范 and Zhonghang 中行 clans will fail first, followed, in order, by the Zhi 智, Han 韓 and Wei 魏 clans. The Zhao clan will survive, however, and Jin will eventually be ruled by the Zhao. When asked for his reasoning, Sunzi replies that the Fan, Zhonghang, Zhi, Han, and Wei clans will all fail because of the harshness of their tax and land regulations on the people over whom they rule. Such stringency will lead to excessive pride and extravagance among an increasingly large number of government officials, which in turn will engender unrealistic ambitions to increase their power through warfare, resulting ultimately in their downfall.

The Zhao clan, however, because its policies toward their people's welfare are more lenient, and because it maintains a small and frugal government, will maintain its integrity and eventually assume control of all the territories in Jin lost by the other clans.[73]

There is also the following excerpt from the "Di xing" 地形 chapter of the *Sunzi bingfa* that contrasts with the amoral tack found elsewhere in the work:

> If the situation is one of victory but the sovereign has issued orders not to engage, the general may decide to fight. If the situation is such that he cannot win but the sovereign has issued orders to engage, he need not do so. And therefore the general who in advancing does not seek personal fame, and in withdrawing is not concerned with avoiding punishment, but whose only purpose is to protect the people and promote the best interests of his sovereign, is the precious jewel of the state.[74]

In brief, there is ambivalence among the military treatises regarding the *ethical* in warfare: the sage-general must have a certain moral regard for the people who are his soldiers and for the people of the states against which and for which he fights. At the same time, he has a duty to treat the soldiers in his army, who also come from the ranks of civil society, as well as the forces against which he fights with a *metaphysical* mindset applying *pragmatic* means for maintaining order in accord with strict military law. A line from the "Jiang de" 將德 chapter of the *Sun Bin bingfa* sums up this ambivalence: "Love them as though they were handsome children, respect them as you would a strict mentor, and employ them as if they were motes of dust."[75]

Looking at the military treatises of the Zhanguo period as a group, we can say broadly that there is a general, though not entirely consistent, leaning toward the *syncretist* solution to the *wen/wu* problem. While not all of the military treatises speak directly about the importance of applying both martiality and civility in a continuously connected way, they nevertheless demonstrate no support for the *militarist* emphasis on martiality to achieve state stability and only sparingly, as we saw in Chapter 1, contain passages echoing the *compartmentalist* idea of divorcing martiality from civility. Instead, the military treatises, in aggregate, place the greatest value on adapting civil concepts to martial purposes and vice versa, and on perfecting civil institutions in tandem with building military potency. At the same time, the military treatises address all of the main perspectives/applications as they apply to the *wen/wu* debate—the *metaphysical*, the *pragmatic*, and the *ethical*. It is perhaps for these reasons that the military treatises constitute such a rich body of thought on the *wen/wu* problem in the Zhanguo period.

Conclusion

This chapter has explored a wide swath of primary sources on the moral dimension of war in the Zhanguo period, illustrating not only a lively debate among civil and military theorists alike, but the importance of the *wen/wu* question in a fractious time. What is critical to remember from this exploration is that none of the solutions forwarded in this debate had the upper hand in the Warring States era. All three of the core solutions had their defenders, and any of them could have become dominant in later times depending on the success of individual leaders and their advisors in bringing interstate strife to an end and establishing renewed stability throughout the old Zhou realm.

When the Qin regime failed to sustain its unified state past a few years and Liu Bang was successful in reasserting a unity in the Sinitic world that it had not seen since the beginning of Western Zhou, the stage was set for a new turn in the longstanding *wen/wu* debate that would lead to new relationships among the three central solutions. We therefore shift in the next chapter to a consideration of the evolution of the *wen/wu* controversy during the Western Han dynasty.

Chapter 5

The Permutations of Western Han

As we proceed from late Zhanquo into the Western Han period and the establishment of a new imperial order, we will be examining some new issues in the evolution of military thought in early China. These include the relationship of the *wen/wu* debate to the competition between Huang-Lao and Legalist-Ruist traditions in the early Han, the evolution of Han foreign policy, and changes in society and institutions from the standpoint of military philosophy.

Realignment of Solutions

In the years leading up to the Qin unification, *militarism* appeared poised to win the philosophical battle with *syncretism* and *compartmentalism* over the most effective way to achieve a stable, unified state. However, after the ignominious fall of the second emperor of Qin, the *militarist* position, perceived as part of the policy of an overly ambitious and ruthless regime, declined as an acceptable solution to the problem of conflict abatement. As a result, the participants in the *wen/wu* debate underwent realignment, with *syncretists* and *compartmentalists* becoming the chief protagonists, while *militarism* ceased during Western Han to have any prominent spokesmen.

At the beginning of the Western Han, perhaps as a partial result of the failure of *militarism*, the predominant trend in the *wen/wu* debate was in favor of the *syncretist* approach to martiality and civility. Speaking in the first century CE, Ban Gu, the main compiler of the *Hanshu*, commented that the founding emperor of the Han, Han Gaozu, "relied on the scholarly civility (*wen*) of Xiao He 蕭何 [d. 193 BCE] and Cao Shen 曹參 [d. 190 BCE], employed the military stratagems of Zhang Liang and Chen Ping 陳平 [d. 178 BCE], promoted the argumentations of Lu Jia 陸賈 [d. 170

BCE] and Li Yiji 酈食其 [d. 203 BCE], and promulgated the ceremonial of Shusun Tong 叔孫通 [d. ca. 188 BCE]. Civility and martiality were complementary and great plans arose among them."[1]

Among the advisors cited by Ban Gu, Lu Jia was particularly exemplary of this *syncretist* tendency in Han Gaozu's time. Lu's famous admonitions to Han Gaozu both reject the *militarist* position and imply a belief in a *wen*/*wu* continuum.

> In his audiences with the emperor, Master Lu Jia on numerous occasions expounded and praised the *Shi* and the *Shangshu*, until one day Gaozu began to rail at him. "All I possess I have won on horseback!" said the emperor. "Why should I bother with the *Shi* and the *Shangshu*?"
>
> "Your Majesty may have won the empire on horseback, but it was by the principle of obedience that past kings assured the continuance of their dynasties. To pay due attention to both civil and military affairs is the way for a dynasty to achieve long life. In the past King Fuchai 夫差 of Wu and Zhi Bo 智伯, minister of Jin, both perished because they paid too much attention to military affairs. Qin entrusted its future solely to punishments and laws without changing with the times, and thus eventually brought about the destruction of its ruling family. If, after it had united the world under its rule, Qin had practiced humaneness and righteousness and modeled its ways upon the sages of antiquity, how would Your Majesty ever have been able to win possession of the empire?"[2]
>
> Master Lu said, "When the world is at peace, all eyes are upon the prime minister, but when the world is in danger, attention turns to the commanding general. If the general and the prime minister are in agreement with one another, then the rest of the officers and officials will gladly follow them and, with all the rest behind them, though trouble and disaffection occur in the empire, there will be no danger of authority slipping from their grasp."[3]

Even during Lu Jia's lifetime, however, the *syncretist* solution was influenced by a burgeoning competition between the two main philosophical positions of the age, Huang-Lao thought and Legalism-Ruism. These two intellectual hybrids rose in prominence as a result of the novel demands that the Qin reorganization of society had created. In striving to found a universal state, covering a larger territory and requiring more complex governmental machinery, the Qin rulers, and the Han emperors after them, found it politically necessary to replace networks of ephemeral personal relations extending over relatively short distances with increasingly legalistic structures that were governable from a single hub. At the same time, the authority of the hub had to be strengthened, not just with military power, but with a political dogma that rendered the emperor continually capable of manifesting his charisma or awesomeness to the empire as a whole.

Ruists in the Western Han, though still committed to the concept of fiduciary community set forth in the "Zhong yong" 中庸 chapter of the *Liji*, realized that a more practicable alliance between an ideal social hierarchy and legalistic modifications could answer the new imperative for imperial integrity without destroying the moral foundations of pre-Qin Ruism.[4] Thus, ministers such as Shusun Tong and Gongsun Hong 公孫弘 (200–121 BCE) began to shed the attitude of independence that Ruists in Zhanguo times had prided themselves in taking vis-à-vis their state-ruler patrons.[5] Instead, they adopted a more ingratiating relationship toward their sovereigns (*zun jun bei chen* 尊君卑臣) by modifying Ruist principles in accord with new imperial institutions. Through their intellectual efforts, the ruler's commands became absolute, constituting legal precedent, not debatable opinion. Han law, which was a development of Qin governmental practice and the theory of forms (punishments) and names (*xingming* 形 [刑] 名)—the assignment of consistent names to appropriate forms (punishments)—became more important for ordering an enlarged social system. Thus it was that Shusun Tong created a court ceremonial for Han Gaozu on the basis of Qin statutes and Lu regulations from the Zhanguo period, while Zhang Tang 張湯 (d. 115 BCE) and Dong Zhongshu 董仲舒 (ca. 179–ca.104 BCE) employed legalistic pronouncements from the *Shangshu* and the *Chunqiu* to supplement penal ordinances.[6] These readjustments demonstrated the merging of Ruist and Legalist ideas that occurred as part of the momentous transition from Zhanguo fractiousness to Qin-Han unity.[7]

This Legalism-Ruism did not, however, evolve unencumbered. Huang-Lao thought, although not as well represented in the documents extant today, nevertheless had considerable impact on the policies of Western Han government. Combining the primitivism of the *Daodejing* and an administrative doctrine resembling the ideas of Shen Buhai and Shen Dao, Huang-Lao thought constituted a strong alternative to Legalism-Ruism in Western Han, through its stress on a spirit-like sage-ruler presiding mystically over a strictly hierarchical society in accordance with a body of uniform procedures.

It is unclear how early Huang-Lao thought first appeared, for aside from a few texts such as the *Huangdi sijing* and the *Heguanzi*, only secondary sources are available to substantiate the existence of such a synthesis of legalistic and mystical thinking in the pre-Han period.[8] Nonetheless, Huang-Lao thought was well known and influential in the Western Han, judging from the number of statesmen said to have studied its tenets and the policies actually adopted by the early Western Han emperors.

The first undeniable exponent of the Huang-Lao doctrine, He Gong 蓋公 (fl. third to second centuries BCE), established a school in the former state of Qi and eventually became master to Cao Shen, who became one of the chief advisers to Liu Bang, later Emperor Gaozu of Han.[9] Huang-Lao thought thence diffused to ministers and rulers alike; Zhang Liang and Chen Ping were major adherents in Han Gaozu's time.[10] Emperor Wen 文帝 (r. 180–157 BCE), besides being a supporter of a Daoist outlook on government, was, as Herrlee G. Creel described, a follower of Shen Buhai's principles of bureaucratic leadership and therefore was probably not only sympathetic to, but a practitioner of, Huang-Lao ideology.[11] Similarly, Emperor Jing 景帝 (r. 157–142 BCE), although willing to entertain Ruist ideas at his court, was under the influence of Empress Dowager Dou 竇太后 (d. 135 BCE), a staunch supporter of Huang-Lao ideas, and so was at least a nominal sponsor of Huang-Lao doctrine throughout his reign.[12] As the *Shiji* reports, "The Empress Dowager Dou was fond of the doctrines of Huangdi and Laozi, so that the emperor [Han Jingdi] along with the heir apparent and the Dou relations could not but study Huangdi and Laozi and honor their methods."[13] As the scholar Zhou Shaoxian 周紹賢 (1908–1993) concluded in his study of Huang-Lao thought, not only were many scholars in Western Han well versed in Huang-Lao philosophy, but the Huang-Lao technique of "using regular methods (*zheng*) to govern a state and irregular measures (*qi*) to employ soldiers" was actually used by emperors Gaozu, Wen, and Jing to quell potential sources of rebellion and effect good government.[14]

Only during the reign of Emperor Wu 武帝 (r. 141–87 BCE), after the death of Empress Dowager Dou, did Huang-Lao thought lose influence relative to that of Legalist-Ruist ideology. Even then, only a gradual decline occurred; several biographies in the standard histories testify to the continuation of the Huang-Lao tradition in political circles, though some of the spokesmen failed or elected not to take government positions.[15] In time, Ruists who saw the futility of Legalism in the face of the overbearing power of the outer clans (*waiqi* 外戚) in the Han regime began to mix the more metaphysical notions of Huang-Lao thought with their own adopted cosmological ideas to develop Daoist mysticism (*xuanxue* 玄學) during the Eastern Han 東漢 period (25–220 CE).

It was earlier suggested that the rivalry between the *syncretists* and the *compartmentalists* in the early Han regarding the *wen/wu* problem paralleled to some extent the larger ideological competition between Huang-Lao and Legalism-Ruism. This does not mean that Huang-Lao adherents necessarily favored *syncretism* and Legalist-Ruists uniformly sided with *compartmentalism*. Partly because military thought in early China never coalesced into a single school of philosophy, individual spokesmen in Han times on the *wen/wu* issue might take a *compartmentalist* tack on particular questions involving the application of *wen* and *wu* but otherwise remain affiliates of Huang-Lao thought. Conversely, Legalist-Ruist thinkers might, in given circumstances, gravitate to a *syncretist* approach to civility and martiality. Notwithstanding this caveat, certain chronological and ideological coincidences can be seen between *syncretism* and Huang-Lao thought and between *compartmentalism* and Legalism-Ruism.

Regarding the first of these pairings, certain resonances between the Huang-Lao synthesis of mystical and practical knowledge and the generally *syncretist* tendency in the military treatises have already been cited. As seen in quotations from the *Huangdi sijing*, Huang-Lao theorists extended the mystical concepts of nonassertion (*wuwei*) and a naturalistic Way in the *Daodejing* to government affairs, absorbing in the process legalistic and other administrative techniques to construct a more comprehensive political ideology, including a philosophy for war. To give yet another illustration, there is evidence in the *Heguanzi* of Huang-Lao thinkers linking metaphysics with practical techniques of government, including applications to martial decision making. Besides giving a description of hierarchical organizations and legal strictures with military applications, the "Wang fu" 王鈇 and "Dao duan" 道端 chapters of the *Heguanzi* give support to a *pragmatic* outlook in a Daoist context.[16]

> For mutual protection in an army, in night combat it is enough that the soldiers trust each other; in day combat it is enough that they match each other [in abilities]. . . . [If so,] then such troops can dominate the field of battle, executing and attacking, and none will dare to resist. Accordingly, if [a ruler] establishes

> punishments but does not implement them, and if he does not fight but his command power is considerable, then, although he does not form his chariots and armored troops, he will have no adversary throughout the world.[17]

> If you do not employ the worthy in [military] actions, you will be unsuccessful and will certainly be defeated. When [an adversary] sets forth, observe his routes of movement; when he withdraws, be alert for sudden changes. When one deploys his army to guard without, disaster may nevertheless occur within; if [an adversary's] defenses are too scattered, you may attack his most valuable position.[18]

In essence, the following matches can be discerned between Huang-Lao philosophy and Zhanguo military thought: (1) both traditions concentrated heavily on the ideal, omniscient sage-leader who makes liberal use of practical measures to actualize his paranormal intentions; (2) the compilers of the military treatises, like their Huang-Lao counterparts, integrated discussions of proper government (*wen*) with admonitions concerning military tactics and strategy (*wu*); (3) both streams of thought lay stress on laws and statutes to ensure order and correct functioning of roles; and (4) both intellectual streams were concerned with the absolute control of subordinate initiative so that the actions of the people/soldiers are harmonious and in accord with the master's demands.

These resonances indicate that the strength of Huang-Lao thought in Western Han politics may have been partially responsible for the sustained interest in military philosophy after the creation of a stable empire. The fact that the military texts found at Yinqueshan were written between 140 and 118 BCE suggests that during at least that period there was a continuing desire to preserve older military treatises and perhaps to compile new ones.[19] We are told in the *Hanshu* "Treatise on Literature" that at the beginning of the Western Han, the generals Zhang Liang and Han Xin were in charge of combing through 182 available works on military methods (*bingfa*) to assemble thirty-five worthy volumes.[20] Such efforts may have been encouraged not only because military manuals were still useful for ongoing campaigns but also because a major political ideology of the time legitimized philosophizing on war and enhanced the effects of the loosely *syncretist* viewpoint that many of the Zhanguo military treatises espoused.

One important Western Han intellectual, Chao Cuo 晁錯 (ca. 200–154 BCE), may exemplify this receptivity to the *syncretic* solution in a time of Huang-Lao influence. Chao's biographies say not only that he was a student of Shang Yang and Han Fei before entering government service as an erudite (*wenxue* 文學), they also suggest that he cultivated a wide knowledge of early military tracts.[21] In one of his major memorials to Emperor Wen, analyzing the relative strategic strengths of the Han and the Xiongnu 匈奴 state to the north, Chao compared in *pragmatic* terms the abilities and weapons of the two adversaries, noting that the horses of the Xiongnu were stronger in hilly country and for crossing rivers; their horsemen were more deft on treacherous roads and sharply inclined ground; and their soldiers were generally more resistant to bad weather, fatigue, hunger, and thirst. The Han, on the other hand, had the edge in open, flat terrain, where light chariots and cavalry charges could more easily disrupt the foe's defenses, and in technology, because Han's crossbows had a longer range than the simple bows of the Xiongnu. Moreover, Han armored infantry, equipped with long and short swords, was more effective in pitched battles than northern tribal warriors, and Han forces were more accurate marksmen with bow and arrow, as well as being more disciplined in dismounted formations. Overall, Chao Cuo gave the Xiongnu three major advantages as compared to five for Han, and went on to suggest briefly how Emperor Wen might benefit militarily from the best use of this analysis of relative strengths, warning at the same time that superiority in manpower, equipment, or terrain does not necessarily mean success; the perspicacity of the ruler and his generals must be equal to the task.[22]

A second memorial to Emperor Wen from Chao Cuo concerned northern border defense. In this discourse Chao Cuo outlined the Qin experience with the use of expeditionary armies in the northwest. Based on the deduction that soldiers who withstand the hardships of fighting in foreign climes demand added compensation, and that other means of creating military potency would be more economical, he suggested the formation on the Han-Xiongnu frontier of resident agricultural-military communities (*tunken* 屯墾, later known as *tuntian* 屯田). These outposts, he proposed, would be populated initially by convicts, but in time they would also be open to any free settlers who chose to migrate. Living conditions would be designed to encourage long-term residence, each compound offering the social services of physicians, shamans, and even matchmakers, as well as proper mortuaries and "complete and peaceful" abodes. At the same time, the inhabitants, organized into traditional military-agricultural hierarchies, would be trained in frontier defense methods. Therefore, although close social harmony and mutual responsibility would be encouraged, rewards and punishments, not Ruist fiduciary cooperation, would be the foundations of community discipline.[23]

If Chao Cuo's writings point to the continuing importance of *syncretism* among scholar-officials in the early Western Han, *compartmentalism* was also represented in this period. Jia Yi 賈誼 (200–169 BCE), for example, though offering practical solutions to instances of conflict, adopted a basically negative attitude toward the use of martiality. To be sure, in his oft-quoted memorial on the "three standards and five baits" (*san biao wu er* 三表五餌) for dealing with the Xiongnu, he promoted a *pragmatic* device—dependent states (*shuguo* 屬國)—for pacifying potentially hostile northern tribes. However, his emphasis was on the influence of Ruist virtue: "I have heard about strong countries and martial wisdom that a true king battles using righteousness and a true emperor battles using virtue."[24] Elsewhere he advocated nonassertion (*wuwei*) in conjunction with humaneness and righteousness and the power of law, which may reveal inclinations toward Huang-Lao thought and/or *syncretism*.

> The reason why Butcher Tan carved twelve oxen in a single morning without dulling the sharp edge [of his knife] was that he always attacked and severed according to the various fibers [in the meat]. When it came to the broad-boned areas, he used either a *jin* 斤-cleaver or a *fu* 斧-cleaver. Now, humaneness, righteousness, compassion, and kindness are the sharp edges of a ruler, while command power, circumstantial power, laws, and institutions are his cleavers.[25]

Importantly, this metaphorical disguising of martial weapons as civil principles is critical to understanding Jia Yi's *compartmentalist* view of *wen/wu*. Essentially, Jia Yi tried to mask the symbols of martiality by claiming they are really civility in other forms. Thus, civility is praised, while martiality—its original meaning distorted—becomes a secondary matter. Outwardly, the idea of dependent states may seem to be an affirmation of the value of martiality through the institution of controlled states peopled by potential enemies as a strategic defense against the enemy. In fact, however, this notion represents an isolation of martiality from civil conduct and a rejection of martiality as a legitimate part of governing the empire.

Wen/wu and Foreign Policy

Compartmentalist ministers clearly had their impact on foreign affairs in the Western Han period, despite counterarguments from *syncretist* critics. It is well known that until the reign of Emperor Wu, Chao Cuo's arguments notwithstanding, the Han dynasty was at a military disadvantage relative to its northern neighbors both for technological and economic reasons. Principally because of this situation, the Han regime, without abrogating its assumed moral superiority, adopted a policy of appeasement (*heqin* 和親) toward the Xiongnu and other northern nomadic tribes. This diplomatic stance was a fundamentally civil attitude that reflected a sheer inability to counteract Xiongnu cavalry tactics as well as a preference to offer gifts rather than create new military or other strategic deterrents.

As its originator, Liu Jing 劉敬, envisioned the appeasement policy, it would be possible to "find harmony in family ties" (*heqin*) with the Xiongnu, based on the conviction, also held by Jia Yi, that virtuous behavior and commercial relations, not martial confrontation, would eventually mollify if not quell aggression from the north. After 141 BCE, however, the limited success of this policy convinced some that Han should dispense with this overly civil approach. In the 135–134 BCE debates between Wang Hui 王恢 and Han Anguo 韓安國 (d. 127 BCE) on the border problem, for example, one sees efforts to move toward more balance in the application of *wen* and *wu*.[26]

On the one hand, Wang Hui argued that the Xiongnu had no fear of Han retaliation and therefore continued their southern raids. Believing that an effective attack would be the best defensive measure, Wang urged the utilization of Han's burgeoning resources to rid the Central Plain (*zhongyuan* 中原) of the barbarian menace and soothe the people's wounds. In brief, the Han regime required, in Wang Hui's view, a shift from a policy of appeasement to one of military potency. While not speaking in *metaphysical* terms, Wang Hui saw the ultimate purposes of martial action in *syncretist* terms and petitioned for a reasoned application of military force to a persistent national security problem.

Han Anguo, on the other hand, was assured that the past successes of the appeasement policy were evidence of its continued usefulness in the present. In his opinion, expeditions to the north were still unfeasible, too costly in human pain and too unrewarding in territory and wealth. War, for Han Anguo, was not an acceptable alternative but must be avoided in favor of a civil approach—that is, a *compartmentalist* tack.[27]

Chang Ch'un-shu commented some years ago that the proponents of the appeasement policy in the years before Emperor Wu had a more convincing case, because of their usually greater military experience and, in general, wiser view of Han-Xiongnu relations. Moreover, the proponents of the appeasement policy at that time constituted a majority in the Han imperial court and therefore could argue more successfully for their point of view against critics of lower rank and less experience in actual encounters with the Xiongnu.[28] As a result, no matter how philosophically attractive the opponents' arguments might have been in the abstract, objective conditions in Emperor Wen's time and earlier, as well as specters of past debacles, easily overwhelmed risky proposals for army mobilization against the northern tribal state. By the time of the debates in 135–134 BCE, however, conditions in the Han economy had measurably improved, a young and ambitious emperor had taken the throne, and Wang Hui, as a high-level official at court, was more persuasive in representing a more martial position vis-à-vis the Xiongnu. The result was that Wang Hui's ideas were accepted and the credibility of the appeasement policy began to erode.

Turning to the arguments for and against appeasement in the *Yantielun* 鹽鐵論, presented in 81 BCE, some fifty years after the Wang Hui-Han Anguo debate, one finds that the strategic situation and the characteristics of the debaters had undergone great change. Sang Hongyang 桑弘羊 (ca. 152–80 BCE), the chief protagonist for a military approach, was a high official with a substantial record in imperial administration, while his competitors were Ruist erudites (*wenxue*), not seasoned field commanders. Also, the Western Han regime had recently completed its furthest territorial expansion and was attempting to recover economically, while maintaining its strength over newly vanquished neighbors. Consequently, the arguments forwarded in the *Yantielun* debates, although resembling those voiced in the conclaves of 135–134 BCE, had different impacts.

One of the main points at issue in the *Yantielun* debates was a concept we have already encountered in this study, that of righteous war or righteous troops (*yibing*). The idea that military expeditions should be waged for righteous purposes had already been discussed for centuries as a legitimate basis for going to war, and spokesmen for all three of the main solutions to the *wen*/*wu* problem had addressed this notion in positive terms. During the Zhanguo period, for example, the "Chi mi" 侈靡, "Ba yan" 霸言, and "Wen" 問 chapters of the *Guanzi*, which discuss martial affairs in generally *syncretist* terms, have this to say:

> One whose troops are strong but has no righteousness will perish.[29]

> This is the way the former kings made punitive expeditions: to raise [troops] required righteousness; to employ them required violence.[30]

> Military ventures are dangerous things. Being untimely in one's victories or unrighteous in one's acquisitions will not lead to good fortune.[31]

Similarly, in the *compartmentalist* approach espoused in the *Xunzi*, we find the following assertion:

> Humaneness is to love others; thus it is evil men who cause damage. Righteousness is to follow ordering principle; thus it is evil men who cause disorder. Accordingly, war is the means for interdicting the violent and eliminating the damaging; it is not [merely] to conflict and conquer.[32]

Finally, the *Lüshi chunqiu*, a work whose composition was supervised by an advisor to *militarist* Qin, contains statements favorable to the use of righteousness in waging war. To cite but one passage:

> In these times, if there was one who could give life to a single dying man, the world would surely fight to serve him. Righteous troops give life to a single man several times over; who would not be elated? Thus, wherever righteous troops arrive, the people of neighboring countries submit to them [unremittingly] like flowing water, and the people of the attacked country look upon them as they would their fathers and mothers.[33]

During the Western Han, this long-addressed concept of righteous war gained heightened importance as a new set of questions regarding the uses of martiality and civility to protect an imperial state came to the fore. In the *Yantielun* discussions of the first century BCE, the Ruist erudites interpreted righteous war, as had been done in the past, as a social-philosophical force essential for maintaining cultural integrity.

> Formerly, Lord Huan of Qi secured the loyalty of the people within and pacified the other lords of the realm without by preserving the dying and aiding the crippled, the world acquiesced to his rule. But afterwards his virtue waned and his deeds lost [their brilliance]. At the Kuiqiu 葵丘 conference [of 651 BCE] he was curt and self-praising with [the lords of the realm], so that nine states revolted.[34] The *Chunqiu* criticized his devaluation of virtue and his paeans to power. Thus, by relying on virtue, powerful Chu announced its submission and, without summons, distant states came of themselves [to show their submission]. By relying on [mere] strength, nearby states became unfriendly and small states would not submit. Such were the results. If you sincerely examine why the Three Sovereigns were prosperous, discuss why Qin perished, and relate why Lord Huan of Qi rose to power; and if you eliminate *wu* and practice *wen*, discard [mere] strength and esteem virtue, put an end to customs barriers and [toll] bridges, dismantle [defense] earthworks and palisades, and use humaneness and righteousness to guide [your policies], then the northern borders will have no worry of [barbarian] bandits and the central states will be free from war.[35]

Thus, the erudites asserted a general abhorrence of the privations the common people had to endure in order that privileged members of society could satisfy their lusts for imperial expansion and increased wealth. They argued that the conquered lands were useless for agriculture and the expenditures ruinous for the imperial economy.[36]

In response to the erudites, Sang Hongyang, as the censor in chief (*yushi dafu* 御史大夫), was consistently sensitive to the factors of realpolitik. While all had been done, he said, to alleviate the burdens of the masses, there remained a manifest need to conduct an aggressive military policy in order to avert later disaster. Sang conceded, however, that righteous troops must continue to be an important ingredient in such a policy.[37]

> Now, the Xiongnu are nibbling into our territory so that even those far away [from the borders] are not separated from the painful effects. . . . If we do not take offensive and defensive measures, then the violence and injury will not stop. Thus the Former Emperor [i.e., Emperor Wu] levied righteous troops to punish their crimes.[38]

Sang Hongyang admired, somewhat romantically, the courage and power of the Qin leaders and saw such military might in a positive light.[39] But at the same time he recognized the moral responsibilities involved. While the erudites made an effective argument against what they saw as Sang's exclusive promotion of physical defenses,[40] Sang's prospectus was more nuanced than the erudites' steadfast adherence to moral force.

> If the matter [of military deployment] is not analyzed in advance, one cannot respond to [enemy] troops; if there are no internal preparations, one cannot resist the adversary. The *Shi* says, "Perfect what concerns your officers and people; / Be careful of your duties as a prince [of the kingdom]— / To be prepared for unforeseen dangers."[41] Therefore, to have a civil situation one must have martial preparations. Formerly, Lord Xiang 襄公 of Song [d. 637 BCE] put his faith in Chu and was not prepared; he was thereby greatly humiliated. He himself was taken prisoner and his state was nearly lost.[42] Thus, although you may have a sincere and trustworthy heart, if you do not know about command power and rapid changes in battle, this is the way of danger and death.[43]

While the erudites adopted a typically *compartmentalist-ethical* position, Sang Hongyang, also aware of *ethical* imperatives, was more *syncretist* in approach. War may be dangerous, but it is as necessary and endemic a part of government activity as political, civil morality.

> Formerly, King Yan 偃王 of Xu 徐 [fl. late Western Zhou] conducted himself with righteousness but was destroyed.[44] Lord Ai 哀公 of Lu [r. 495–467 BCE] was fond of Ruist [principles] but was slain.[45] To know civility but not martiality is to know one but not two. Thus a true gentleman is devoted to humaneness in his conduct, but against those who are not humane and may harm him he must construct fortress walls for protection and build [siege] equipment for defense.[46]

It is possible to say, then, that new circumstances during the Western Han had altered over a period of years the relative attractiveness of a *compartmentalist* foreign policy of appeasement toward the threat from northern tribes. Such factors as the development by the Western Han of a high-quality iron industry capable of producing superior weapons, the disintegration of a once-solid Xiongnu state, the building of an effective cavalry force by the Han to counteract former Xiongnu dominance in horse warfare, and the establishment of a strategic defense network of agricultural colonies and dependent states all played a part in this shift. While Sang Hongyang, eager to accrue power, misjudged the willingness of the common people to sacrifice for the Han regime and wrongly predicted the economic gains from foreign trade, he and others of like conviction nevertheless discerned the need for continued military potency, without losing sight of *ethical* verities.[47]

In addition to addressing the moral aspects of Han foreign policy, the debates of 135–134 and 81 BCE supplied ideological justification for the tributary system that developed after Emperor Wu. Whereas Western Han formerly found it necessary to maintain a *compartmentalist* attitude in its relations with the outside world, these debates suggested that Han could adopt a more *syncretist* arrangement, built on the assumption of a militarily and culturally dominant Sinitic state with lesser foreign states acknowledging suzerainty. This new system provided that, like the sage-general described by Zhanguo thinkers, the Han ruler should use his cultivated awesomeness and manifest generosity to prevent the occurrence of conflict in the world order, and to intervene militarily to correct a wayward rebel only if his awesomeness was insufficient. The chief purpose of the tributary system was not so much to enhance Han power, though that was surely one consequence; rather, the objective was to prevent the loss of any power because of external violent incursions or economic warfare. In his discussion of the tributary system, the modern China scholar Yu Ying-shih noted several years ago that, on the one hand, the system was capable of keeping the various barbarian groups on China's border in a state of relative equilibrium, but on the other hand, the system set limits on China's trade and expansion because it afforded little incentive for Chinese merchants to seek wealth outside China or for Chinese rulers or generals to seek the acquisition of additional territories.[48]

Although Yu was not writing of martial philosophy, the essential qualities of the tributary system he outlined align with the tradition of military thought presented in this study. The tributary system can be interpreted as a means of equalizing vital energy (*qi*) among potentially contending parties while at the same time retaining sufficient vital energy of one's own to be in absolute control of international relations. The appeasement policy, by not allowing Western Han to direct its power positively and by draining the dynasty of its vital energy vis-à-vis the northern tribes, would probably not have been acceptable to the writers of the military treatises in the Zhanguo era, who argued generally for a *syncretist* approach. By contrast, the tributary system, by setting parameters for martial activity, accorded with these principles and thus would have been seen by the Zhanguo military thinkers as constituting a more viable theory of conflict prevention.[49]

A Double Paradox

Based on the above discussion of the interaction of military thought with Western Han foreign policy debates and the ideological convictions of participants in those debates, one can see that the main alternatives in these controversies—an appeasement policy and a tributary system—were but two new ways of addressing the same *wen/wu* problem that existed in pre-Han times. Moreover, one can detect intellectual links between each of these solutions and compatible solutions in the military treatises of the Zhanguo period.

These theoretical connections between Huang-Lao thought and *syncretism* and between Legalism-Ruism and *compartmentalism* did not necessarily mean that individual officials in Han government who generally adhered to Huang-Lao or Ruist viewpoints applied the principles of their parallel outlooks on the *wen/wu* issue in a consistent way. Nevertheless, even allowing for these inconsistencies, one encounters a double paradox in examining the fates of the appeasement and tributary system policies as compared to their philosophical counterparts—*compartmentalism* and *syncretism*. Whereas the tributary system became the dominant model of foreign diplomacy in the Han dynasty after Emperor Wu, the *syncretist* view of *wen/wu* that would seem to inhere in that model underwent a decided decline in the latter years of Western Han. Conversely, the rejection of the appeasement policy coincided with the flowering of its apparent philosophical rationale, the *compartmentalist* view.

To explain this double paradox, one can first look at the trends that helped to create the situation. Once again, chronological parallels between military thought and greater intellectual systems are important to observe. Sima Qian asserted in the *Shiji* in the early first century BCE that the rise in the status of Legalist-Ruist ideas was delayed by the military consolidation of imperial rule and the influence of Huang-Lao thought.

> [In the early years of Western Han] there was still military activity to pacify and settle the empire, and certainly there was not yet the leisure for regularized education. In the time of Emperor Hui 惠帝 and Empress Lü 呂后 princes and high ministers all gained merit by military efforts, and although Emperor Wen drafted and employed many [Ruists], he was basically fond of forms and names (*xingming*) doctrine. Emperor Jing did not rely on Ruists and, furthermore, Empress Dowager Dou was fond of Huang-Lao methods. Thus the erudites [of Ruist learning] filled official posts and waited for imperial consultation, but none were yet advanced.[50]

However, in Emperor Wu's reign, Tian Fen 田蚡 (d. 130 BCE) and others, having finally gained the confidence of the sovereign after Empress Dowager Dou's death, began to rid the court of ministers who did not espouse the philosophy of Legalism-Ruism. At the same, a new synthesis of political philosophy was being created that eventually superseded Huang-Lao thought in scope and practicability. Thereafter Legalist-Ruist ideology began gradually to dominate Han intellectual life. In military thought, this change seems to have had a subtle but decisive impact, as can be seen in a number of texts from the later Western Han period and the first decades of the Eastern Han period.

The first of these texts for our consideration is the "Bing lüe" 兵略 chapter of the *Huainanzi* 淮南子, whose collected lore probably reflects in general the ideas of a frustrated would-be usurper of the Han throne, Liu An 劉安, in the mid–second century BCE as well as the scholars Liu An assembled to compile the work.[51] The chapter begins with the primordial causes of conflict. At the outset, war is seen as an altruistic agent, a moral means. "In ancient times the military was employed not to profit from enlargement of territory or to lust after the seizure of gold and jewels. Rather, it was for preserving dying [regimes], aiding interrupted [lines of succession], removing disorder in the world, and eliminating scourges from among the people."[52] Afterward, the chapter highlights the now-familiar theory of martial origins, in which men, lacking natural weapons, devised their own for self-protection and fulfillment of instinctual desires. The formation of organized armies, however, led to moral criteria for employment.

> Now, the reason for weapons is to interdict the violent and punish the disorderly. Yandi 炎帝 caused fire disasters and

therefore Huangdi arrested him. Gong Gong caused flood damage and therefore Zhuan Xu 顓頊 executed him. [A sage-ruler] instructs by means of the Way and leads by means of virtue. But if [his inferiors] do not comply, then he approaches them with awesomeness and martiality. If, by approaching them with awesomeness and martiality, they still do not follow [instructions], then he disciplines them with weapons and armor. Thus the employment of weapons by a sage is like combing the hair or hoeing away weeds. What is eliminated is slight, but what is profited is great.[53]

Once again the notions of righteous war and of war as a method of conserving potency are affirmed. War should be conducted in the name of civility; violence should be applied only against offending leaders, while the people, undisturbed, are free to carry on their civil activities. "Thus the ultimate of righteous war is simply the attainment of no war."[54] In line with the *Daodejing*, "no war is best." Having said this, the "Bing lüe" chapter assigns proper control of martiality to the civil ruler. "He who fights from the ancestral temple is an emperor; he who transforms with psychical power (*shen*) is a king."[55] Success in war, says the *Huainanzi*, depends not on a sage-general's psychical power but on the cultivation of psychical power by the sage-ruler. On leading the people into war, the goals of harmony and public-mindedness (*gong* 公) are important, with a sustained emphasis on civility. Combining Ruist moralism and law, the chapter juxtaposes Legalist discipline with the powers of virtue and, in the process, also gives prominence to both the *metaphysical* and the *pragmatic*.

In military [strategy] there are three important [responsibilities]: to govern the country and put all within the borders in order; to conduct affairs with humaneness and righteousness and demonstrate virtue and kindness; and to establish upright laws and block evil subterfuges. If the ministers are in close agreement and the people are in harmonious unity; if superior and inferior are of one mind and ruler and subject exert themselves in concord; if subordinate lords submit to [the ruler's] awesomeness and the entire realm cherishes his virtue; if he cultivates government in the ancestral temple and audience hall, and yet can cut off [enemy] penetrations a thousand *li* away; if he is reverent in his leadership so that the empire responds [to his orders]—this

> is the best employment of war. If the territory is extensive and the people numerous, the ruler worthy and the generals loyal, the state prosperous and the army strong; if treaties and pacts are trusted and commands and orders are clear; if, when two armies face each other, drums and bells mutually responding, the enemy flees in defeat before weapons have clashed and blades have met—this is the second best employment of war. If [the ruler] knows the most suitable terrain, is versed in the advantages of cliffs and defiles, understands rapid changes between irregular and regular deployments, and has studied the methods for military formations, their proper division and linkage, he has only to [lift] his attached drumsticks and drum [the signal for advance]. Then, with naked blades clashing and flying arrows meeting, he will make his way through blood and guts, cart away corpses and prop up the wounded; and with blood flowing for a thousand *li*, and exposed skeletons filling the battleground, he will be decisively victorious—this is the least best employment of war.[56]

Consistent with this largely Ruist interpretation of the seat of primary influence in martial activities, the Way of the sage-general now receives second-place mention. Although the basic position of the military treatises regarding the role of the sage-general is maintained in the *Huainanzi*, the brevity of the description of the sage-general, as compared to the lengthy narrative on the attributes of a sage-ruler, indicates a certain ideological predisposition: "That by which a good general will surely be victorious is his constantly unfathomable knowledge and his indescribable way; with these, it would be difficult to compare him with the multitude."[57] This observation is validated by the immediately following passages, supported by examples, that assure the reader that large territories and populations, strong armies and fortifications, and strict laws and regulations are not enough to ensure survival. Rather it is good government that will preserve a state's integrity.[58] Once more, virtue is thought to be necessary and sufficient for victory in war. And yet, this argument is sometimes conjoined with features of the *metaphysical* perspective.

> Psychical power expresses itself with unerring swiftness and, embodied in a sincere and unified armed force it will lead one to seemingly effortless victory. Though practical measures and the demonstration of unswerving awesomeness are critical to a

> successful engagement, the optimum situation is one in which no battle ensues; it is the distribution of vital energy which determines the outcome. . . . Victory is in attaining awesomeness; defeat is in losing vital energy.[59]

It is important to note, however, that the, distribution of vital energy, as described in the *Huainanzi*, is not to be effectuated in amoral fashion, as in the military treatises, but in accord with the priorities of the civil ruler—that is, by force of *Mengzi*-like mind.

Because of the substantial volume of data in the "Bing lüe" chapter supporting the *syncretist* idea of *wen*/*wu* balance, it is difficult to call the overall intention of the chapter *compartmentalist*. However, the *ethical* element, which has so often been linked to the *compartmentalist* solution, is certainly more pronounced here than in the military treatises of the Zhanguo period. This judgment is strengthened if one considers the chapter's conclusion. There we find in the descriptions of the traditional ceremonies for commissioning a general and hailing his return a tendency to promote the separation of military and civil on moral grounds. In the case of the return ceremony:

> [The general] unfurls his banner to present his battleax and halberd. Reporting the end [of hostilities] to the sovereign, he says, "The army having no further control I now retire in white silk mourning garments. I request Your Highness to define my guilt." The sovereign replies, "You are pardoned. Withdraw in mourning garments."[60]

The description draws a sharp line between civility and martiality, as well as suggesting that military generals participate in an immoral activity for which they must be pardoned. Whether the description of the ceremony is original with the *Huainanzi* or borrowed from an earlier text is unclear, but the presence of this long section on ceremonies at the end of the "Bing lüe" chapter bespeaks a focus on the ethical consequences of war. This is even more evident in the moralistic tone of the final lines of the chapter, which seem to reflect the convictions of its author as much as the content of its sources.

> The country to which warfare is applied must be without the Way. Thus one may battle to victory and not for revenge, seize

> territory and not return it. The people will not suffer pestilence and the general will not die before his time. The five grains (*wugu* 五穀) will be flourishing and abundant; the winds and rains will come in their proper season. Battles will be won without and blessings will appear within. Hence renown will certainly be achieved and there will be no later harm.[61]

The general attitude of the "Bing lüe" chapter of the *Huainanzi* toward the *wen*/*wu* problem can be interpreted as *syncretist*; however, mixed into the chapter's arguments are favorable words for the *compartmentalist* approach, along with an *ethical* emphasis and both *metaphysical* and *pragmatic* characteristics. Appearing in about 139 BCE, before Legalism-Ruism took a solid grip on intellectual opinion in the Han capital, the "Bing lüe" chapter can be said to suggest the growing strength of Ruist ideology, with its proclivity to cast military-political affairs in moral terms.[62]

A second text of significance for trends in military thinking in the Western Han is the *Huangshigong Sanlüe* 黃石公三略 (hereafter *Sanlüe*).[63] This short work, which probably dates from the end of the Western Han, is concerned with the role of the military primarily from the viewpoint of a civil ruler. The emphasis is on methods of administrative control, the management of command power (*quan*), and the judicious use of military means to correct disorder. Running through the text is much advice familiar to readers of the Zhanguo military treatises. Occasionally, there are hints of *metaphysical* or Daoist approaches to generalship. "The *Military Portents* (*Jun chen* 軍讖) states: 'The soft can control the hard, the weak can control the strong.' "[64] But the major portion of the *Sanlüe* is on the *pragmatic* application of awesomeness (*wei*) and the *ethical* treatment of the people—whether high officials, soldiers, or the common masses—to effectively maintain tranquility.

These characteristics can be seen in the *Sanlüe* compiler's outline of the intentions of the three parts of the work:

> The sage (*shengren* 聖人) embodies heaven, the worthy (*xianren* 賢人) models on earth, and the wise man (*zhizhe* 智者) finds his teachers in antiquity. Thus the *Sanlüe* has been written for a period of decay. The Upper Strategy (*shang lüe* 上略) establishes the rules of propriety and rewards, distinguishes between evildoers and heroes, and makes clear success and failure. The Middle Strategy (*zhong lüe* 中略) distinguishes virtue (*de*) and action and

> examines command power (*quan*) and changes [in circumstances]. The Lower Strategy (*xia lüe* 下略) lays out the Way (*dao*) and virtue, investigates security and danger, and illuminates the errors of harming the worthy. Thus, if a ruler deeply understands the Upper Strategy he will be able to employ the worthy and seize his enemies. If he deeply understands the Middle Strategy he will be able to control his generals and unite the people. If he deeply understands the Lower Strategy he will be able to discern the sources of flourishing and decay and examine the institutions for ordering a state.[65]

In this description are suggestions of the same Legalist-Ruist mindset that we have seen in other Han sources. Martial methods, according to the *Sanlüe*, are inherently unsavory and must be compartmentalized unless deemed necessary to preserve good order in society. A ruler must maintain a grip on the circumstantial power (*shi*) of the state through meritorious rewards and legalistic punishments. When that grip is lost he must then turn to corrective military measures—but only in accordance with moral principle.

> The sage king does not take pleasure in using the weapons of war, but does so only to execute the violent and punish the disorderly. Now, using the righteous to execute the unrighteous (*yi yi zhu bu yi* 以義誅不義) is like releasing the Yangzi and Yellow rivers to extinguish a torch, or pushing over someone at the edge of an abyss. Success is inevitable! That is why those who hesitate and remain idle [in such situations], failing to move forward, wreak serious harm on all men. Weapons are inauspicious instruments abhorred by the Way of Heaven, and yet their employment is unavoidable. This is Heaven's Way.[66]

So saying, the *Sanlüe* bespeaks the evolution of ideas on the uses of martiality in the service of civility that had been occurring since the reign of Emperor Wu.

One final text to examine in this context is the *Wenzi* 文子, also called the *Tongxuan zhenjing* 通玄真經, a version of which was circulating in the second century BCE and contains notable commentary on military affairs.[67] With respect to the *wen*/*wu* debate, the received version of the *Wenzi* contains expansions on *Daodejing* arguments for an avoidance of war and the segregation of martial behavior from preferable civil behavior.[68] On the other hand, the *Wenzi* cites the importance of coupling righteousness and martial awesomeness (*wei*).

> That by which a state is strong lies in a commitment to die for the state, and that by which there is a commitment to die for the state lies in righteousness. Righteousness is effectuated through awesomeness. Thus, a ruler should direct his people with civility and unify them with martiality; by so doing he will surely succeed. He should demonstrate both awesomeness and righteousness; by so doing he will surely be strong. . . . Thus, internally a righteous ruler cultivates good order to accrue virtue, while externally he fends off evil influences to heighten his circumstantial power (*shi*). He keeps apprised of whether the people are well-employed or idle, undernourished or well-fed. When the day comes to wage war, and the people willingly fight to the death for the state, he treats them with kindness.[69]

In addition to this *syncretist* linkage, the received version of the *Wenzi* and corresponding passages in the *Wenzi* fragments discovered in Hebei in 1973 include a listing of the types of war that closely resembles the *ethical* list in the *Wuzi*, giving pride of place to righteous war.[70] Moreover, elsewhere in the received version of the *Wenzi* are paraphrases of *metaphysical* advice from the *Sunzi bingfa* and the *Sun Bin bingfa* with regard to irregular (*qi*) and regular (*zheng*) forces.

> Laozi said: "Use regular means to govern a state; use irregular means to go to war." First put into effect a state administration that cannot be conquered, and only then seek to overpower an enemy. To use a state that is not well ordered to attack another in chaos is like using fire to respond to fire, or water to respond to water. In both cases it will not be sufficient to exert good order, so use a different approach as an irregular means. The irregular for calm is rash; the irregular for well-ordered is chaotic; the irregular for well-fed is undernourished; and the irregular for well-employed is idle. Irregular and regular mutually respond like the mutual overcoming of water, fire, metal, and wood. In all cases there will be success.[71]

Overall, then, the treatment of the *wen/wu* issue in the received version of the *Wenzi*, as well as in the unearthed *Wenzi* fragments, largely underscores views attributed to Laozi. But this general alignment of views is modified by an admixture of *compartmentalist* and *ethical* ideas, blended with occasional statements reminiscent of Huang-Lao or *syncretist* viewpoints. Like other works of its time, the *Wenzi* reflects the fluidity of opinion in early China regarding how to use civility and martiality, both individually and together, in sustaining a state.

To summarize the foregoing, the last hundred years or so of Western Han saw a general decline in the value ascribed to the balanced *syncretist* view of *wen*/*wu* by prominent literati, and this decline paralleled chronologically the weakening of Huang-Lao influence in government affairs. While there continued to be mutual borrowings of ideas between the two remaining *wen*/*wu* solutions, as well as various matchings with *metaphysical*, *ethical*, and *pragmatic* elements, increasingly the synthesis developed by a variety of Legalist-Ruists provided a new authority for the control of conflict—one characterized primarily by a combination of *compartmentalist* and *ethical* approaches.

Effects of Social and Institutional Changes

Concurrent shifts in sociopolitical conditions in Western Han contributed to this movement toward a more *wen*-centric ideology. As noted in Chapters 1 and 3, with the gradual disappearance of aristocratic warfare, commoners and low-level officials gradually became the protagonists in battle. Especially in pre-imperial Qin under the influence of Shang Yang, war was clearly a duty of the populace at large, except for those who had been attracted from abroad to open up new agricultural lands.[72] In this respect, Qin probably was more efficient than other states in organizing its population for war. Nevertheless, other sources suggest that warfare was an occupation for lower classes as well as so-called good families (*liangjia* 良家) in Zhanguo times, and that aside from possible patriotic motives, the army offered opportunities to the bold, athletic, and intelligent for rapid social advancement.[73]

After the various remaining states had been welded into an empire, however, the character of soldiering began to change more fundamentally. Despite a lack of precise data, it appears that gradually larger numbers of lower-class men were being absorbed into the military and that in contrast to their Zhanguo counterparts, these warriors, with little sense of state loyalty, sought only personal security and/or high rewards.[74] The influx of such ignoble newcomers eventually caused a situation in which sons of wealthier families refused to enter military service, thereby forcing the imperial government to recruit increasing numbers of lower-class men.[75]

With the fall of the Qin regime came attempts in early Western Han to reestablish independent states as existed in the Chunqiu and Zhanguo periods. Chu, having avoided less of the destruction visited on other regions during Qin unification, made the strongest claim for independence by forging a close-knit army, led by talented nobles Xiang Liang 項梁 (d. 208 BCE) and Xiang Yu 項羽 (232–202 BCE), which was reminiscent of an older martial excellence. This was a vain effort, however. The Han regime nullified this vestigial tradition of armies loyal to individual states and founded in its place a Qin-inspired, impersonal army organization consisting of individual draftees. In general, this system, as it existed in theory before Emperor Wu's time, consisted chiefly of a small core of active-duty personnel for capital guard duty and/or border service.[76] This core was supplemented by two categories of inactive reserve troops drawn from all able-bodied males in the empire: those who, after performing two years of continuous duty, returned to border stations for limited training/duty each year; and those who performed one month of border service per year, usually in maintenance, construction, or supply work.[77] However, due to the rise of various classes of exemptions and a system of commutation and substitution, such universal conscription did not apply in practice to all eligible men. Unless the patriotism of the population at large was intense, only those who were least able to pay the commutation fee or find a suitable proxy actually served in Han armies, either in active or reserve status. Moreover, indigent reserve soldiers frequently remained as border troops after the expirations of their terms of service, either because they were persuaded to be proxies or because they preferred permanent residence on the frontier to expensive moves across the empire. Many brought their families to frontier posts and essentially became career military personnel.[78]

This system, with minor modifications, pertained only to regular defense missions on the northern, northwestern, and southern borders of the Han realm. In times of hostilities special levies were required to augment already mobilized troops, and these recruitments, especially in Emperor Wu's time and afterward, tended to draw on population groups not normally liable for army duty during peacetime—that is, convicts and foreigners.[79] This was particularly true in the latter years of the campaigns against the Xiongnu, when manpower became less and less available. In addition, the establishment of dependent states and the adoption of a loose-rein (*jimi* 羈縻) policy to control Xiongnu incursions served to bolster the trend toward a low-grade rank and file by increasing Han's reliance on outcasts and, especially in Eastern Han, barbarians to fight its wars.[80]

In the early Han consolidation period the ill effects of this downward trend in the social makeup of the military on the security of the empire were probably not serious. By Emperor Wu's time, however, one begins to see failures in leadership that were probably related to the long-term decline in social standing of ordinary soldiers. The backgrounds of early Western Han generals were not uniform: some came from nobility, others originated in military families, and still others were poor or had criminal records.[81] But judging from the number of defeats suffered against foreign adversaries and the large estimates of casualties sustained by Western Han armies during battles with the Xiongnu, talented military commanders were difficult to find.[82]

The details of this apparent lapse in military proficiency are still obscure, but it is clear that along with the overall decrease in the prestige of military service, the central government, beginning in Emperor Jing's time, allowed the appointment of generals to be based often on other than military competence. Besides ordering that no one would be enfeoffed a king (*wang*) unless he was a member of the Liu clan, Emperor Gaozu proclaimed that no one would be selected a marquis (*hou*), that is, a potential commander in chief during wartime, unless he had distinguished himself in combat.[83] A half-century later, however, during Emperor Jing's time, these admonitions from the dynastic founder were being disregarded. Significantly, it was Zhou Yafu 周亞夫 (d. 143 BCE), the chief general for Han during the Seven Kingdoms Rebellion (154 BCE), who most vocally criticized Emperor Jing for not observing his ancestor's wishes.[84] Emperor Wu exacerbated the situation during his reign when he attempted to concentrate power in his hands by shifting the locus of decision making from the outer to the inner court. As a result of this move, the emperor's outer clans and other favorites rose steadily to positions of military power.[85] This was a trend which, especially after the assumption of both martial and civil duties by Huo Guang 霍光 (d. 68 B.C.E), only aggravated the fall in the quality of army leadership.[86] Though some commanders appointed from among the consort families did distinguish themselves during Western Han—notably Wei Qing 衛青 (d. 106 BCE) and Huo Qubing 霍去病 (140–117 BCE)—their appointments were probably due in large part to either blood relationships or perhaps individual physical skill, rather than to an institutionalized policy like that in the civil realm for selecting those with the greatest potential for leadership.[87] Curiously, it is after 135 BCE, during the period of greatest territorial expansion in Western Han, as militarily untrained favorites and imperial relatives moved into influential inner-court roles, that one sees more clearly the low esteem with which the military was viewed by government official and peasant alike.[88]

Thus, in both social-institutional and intellectual terms, martiality was being eroded as a vital component of government policy-making. Once again it is worth stressing that this downward movement, beginning in Western Han, was not precipitous. The directives of Emperor Wu to Yang Pu 楊僕 (d. ca. 108 BCE) and of Emperor Jing to Ren Hong 任宏 to collect military treatises, as well as the decision by Emperor Wang Mang 王莽 (r. 9–23 CE) of the Xin 新 dynasty to assemble sixty-three works on military methods (*bingfa*), are but three instances of a certain amount of imperial interest during this period in the maintenance of a martial tradition.[89] Still, the rapid decline in new military thought, combined with the intellectual flowering of Han classical studies, demonstrates that in the realm of philosophical inquiry there was a dismissal of martiality and a concentration on civility. An army career per se was no longer a route to fame and wealth; indeed, soldiering had become socially debased. The ability of powerful clans to appoint military leaders based on family links or political influence rather than an aptitude for military leadership; the fall of Huang-Lao thought and the rise of a state-sponsored Ruism unsympathetic to the military; and the development of an Imperial Academy (*taixue* 太學) recommendation system for civil officials, which stimulated intelligent men to devote their energies to government service and *belles lettres* rather than military careers—all of these were factors that discouraged excellence in military affairs and retarded the further development of a vibrant philosophy of war.

In view of this confluence of factors, it is now possible to explain the apparent contradiction between a *syncretist* tributary system and a *compartmentalist* attitude toward *wen*/*wu* beginning in the latter part of Western Han period. As has been noted, for various reasons armies designed to constitute the potency for controlling external violence and for enabling the emperor to arbitrate a new world order were populated by foreigners and outcasts of Han society. In accord with the loose-rein policy and a policy of "using barbarians to attack barbarians" (*yi yi fa yi* 以夷伐夷), a *compartmentalist* statesman could argue for the use of low-ranking, segregated men of war stationed on the fringes of the Han domain to fulfill higher, civil purposes. Rather than recognize the *syncretist* nature of the tributary system as envisioned in Emperor Wu's time—a balanced application of *wen/wu* to control aggression—*compartmentalist* officials could employ sanitized, isolated martial elements as disguised tools of civility. Martiality was thereby placed under civility and disallowed from becoming a positive element in the governance of the state.

One way to corroborate this evolving *compartmentalist* relationship between civility and martiality is to observe the employment of what were labeled harsh officials (*kuli* 酷吏) to counteract the centrifugal forces of powerful local magnates and knights-errant (*youxia* 游俠). Knights-errant appeared initially in Zhanguo times as guests (*ke* 客) of state lords. As Sima Qian portrayed them, model knights-errant were more than just henchmen.

> Although their actions may deviate from proper righteousness, they always keep their word; resolute in action, they are faithful in carrying out a promise; caring not about their own lives they go to the assistance of those in distress; and when they have preserved others from perishing, they do not brag of their ability and will feel ashamed in boasting of their kindness to others.[90]

They were engaged, therefore, to be loyal and righteous soldiers, ready to carry out the violent tasks required by their patrons and the power politics of the times in ways that reflected the idea of righteous war. These agents of *wu* were complemented at the courts of such Zhanguo strongmen as Lords Mengchang 孟嘗, Chunshen 春申, Pingyuan 平原, and Xinling 信陵—known as the Four Lords (*si gongzi* 四公子) or the Four Gentlemen (*si junzi* 四君子)—by disputers (*bianshi* 辯士) who were deft in rhetoric, strategic planning, and scholarly, civil, affairs.[91] There were, in other words, both martial and civil components in a regional strongman's collection of guests, which might be employed as needed to implement their lord's commands.[92]

Coupled with the rise of knights-errant in Zhanguo times was the use of assassins (*cike* 刺客) to deal with political or personal grievances. These were not seen as mere mercenaries or hit-men, but as nonprofessional military men who volunteered to kill for others' righteous purposes. The rationale was that, by hiring an assassin to kill an enemy, one could avoid a long and costly conflict with an unrighteous rival who was too strong to confront directly.[93]

In the pre-Qin period, when state rulers and lesser strongmen could apply their own interpretations of righteous war, such instruments of martiality as assassins and knights-errant were accepted instruments of power.

But once the unified Han regime was established, the legitimacy of assassins and knights-errant came into question. Neither the adherents of Huang-Lao thought nor the proponents of Legalism-Ruism found value in such elements, for they could no longer be justified as agents of righteousness. Instead they were threats to a new imperial order. Even in pre-Qin times, Han Fei considered such men, along with Ruists, dangerous to government and society.

> The Ruists with their learning bring confusion to the law; the knights-errant with their military prowess violate the prohibitions. Yet the ruler treats both groups with respect, and so we have disorder. People who deviate from the law should be treated as criminals, and yet scholars actually attain posts in the government because of their literary accomplishments. People who violate the prohibitions ought to be punished, and yet the bands of knights-errant are able to make a living by wielding their swords in a private case. Hence those whom the law condemns the ruler accepts, and those whom the magistrates seek to punish the higher officials patronize. Thus law and practice, high official and lowly magistrate, are all set at odds, and there is no fixed standard. Under such circumstances even ten Huangdis could not bring the state to order. Those who practice humaneness and righteousness should not be praised, for to praise them is to cast aspersion on military achievements. Men of literary accomplishment should not be employed in the government, for to employ them is to bring confusion to the law.[94]

Three centuries later, Ban Gu expressed similar disapproval, though for Legalist-Ruist reasons.

> As for standard laws in ancient times, the Five Hegemons were the offenders against the Three Sovereigns and [the rulers of] the Six States were the offenders against the Five Hegemons. Now, the Four Lords were the offenders against [the rulers of] the Six States, and this is all the more the case for the likes of Guo Xie 郭解, who, with the slight station of horse groom, usurped the power of life and death; their offenses were more insufferable than capital crimes. [True,] they demonstrated warm kindness and broad affection; assisted the poor and aided the distressed;

> withdrew humbly and did not attack [when they thought it unrighteous]—certainly each had outstanding endowments. But, alas, they did not enter [the company of] those who accord with the Way and virtue; instead they recklessly gave themselves over to debased social elements, killing themselves and destroying their family lines—it was not mere misfortune.[95]

To be sure, knights-errant at the beginning of the Western Han continued to be important for the military consolidation of the empire. Without the military skills and large following of Ju Meng 劇孟, an exceptionally powerful knight-errant, the Seven Kingdoms Rebellion in 154 BCE might have been successful.[96] But increasingly, both Huang-Lao and Legalist-Ruist statesmen at the imperial court were effective in promoting a new institutional framework for the empire that would displace the concatenation of power centers that had previously existed. The decentralized state structure that had nourished the rise of knights-errant came under attack, as the government moved to uproot great regional families (*haozu* 豪族) who, by commerce, imperial connection, or sheer coercion, had carved out spheres of influence for themselves. Rationalizing that these powerful elements were not fulfilling their proper roles in society, or that they prevented the actualization of an effortless, universal rule, the Han government attempted to subjugate these elements and the martial traditions that had sustained them in pre-Qin times. The criterion of public-mindedness (*gong*) was important in legitimizing this effort: whereas public-mindedness was conducive to political unity and civil harmony, the remaining strong families and their affiliated knights-errant represented private-mindedness (*si* 私), being concerned only with benefits to themselves.

To carry out this task of eliminating martial power centers, however, martial means were necessary. In the case of the Seven Kingdoms Rebellion, whole armies had to be deployed. But even in cases of powerful clans and knights-errant who had accumulated large numbers of cohorts and maintained de facto hegemony over territory in the countryside or even a few wards in large cities, the Han central government had to dispatch men of martiality—harsh officials—to weed out the separatists. These harsh officials were, in many instances, unscrupulous, unsavory characters, aided by ruthless assistants known as "claws and teeth" (*zhaoya* 爪牙), who had to be restrained by the very penal laws they were supposed to enforce.[97] Moreover, although these proxies of the central government effectively destroyed the power bases of offending great clans and knight-errant brotherhoods, they often gave rise to reigns of terror that were nevertheless viewed externally as evidence of stability and civil peace. Hence the Han court, especially under Emperors Wen, Jing, and Wu, was prepared to use agents of martiality to carry out its policy of consolidation and moral correction.[98] In this way, Western Han rulers, with varying degrees of will, chose to use *wu* in the name of *wen*.

As with the earlier double paradox in foreign-military affairs, one could interpret this employment of harsh officials, especially in post-Emperor Wu times, as both an abrogation of the now-dominant *compartmentalist-ethical* idea that virtue in itself could bring recalcitrant reactionaries to heel and as proof that a *syncretist* view was still in favor. To some extent, that was the case. However, the use of harsh officials could also be rationalized on *compartmentalist* grounds, since these functionaries were not men of civility or even upstanding military professionals but often undesirable, clever men who, because they were loyal to the throne and ruthless in their effectiveness, were useful to the Han government in its consolidation efforts. From an ideological standpoint, they symbolized the distaste with which martiality was perceived by many Legalist-Ruists. Just as disreputable, foreigner-manned border armies were utilized to achieve civil goals in a new tributary system, the task of suppressing separatist martial elements inside the empire was assigned to harsh officials. As a result, *wu* could be figuratively segregated from *wen*. Government-sponsored men of martiality would not be held in high popular esteem, private-minded men of martiality—whether foreign aggressors, knights-errant, or regional strongmen—would be eliminated, and civil society would be ostensibly enhanced. The use of harsh officials as well as barbarian-outcast armies, at least for the late Western Han and Eastern Han periods, can therefore be seen as an outcome of the *compartmentalist-ethical* approach to the *wen-wu* problem.

Conclusion

It may be useful now to retrace briefly the intellectual movements in the history of Western Han military thought as presented in this chapter.

With the imminent political unification of the Zhanguo states, the proponents of the three major streams of martial thinking approached the inevitability of conflict during Zhanguo times in various ways, sometimes changing the emphases of their respective convictions. The *militarists* developed their theory of an agricultural-legalist-military nexus into a model for empire building; the *compartmentalists* continued to emphasize the notion of segregating martial activity in order to preserve civil virtues and thereby create a harmonious society; and the *syncretists* continued to argue for balanced application of martiality and civility, stressing that the ultimate purpose of war is to conserve civil peace.

After the success of Qin, the *militarist* view became temporarily dominant. However, the Qin regime's belief in the brutal application of legal strictures in the name of state power proved untenable, and the militarist solution that adhered to the Qin dynasty died with the empire's demise. A new empire, the Western Han, resumed the program of imperial consolidation started by Qin, but with a clear awareness of the civil features that must be incorporated into government in order for that consolidation to endure. As a result, the *syncretist* solution, which drew many of its elements from Huang-Lao thought, and the *compartmentalist* solution, which derived most of its tenets from Ruism, vied for prominence in the Western Han in a fashion parallel, but not equivalent, to the competition between Huang-Lao and Legalist-Ruist thinkers to establish a dominant ideology for the new imperial order.

Until the reign of Emperor Wu, these two approaches to the *wen*/*wu* problem each had effects on the military-foreign policies of the Western Han. The appeasement policy, pursued early in the regime's history, was based on a *compartmentalist* view, while the tributary system, established later in the Western Han period, was the outcome of a *syncretist* response to external threats. With the creation of a new intellectual synthesis supported by Emperor Wu, Huang-Lao thought began to decline, and the *syncretist* view, whose elements overlapped with those of Huang-Lao thought, went into dormancy. Concurrently, the *compartmentalist* solution began to ascend in importance as a means for preserving civil order within the imperial state and to block potential foreign encroachments. The downgrade in the social status of military servicemen and the rise of imperial favorites and men of the outer clans to positions of civil and military power, most of whom were uninterested in preserving a high level of military competence, contributed to a general intellectual distaste for martial affairs and an indifference to the idea of a balanced *wen*/*wu* continuum. The *compartmentalist* solution supported these attitudes and legitimized the use of low-status tools of martiality, such as harsh officials and conscript soldiers, to carry out necessary tasks of punishment against bad elements, foreign and domestic, without allowing such activities to impinge on the socially and politically more important tasks of civil government.

Even as the relationships among the three main solutions to the *wen/wu* problem changed over the course of the pre-Han and Western Han periods, the three principal perspectives pertaining to the problem—the *metaphysical*, the *pragmatic*, and the *ethical*—were still being applied. The *metaphysical* features of the sage-general continued to be stressed throughout these centuries as the acme of military leadership. Practical and metapractical techniques of the *pragmatic* perspective on waging war remained important for the prosecution of war. And *ethical* standards for the use of military might, such as the enduring notion of righteous war, grew in stature as critical principles in the use of martial means for civil ends.

Throughout the long history of military thought, from Shang through Western Han, one sees a continual realignment of ideas, yielding new permutations of outlooks on the *wen/wu* problem. In response to sociopolitical conditions, intellectuals created new combinations of ideas and different emphases within these combinations, in attempts to resolve the recurring issue. This process did not languish with the passing of the Western Han dynasty, but was renewed in Chinese history whenever conflict threatened to overturn a stable society.

Epilogue

Based on the foregoing, it is clear that the development of military thought in early China richly contributed to an understanding of the perennial question of how to use civility and martiality properly for the achievement of social harmony. By the end of the Western Han, the overall structure of Chinese military thought as it had grown from ancient times began to stabilize into what would be a relatively unchanging body of military lore. Portions of this lore, along with a work of the early Tang dynasty, were eventually assembled and standardized in about 1078 to create the *Seven Military Classics* (*Wujing qishu* 武經七書).[1] Nevertheless, this corpus of wisdom and technique never really cohered into a unified theory or school. Instead, Chinese military thought continued during post-Han times to be characterized by varying combinations of the elements set forth in this study. As problems affecting war and peace evolved after the Western Han, solutions and perspectives formed earlier were revisited in order to respond to new political-military crises or reinforce new regimes.

As some evidence of this trend during the Eastern Han dynasty and the Sanguo period, a *compartmentalist-ethical* approach can be seen in a discussion of martial and civil matters during the White Tiger Hall conference of 79 CE as summarized in the "San jun" 三軍 and "Zhu fa" 誅伐 chapters of the *Baihu tongyi* 白虎通義.[2] Later in Eastern Han, Wang Fu 王符 (ca. 85–ca. 163), seeing the inevitability of war in his time and the need for legalistic encouragement of troops and commanders, took a *syncretist-pragmatic* stance in his *Qianfu lun* 潛夫論 by outlining possible defense procedures in the manner of Chao Cuo in the Western Han. In addition, Wang expressed an *ethical* regard for the deprivations suffered by the common people in a time when external security was poor and uncontrolled troops were allowed to ravage the countryside.[3] At about the same time, Cui Shi 崔寔 (ca. 103–170) argued in *pragmatic* fashion in his

Zheng lun 政論 for a revitalization of military proficiency in order that potential invaders of the Eastern Han might be deterred.[4] A few decades later Zhongchang Tong 仲長統 (179–220) similarly affirmed in his *Changyan* 昌言 the *pragmatic* necessity of a strong arsenal of weapons and sufficient stockpiles of provisions in case of war.[5] Cao Cao 曹操 (155–220), the noted general at the end of the Eastern Han, also championed *pragmatic* views in his commentary on the *Sunzi bingfa*. During the Sanguo 三國 (Three Kingdoms) period, Huan Fan 桓範 (d. 249) touted the selection of generals based on their strategic knowledge and awesome bearing, and demonstrated a preference for the *compartmentalist-ethical* by assigning greater value to virtuous government than to martial strength.[6] Finally, writings attributed to the military strategist and statesman Zhuge Liang 諸葛亮 (181–234), including the *Bingyao* 兵要, the *Junling* 軍令, the *Bianyi shiliuce* 便宜十六策, and the *Jiangyuan* 將苑 (also called *Xinshu* 新 [or 心] 書), elaborate on key themes of the Zhanguo military treatises, stressing *pragmatic* means for waging war, with occasional references to the *metaphysical* faculties of the sage-general.[7]

The above are only a few examples, as it is beyond this study to address all of the re-examinations of early military thought that Chinese writers produced in post–Western Han times.[8]It is important to say, however, that this body of martial thinking continued to be significant in later imperial China not only because of the recurring *wen*/*wu* debate, but also because of the relevance of its multiple approaches to other fundamental problems in Chinese culture. As we have seen, military theory in early China appeared in writings across the whole corpus of intellectual inquiry, not just in works by military specialists.[9] Similarly, in later imperial China, the interpretations of key ideas in the military treatises and in other works addressing military matters in the pre-Han and Western Han eras were reapplied in different ways to issues in Chinese society in succeeding regimes, to include such perennial questions as what is the best use of punishments (*xing*) and virtue (*de*) in governing a state and what is the most effective method for responding to potential geo-political threats from outside China's perceived sphere of influence.[10] It is for this reason that military thought in early China has continuing usefulness in modern-day China, just as it had for the Sinitic realm many centuries ago. Indeed, one can plausibly argue that many of the ideas argued in this ancient debate on martiality and civility have relevance to other world states seeking to develop and sustain strong and harmonious societies.

Notes

Prologue

1. The military book section ("Bingshu lüe" 兵書略), one of six such sections in the *Hanshu* 漢書 "Treatise on Literature" ("Yiwen zhi" 藝文志), contains four subsections: strategic planning (*quanmou* 權謀), dispositions and circumstantial power (*xingshi* 形勢), *yinyang* calculations (*yinyang* 陰陽), and military skills (*jiqiao* 技巧). The Daoists (*daojia* 道家), Legalists (*fajia* 法家), eclectics (*zajia* 雜家), storytellers (*xiaoshuojia* 小說家), and rites (*li* 禮) divisions of the *Hanshu* "Yiwen zhi" also list titles of now nonextant works that appear to pertain to military affairs—e.g., the *Tai Gong* 太公 in 237 *pian* 篇 (*Hanshu* [Yiwen yinshuguan ed.] 30.33b–34a); the *Chao Cuo* 晁錯 in thirty-one *pian* (*Hanshu* 30.41b); the *Wu Zixu* 五子胥 in eight *pian* (*Hanshu* 30.46b); the *Shi Kuang* 師曠 in six *pian* (*Hanshu* 30.50a); the *Weiliaozi* 尉繚子 in twenty-nine *pian* (*Hanshu* 30.46b), whose relationship to the *Weiliao* 尉繚 in thirty-one *pian* mentioned in the military philosophers (*bingjia*) division [*Hanshu* 30.61a] as well as the received text of the *Weiliaozi* is not certain; and the *Junli simafa* 軍禮司馬法 in 155 *pian* (*Hanshu* 30.12a). For statistics on military texts listed in the various bibliographies of the standard histories (*zhengshi* 正史), see Lennart Frantzell, *Dr. Her's Comprehensive Essays on the Art of War, the Her Bor-shyh Bey Luenn* (Stockholm: Stockholms Universitet Institutionen för orientaliska språk, 1973), 166–170. For catalogs of military texts in China from antiquity through the imperial era, see Lu Dajie 陸達節, *Lidai bingshu mulu* 歷代兵書目錄 (Taibei: Guting shuwu, 1970), and Liu Shenning 劉申寧, *Zhongguo bingshu zongmu* 中國兵書總目 (Beijing: Guofang daxue chubanshe, 1990).

2. The texts discovered during the last few decades and relevant to this study include the military treatise *Sun Bin bingfa* 孫臏兵法; alternate versions of the military treatises *Sunzi bingfa* 孫子兵法, *Weiliaozi* 尉繚子, and *Liutao* 六韜; the military treatise *Wang bing* 王兵; the collection of Huang-Lao texts *Huangdi sijing* 黃帝四經, comprising the *Jingfa* 經法, the *Jing* 經 (previously interpreted as *Shidajing* 十大經 or *Shiliujing* 十六經), the *Cheng* 稱, and the *Daoyuan* 道原; the silk manuscript on cloud prognostications that has been given the title *Tianwen qi xiang za zhan* 天文氣象雜占; the Yin-Yang military prognostication

texts *Gai Lu* 蓋廬 (*He Lu* 闔廬 or *He Lü* 闔閭) and *Didian* 地典; the political-military treatise *Cao Mo zhi zhen* 曹沫之陳; and fragments of the philosophical text, the *Wenzi* 文子. For general descriptions of the excavations and discoveries at Yinqueshan and Mawangdui, see Shandong sheng bowuguan Linyi wenwu zu 山東省博物館臨沂文物組, "Shandong Linyi Xi Han mu faxian *Sunzi bingfa* he *Sun Bin bingfa* deng zhujian de jian bao" 山東臨沂西漢墓發現《孫子兵法》和《孫臏兵法》等竹簡的簡報, *Wenwu* 文物1974 (2): 15–26; Wu Jiulong 吳九龍, *Yinqueshan Han jian shiwen* 銀雀山漢簡釋文 (Beijing: Wenwu chubanshe, 1985); and Jeffrey K. Riegel, "A Summary of Some Recent *Wenwu* and *Kaogu* Articles on Mawangdui Tombs Two and Three," *Early China* 1 (1975): 10–15. For a description of the excavation of the *Gai Lu* (*He Lu*/*He Lü*), see Olivia Milburn, "*Gai Lu*: A Translation and Commentary on a Yin-Yang Military Text Excavated from Tomb M247, Zhangjiashan," *Early China* 33–34 (2010–2011): 101–107. For a description of the excavation of the *Didian*, see Robin D.S. Yates, "The Yin-yang Texts from Yinqueshan: An Introduction and Partial Reconstruction, with Notes on their Significance in Relation to Huang-Lao Daoism," *Early China* 19 (1994): 75–144. For a description and transcription of the *Cao Mo zhi zhen* 曹沫之陳, acquired by the Shanghai Museum in 1994, see Li Ling 李零, *Cao Mo zhi zhen* 曹沫之陳, in *Shanghai bowuguan cang Zhanguo Chu zhu shu* 上海博物館藏戰國楚竹書, ed. Ma Chengyuan 馬承源 (Shanghai: Shanghai guji chubanshe, 2001–), 4: 239–285. For a description of the excavation of the *Wenzi* fragments, see Dingxian Han mu zhujian zhengli zu 定縣漢墓竹簡整理組, "Dingxian 40 hao Han mu chutu zhujian jian jie" 定縣40號漢墓出土竹簡簡介, *Wenwu* 1981 (8): 12.

3. Even in the late twentieth century, efforts were being made by some Chinese scholars to identify the members and locus of a military school (*bingjia* 兵家) in ancient China. In the 1970s, for example, Yan Gengwang 嚴耕望 (1916–1996) attempted to locate the geographical centers of influence for various schools of thought in the Zhanguo period, based on what was known of the putative authors of works listed in the *Hanshu* "Treatise on Literature." Yan concluded that, of fourteen ostensible adherents to the military school for whom data was sufficient, four each derived from the states of Qi 齊 and Chu 楚, and two each from the states of Wei 魏, Wei 衛, and Zhao 趙. The prominence of the *Simafa*, the *Sunzi bingfa*, and the *Sun Bin bingfa* in Qi led Yan to choose Qi as the most important seat of military school influence. See Yan Gengwang, "Zhanguo xueshu dili yu rencai fenbu" 戰國學術地理 與人才分佈, *Xinya shuyuan xueshu niankan* 新亞書院學術年刊 18 (1976), 10.

4. For similar viewpoints on the difficulties of using schools to understand Han and pre-Han philosophical developments, see Mark Csikszentmihalyi and Michael Nylan. "Constructing Lineages and Inventing Traditions through Exemplary Figures in Early China," *T'oung Pao* 89 (2003): 59–99, and Jens Østergård Petersen. "Which Books Did the First Emperor of Ch'in Burn? On the Meaning of Pai Chia in Early Chinese Sources," *Monumenta Serica* 43 (1995): 1–52, esp. 33–37.

5. For a discussion of these two battles and the larger issue of battle accounts in early Chinese histories, see Frank A. Kierman Jr., "Phases and Modes of Combat in Early China," in *Chinese Ways in Warfare*, ed. Frank A. Kierman Jr. and John K. Fairbank (Cambridge, MA: Harvard University Press, 1974), 27–66.

6. Because the focus of this study is on the changing currents of early Chinese military thought, the sometimes complex and controversial issues regarding dating, authorship, and filiation for each of these six treatises will not be addressed at length. The reader is referred to the following useful discussions: Ralph D. Sawyer, *The Seven Military Classics* (Boulder, CO: Westview Press, 1993), 35–37 (*Liutao*), 111–115 (*Simafa*) 149–153 (*Sunzi bingfa*), 191–202 (*Wuzi*), 229–232 (*Weiliaozi*); D.C. Lau and Roger T. Ames, *Sun Pin: The Art of Warfare* (New York: Ballantine Books, 1996), 1–5; Krzysztof Gawlikowski and Michael Loewe, "*Sun tzu ping fa*," in *Early Chinese Texts: A Bibliographical Guide*, ed. by Michael Loewe (Berkeley, CA: Society for the Study of Early China, 1993), 446–455; Victor H. Mair, trans., *The Art of War: Sun Zi's Military Methods* (New York: Columbia University Press, 2007), 1–23; Jens Østergård Petersen, "What's in a Name? On the Sources Concerning Sun Wu," *Asia Major*, 3rd ser. 5, no. 1 (1992): 1–31; Li Ling 李零 et al., comps., *Zhongguo bingshu ming zhu jin yi* 中國兵書名著今譯 (Beijing: Junshi yiwen chubanshe, 1992), 21–22 (*Simafa*; commentary by Li Ling), 51–53 (*Liutao*; commentary by Sheng Dongling 盛冬鈴), 122–124; commentary by Lou Xiyuan 婁熙元), 138–139 (*Weiliaozi*; commentary by Gao Ke 高可 and Li Zhaoxiang 李肇翔); and Zhang Lie 張烈, "*Liutao* de chengshu ji qi neirong" 《六韜的成書及 其內容, *Lishi yanjiu* 歷史研究 1981 (3): 122–126.

7. Unless otherwise noted, all translations from Chinese-language texts in this study were prepared by the author.

Chapter 1

1. The *Shiji* 史記, the first of the standard histories, contains no treatise for military affairs, although information on military principles is included in the "Treatise on Pitch Pipes" ("Lü shu" 律書). The *Hanshu* likewise has no treatise (*zhi* 志) for military affairs but does provide some important ideas in the "Treatise on Penal Administration" ("Xingfa zhi" 刑法志). After the Han dynasty, no systematic treatment is given of military affairs in the standard histories until the *Xin Tang shu* 新唐書 by Ouyang Xiu 歐陽修 (1007–1072). Thereafter, treatises on military matters appear in the *Song shi* 宋史, the *Jin shi* 金史, the *Yuan shi* 元史, the *Xin Yuan shi* 新元史, the *Ming shi* 明史, and the *Qing shi gao* 清史稿. However, few of the latter treatises comment on military ideology; instead they are concerned principally with changes in military institutions. General encyclopedias (*leishu* 類書) in the imperial age are similar in this regard, although there are exceptions. Information on martial affairs in the *Cefu yuangui* 冊府元龜, compiled in the Song

宋 dynasty (960–1279), and the *Yuhai* 玉海, compiled by Wang Yinglin 王應麟 (1223–1296), is almost entirely related to the development of military institutions. On the other hand, the *Beitang shuchao* 北堂書鈔 and the *Yiwen leiju* 藝文類聚 of the Tang 唐 dynasty (618–907), as well as the *Taiping yulan* 太平御覽 of the Song dynasty, supply numerous quotations of significance for the study of military philosophy—some originating from now nonextant texts of earlier times. Also, among the encyclopedic histories of institutions, the *Tongdian* 通典, by Du You 杜佑 (735–812), draws from the pre-Han military treatises, as well as other Han and pre-Han works, to illustrate not only the evolution of military organization, but also strategic and tactical principles.

2. *Boshu Laozi* 帛書老子 (Taibei: He-Le tushu chubanshe, 1975), 214 (nos. 91–95). These citations of Yanran and Shancai are the first known occurrences in early Chinese writings. Further citations of the four components of the *Huangdi sijing*—the *Jingfa* 經法, the *Jing* 經, the *Cheng* 稱, and the *Daoyuan* 道原—will list the relevant work, the appropriate page number in the above edition, and the number(s) in parentheses of the original strips in their recovered order. Although there is still some question about the proper title to be assigned to the group of four works and the titles of each of the works, accepted here is Tang Lan's 唐蘭 conclusion that the four works constitute the *Huangdi sijing* listed in the *Hanshu* "Treatise on Literature" (*Hanshu* 30.30b; Tang Lan, "*Huangdi si jing* chu tan"《黃帝四經》初探], *Wenwu* 文物 1974 (10): 48–52; Tang Lan, "Mawangdui chutu *Laozi* yi ben qian yishu de yanjiu" 馬王堆出土《老子》乙本卷前古佚書的研究, *Kaogu xuebao* 考古學報 1975 (1): 7–27). For other discussions of the *Huangdi sijing*, see R.P. Peerenboom, *Law and Morality in Ancient China: The Silk Manuscripts of Huang-Lao* (Albany: State University of New York Press, 1993), 1–19, and Robin D.S. Yates, trans., *Five Lost Classics: Tao, Huang-Lao, and Yin-Yang in Han China* (New York: Ballantine Books, 1997), 193–202.

3. For background on the composition of the *Shiji* 史記, see A.F.P. Hulsewé, "*Shih chi* 史記," in Loewe, *Early Chinese Texts*, 405–414.

4. *Shiji* (Yiwen yinshuguan ed.) 24.31a.

5. *Shi* 詩, "Shu yu tian" 叔于田 (trans. James Legge, *The Chinese Classics* [Taibei: Jinxue shuju, 1958; reprint of the last editions of Oxford University Press], 4: 127–128). For a discussion of the content and dating of the *Shi*, see Michael Loewe, "*Shih ching* 詩經," in Loewe, *Early Chinese Texts*, 415–423.

6. *Shi*, "Qi yue" 七月 (trans. Legge, *Classics*, 4: 229–230).

7. For recent discussions of the dating and composition of the *Zuozhuan* 左傳, see David Schaberg, *A Patterned Past: Form and Thought in Early Chinese Historiography* (Cambridge, MA: Harvard University Asia Center, 2001), Appendix; Yuri Pines, *Foundations of Confucian Thought: Intellectual Life in the Chunqiu Period (722–453 B.C.E.)* (Honolulu: University of Hawai'i Press, 2002), chapter 1; A. Taeko Brooks, "Heaven, *Li*, and the Formation of the *Zuozhuan* 左傳," *Oriens*

Extremus 44 (2003–2004): 51–100; and Barry B. Blakeley, "'On the Authenticity and Nature of the *Zuozhuan*' Revisited," *Early China* 29 (2004): 217–267.

8. The precise meanings of these two terms are in doubt. The *Erya* 爾雅 ([*Sibu congkan chubian* 四部叢刊初編 ed.] B.9a) defines *zhibing* 治兵 and *zhenlü* 振旅 as activities engaged in before and after a battle, respectively. The *Chunqiu Gongyang zhuan* 春秋公羊傳 (Zhuang 莊 8) provides the following partial explanation: "When setting forth [for battle], it is called *cibing* 祠兵; when returning [from battle], it is called *zhenlü*. The ceremonies performed are identical." This gloss suggests that *zhenlü* was a particular rite, and not merely, as in Legge's translation, a returning of troops. In another passage from the *Zuozhuan* (Xi 僖 28) we see the following: "In autumn, on the *bingshen* 丙申 day of the seventh month, [the troops of Jin 晉] had a *zhenlü* and triumphantly entered the Jin [capital]." It can be hypothesized that *zhibing* and *zhenlü*, in these contexts, were assembly formations before and after a battle and the occasions of specific rites. This interpretation is consistent with a passage in the *Zhouli* 周禮 ([*Sibu congkan chubian* ed.] 7.12b–18a), a work written sometime before the first century BCE, which describes training procedures for the four seasons; two of these procedures are named *zhibing* and *zhenlü*. For background on the text of the *Zhouli*, first known as *Zhouguan* 周官, see William G. Boltz, "*Chou li* 周禮," in Loewe, *Early Chinese Texts*, 24–32.

9. *Zuozhuan* (Yin 隱 5; trans. Legge, *Classics*, 5: 19; translation modified by author for style). Also see *Zuozhuan* (Huan 桓 6). The "Yue ling" 月令 chapter of the *Liji* 禮記 ([*Sibu congkan chubian* ed.] 5.15a, 5.18b, 5.21a) speaks similarly of teaching hunting methods and the use of the five weapons (*wurong* 五戎) in late autumn, and of combat training in early winter. Cf. *Huainanzi* 淮南子 (*Sibu congkan chubian* ed.) 5.8a, 5.10b, 5.12a.

10. *Guoyu* 國語 (*Sibu congkan chubian* ed.) 1.9a. Also see Derk Bodde (1909–2004), *Festivals in Classical China* (Princeton, NJ: Princeton University Press, 1975), 349–359, 381–386. For background on the text of the *Guoyu*, see Chang I-jen, William G. Boltz, and Michael Loewe, "*Kuo yü* 國語," in Loewe, *Early Chinese Texts*, 263–268.

11. *Liutao* (*Sibu congkan chubian* ed.) 3.25a–b.

12. *Shi*, "Gong Liu" 公劉 (trans. Legge, *Classics*, 4: 483–484).

13. This characteristic of the cultural hero in ancient China had a long-lasting effect on aristocrats even through the Chunqiu period. As the Chinese scholar Lei Haizong 雷海宗 (1902–1962) pointed out, sons of royal lineage were taught both military and administrative-ritual skills. The relatively loose governmental procedures and the simplicity of battle tactics made this dual training possible, and even necessary, in order to prepare future rulers for the duties that their roles entailed. It might happen that some ruling-class sons would become more concerned with scribal and ceremonial duties than others of their peers, but these same nobles were

always expected to be ready for military service if they were required. Lei Haizong, "Zhongguo de bing" 中國的兵, *Shehui kexue* 社會科學 1, no. 1 (October 1935): 5–6. Also see Mark Edward Lewis, *Sanctioned Violence in Early China* (Albany: State University of New York Press, 1990), 15–52.

14. Several decades ago, the American political scientist Quincy Wright (1890–1970), in his investigation of war in the Western context, spoke of the positive nature of warfare in early stages of societal development. In his view, primitive warfare was an important factor in developing civilization, since it cultivated the virtues of courage, loyalty, and obedience, and also created solid social groups and a method for enlarging the area of such groups. Over time, however, the value of war in developing social virtues and social organization was increasingly offset by its evils in eliminating human sympathy, preventing cooperation beyond those engaged in war, and increasing destructiveness. See Quincy Wright, *A Study of War* (Chicago: University of Chicago Press, 1942), 1: 98–99.

15. *Shi*, "Yi jie" 猗嗟 (trans. Legge, *Classics*, 4: 161–162). Another example of an ancient verse suggesting high regard for martial prowess is the "Er shi" 而師 inscription found fragmentarily among the so-called Stone Drums (*shigu* 石鼓), a collection of ten drum-shaped, engraved stones unearthed in northern China sometime before the early seventh century CE and dating from perhaps the fifth century BCE in what was then the state of Qin. See Gilbert Louis Mattos (1939–2002), *The Stone Drums of Ch'in* (PhD dissertation, University of Washington, 1973), 20–41, 391–415, 498–501

16. *Shi*, "Pan shui" 泮水 (trans. Legge, *Classics*, 4: 616–620). Cf. *Shi*, "Song gao" 崧高.

17. See C.H. Wang, "Towards Defining a Chinese Heroism," *Journal of the American Oriental Society* 95, no. 1 (1975): 25–35.

18. This, of course, was not the first time that the characters *wen* and *wu* were used in posthumous royal titles. The Shang rulers known as Wu Dng 武丁, Wu Yi 武乙, and Wen Wu Ding 文武丁 all appear by those names in Shang-era oracle bones. For a comprehensive study of the oracle bones of Shang, see David N. Keightley, *Sources of Shang History: The Oracle-Bone Inscriptions of Bronze Age China* (Berkeley and Los Angeles, CA: University of California Press, 1978).

19. Muye 牧野 was located in the vicinity of present-day Xinxiang 新鄉 Municipality, Henan Province.

20. Shangfu 尙父 can be identified as Tai Gong of Qi (Qi Tai Gong 齊太公; also known as Taigong Wang 太公望, Lü Shang 呂尚, Jiang Ziya 姜子牙, and Jiang Shang 姜尚) of the *Liutao* and other texts. See Sarah Allan, "The Identities of Taigong Wang in Zhou and Han Literature," *Monumenta Serica* 32 (1972–1973): 57–99.

21. *Shi*, "Da Ming" 大明 (trans. Legge, *Classics*, 4: 435–436; translation slightly modified by author for style).

22. *Shi*, "Shi mai" 時邁 (trans. Legge, *Classics*, 4: 577–578).

23. Herrlee G. Creel, *The Origins of Statecraft in China, Volume One: The Western Chou Empire* (Chicago and London: University of Chicago Press, 1970), 64–65. For additional background on the text of the *Shangshu* 尙書, see Edward L. Shaughnessy, "*Shang shu* 尙書 (*Shu ching* 書經)," in Loewe, *Early Chinese Texts*, 376–389.

24. Creel, *Origins*, 447–463.

25. Creel, *Origins*, 450.

26. As background, Jizi 箕子, born Zi Xuyu 子胥余, was son of King Wen Ding 文丁 of Shang, younger brother of King Di Yi 帝乙 of Shang, and a paternal uncle of King Zhou 紂王 of Shang. A grantee of lands in Ji 箕, located in present-day Taigu 太谷 County, Shanxi Province, Jizi was appointed a senior advisor to King Zhou and was said to have lodged forceful remonstrations against King Zhou's ill behavior as Shang sovereign. As a result, King Zhou placed Jizi under arrest. When King Wu of Zhou overthrew King Zhou, the new king ordered the Duke of Shao 召公 to release Jizi from captivity. Evidence of King Wu thereafter consulting Jizi on government matters appears in the "Hongfan" 洪範 document of the *Shangshu*. Bi Gan 比干, also a son of King Wen Ding and a paternal uncle of King Zhou, became a senior minister to King Zhou and, like Jizi, a candid critic of King Zhou's malfeasance. The circumstances of Bi Gan's death are unclear, but Bi Gan apparently lost his life during the Shang-Zhou struggle for power and was buried after the Battle of Muye. He was later officially honored by the Zhou regime as a meritorious "spirit of the state" (*guo shen* 國神). Much later in Chinese history he was transformed by religious Daoism into a god of wealth (*cai shen* 財神). Little of certainty is known of Shang Rong 商容, except that, according to the "Treatise on Music" ("Yue shu" 樂書) in the *Shiji*, he was a music official in the court of King Zhou. Like Jizi and Bi Gan, he was reportedly openly critical of the king's errant ways.

27. Lu Tower (Deer Tower) is described in the "Yin Basic Annals" ("Yin benji" 殷本紀) of the *Shiji* as being the site of a storehouse of treasures gleaned from "heavy taxation" during the reign of King Zhou of Shang. The tower was located in Zhaoge 朝歌, in present-day Henan Province. Juqiao 鉅橋 (Great Bridge) was the name given to a grain storage facility located northwest of present-day Quzhouxian 曲周縣, Hebei Province. The implication of the reference is that the grain stored at Juqiao was being hoarded by King Zhou when it should have been distributed to needy people in the kingdom.

28. *Shangshu*, "Wu cheng" 武成 (trans. Legge, *Classics*, 3: 314–316; translation modified by author for style).

29. *Shangshu*, "Mu shi" 牧誓 (trans. Legge, *Classics*, 3: 304).

30. *Shi*, "Zhuo" 酌 (trans. Legge, *Classics*, 4: 606).

31. *Shangshu*, "Zhonghui zhi gao" 仲虺之誥 (trans. Legge, *Classics*, 3: 181; translation slightly modified by author for style).

32. See *Shangshu*, "Luo gao" 洛誥, "Duo shi" 多士, and "Duo fang" 多方. King Cheng 成王 of Zhou has also been identified as a worthy mediator between civility and martiality. As the *Guoyu* (3.12b) described him, "King Cheng is one capable of manifesting his civility and [making it] glorious, and of establishing his martiality and [making it] awesome."

33. *Guoyu* 6.14a.

34. *Zuozhuan* (Xiang 襄 14); trans. Legge, *Classics*, 5: 467).

35. This interpretation of the character *wu* 武, though philosophically interesting and accepted by many imperial-era Chinese commentators, is probably faulty. The Qing dynasty scholar Qian Dian 錢坫 (1744–1806) convincingly argued in his commentary on this character in the *Shuowen jiezi* 說文解字, the etymological dictionary by the Eastern Han 東漢 (25–220 CE) philologist Xu Shen 許慎 (ca. 58–ca. 147), that *zhi* 止 does not mean "stop" in this context but is equivalent to the modern character *zhi* 趾, meaning "foot." Hence the character *wu* was probably derived from an ancient pictograph consisting of a shafted spear and a foot, signifying an armed man. See Qian Dian, *Shuowen jiezi jiaoquan* 說文解字斠詮 in *Shuowen jiezi gulin* 說文解字詁林, ed. Ding Fubao 丁福保 (Taibei: Commercial Press, 1970), 9: 5694.

36. *Zuozhuan* (Xuan 宣 12) (trans. Legge, *Classics*, 5: 320–321). The *Guoyu* (9.9b) may also be cited to illustrate this normative view of martiality: "Exi 蛾析 said: 'I have heard that for a minister who hastens to punish, it is best to pardon him in order for him to take revenge [for you]. Why don't you pardon him to take revenge on Qin?' Liang Youmi 梁由靡 said: 'No. If we could do such a thing, why couldn't Qin? Furthermore, to use brigands to take revenge after having lost a battle is not martiality and to be unsuccessful in battle or not pacifying in occupation is not knowledge.' "

37. *Guoyu* 1.1a.

38. See *Zuozhuan* (Xuan 12).

39. *Zuozhuan* (Xiang 27) (trans. Legge, *Classics*, 5: 534; translation modified by author for style and accuracy).

40. *Shi*, "Si wen" 思文.

41. *Zuozhuan* (Cheng 成16) (trans. Legge, *Classics*, 5: 395–396; translation modified by author for style).

42. For commentary on this point, see Frank A. Kierman Jr., "Phases and Modes of Combat in Early China," in Kierman, *Chinese Ways in Warfare*, 30–31.

43. As background, the Jade Academy (*biyong* 辟雍 [璧廱]) cited here was an institution established in Zhou times for instructing aristocratic scions in such subjects as rites, music, dance, and horsemanship. It became linked in function to the Bright Hall (*ming tang* 明堂), an institution of ancient vintage devoted to royal religious ceremonies and other court assemblies.

44. *Liji* 4.5b (trans. James Legge, *Li Ki*, vol. 27 of *Sacred Books of the East*, ed. F. Max Muller [Oxford: Clarendon Press, 1885], 220).

45. *Zuozhuan* (Cheng 13) (trans. Legge, *Classics*, 5: 382).

46. *Zuozhuan* (Xiang 3) (trans. Legge, *Classics*, 5: 420; translation slightly emended for style).

47. See, e.g., Herrlee G. Creel, "The *Fa-chia*: 'Legalists' or 'Administrators'?" in *Studies Presented to Tung Tso Pin on his Sixty-fifth Birthday*, *Zhongyang yanjiuyuan lishi yuyan yanjiusuo jikan* 中央研究院歷史語言研究所集刊, Extra Volume No. 4 (Taibei, 1961), 607–636 (reprinted in *What is Taoism? And Other Studies in Chinese Cultural History* [Chicago and London: University of Chicago Press, 1970], 92–120); Herrlee G. Creel, *Shen Pu-hai: A Chinese Political Philosopher of the Fourth Century B.C.* (Chicago and London: University of Chicago Press, 1974); Paul M. Thompson, "The *Shen-tzu* [Shen Dao 慎倒] Fragments" (PhD dissertation, University of Washington, 1970), 1–2; Tang Lan, "*Huangdi si jing* chu tan"《黃帝四經》初探, *Wenwu* 1975 (10): 48–52; Cheng Wu 程武, "Han chu Huang Lao sixiang he fajia luxian—Han Changsha Mawangdui san hao Han mu chutu boshu zhaji" 漢初黃老思想和法家路綫—漢長沙馬王堆三號漢墓出土帛書扎記, *Wenwu* 1974 (10): 43–47, 64; Kang Li 康立 and Wei Jin 衛今, 法家路綫和黃老思想—漢帛書《經法》, *Wenwu* 1975 (7): 1–7; Tang Xin 湯新, "Fajia dui Huang Lao zhi xue de xishou he gaizao—Han Mawangdui boshu *Jingfa* deng pian" 法家對黃老之學的吸收和改造—漢馬王堆帛書《經法》等篇, *Wenwu* 1975 (8): 18–22.

48. For background on the text of the *Shangjunshu* 商君書, see Jean Levi, "*Shang chün shu* 商君書," in Loewe, *Early Chinese Texts*, 368–375.

49. See *Shangjunshu* (*Sibu congkan chubian* ed.) 4.8b. Cf. *Simafa* (*Sibu congkan chubian* ed.) A.1a

50. *Shangjunshu* 4.9a (trans. Duyvendak, *Lord Shang*, 286).

51. *Shangjunshu* 1.14a–b (trans. Duyvendak, *Lord Shang*, 205).

52. *Shangjunshu* 1.8b–9a (trans. Duyvendak, *Lord Shang*, 190).

53. Guan Zhong 管仲 (ca. 720–645 BCE; born Ji Yiwu 姬夷吾 of the Guan 管 lineage), was the celebrated chief minister to Lord Huan 桓 of Qi (r. 686–643 BCE).

54. *Hanfeizi* 韓非子 (*Sibu congkan chubian* ed.)19.5a-b (trans. Burton Watson, *Han Fei Tzu, Basic Writings* [New York: Columbia University Press, 1964], 110). The received version of the *Hanfeizi* contains at least one suggestion that its author, who was probably Han Fei himself, may not have been committed entirely to the kind of militaristic approach espoused in the *Shangjunshu*. In the "Wang zheng" 亡徵 chapter of the *Hanfeizi* is a caution against unbridled war: "If the ruler is often angry and fond of using weapons; if he demeans fundamental instruction [and tactics] and takes offensive war lightly, then he may perish" (5.2a).

55. For background on the text of the *Daodejing* 道德經, see William G. Boltz, "*Lao tzu Tao te ching* 老子道德經," in Loewe, *Early Chinese Texts*, 269–292.

56. *Daodejing* 31 (trans. D.C. Lau, *Lao Tzu, Tao Te Ching* [Penguin Books, 1963], 89–90). Also see the *Zuozhuan* (Cheng 2) for a passage describing the inauspiciousness of generalship.

57. This impression of the ill destiny attached to military leaders is also seen in the *Shiji* account of Wang Li 王離, grandson of the famous Qin general, Wang Jian 王翦: "Someone said: 'Wang [Li] is a noted general of Qin. Surely he will be recommended to command the troops of mighty Qin in an attack on the newly formed state of Zhao.' But a subordinate said: 'Not so. One [from a family] which has supplied generals for three generations will surely be defeated. Why will he surely be defeated? It is because [his forebears] killed and slaughtered greatly and their descendants have inherited their inauspiciousness (*buxiang* 不祥). Now, Wang Li is already a third-generation general. There is no hope for him.' Xiang Yu 項羽 went to the rescue of Zhao, attacking the Qin army and finally capturing Wang Li" (73.9a).

58. The argument for separation between *wen* and *wu* in Zhanguo thought is echoed in later descriptions of historical prohibitions against sovereigns overruling generals in the latter's jurisdictions during times of hostilities. In the *Shiji* (64.2a–b), the Chunqiu-era general Tian Rangju 田穰苴 (Marshal Rangju 司馬穰苴) is reported to have supported the principle that when a representative of the ruler enters his domain, such an envoy must obey military law (*junfa* 軍法) or suffer the consequences. Also, the Han general Zhou Yafu 周亞夫 is reported in the *Shiji* (57.7b) as promoting the rule that "in the army one complies with the orders of the commander in chief, not the edicts of the emperor." Even Emperor Jing 景帝 of Han 景帝, it is said, acknowledged the priority of military law when he entered Zhou Yafu's encampment.

59. In his history of the Zhanguo period the modern Chinese scholar Yang Kuan 楊寬 summarized the changes leading to the establishment of the two separate occupations of general (*jiang* 將) and minister (*xiang* 相). See *Zhanguo shi* 戰國史 (Beijing: Renmin chubanshe, 1955), 108.

60. See Hsu Cho-yun, *Ancient China in Transition: An Analysis of Social Mobility, 722–22 B.C.* (Stanford, CA: Stanford University Press, 1965), esp. chapters 4 and 6.

61. The only anomaly in this regard was Mozi 墨子 (fl. late fifth century BCE), who seems to have had considerable experience with defensive warfare and was continually opposed to offensive combat. A discussion of Mozi's contribution to the *wen*/*wu* debate is in Chapter 4.

62. It is important to note that some of the military treatises also argue in favor of segregating martial and civil activities, but in doing so they do not explicitly subordinate *wu* to *wen*. The *Simafa* (A.2b–3a) states, for example: "Anciently state matters did not overlap the military, and military matters did not overlap the state. Thus virtue and righteousness [pertaining to state and military, respectively] did not overstep one another. . . ." Similarly, the *Liutao* (3.18a–b), in a description of the commissioning ceremony for a general, illustrates the necessity for a strict separation between the controllers of military troops and civil government, but the treatise does not go further to assert that *wen* is superior to *wu*. Cf. *Weiliaozi* (*Wujing qishu zhijie* 武經七書直解 ed.) 4.7b–8a, and *Huainanzi* 15.16a–b. Also see the

description of a general's departure ceremony in Wang Zongyi 汪宗沂, comp., *Tai Gong bingfa yiwen* 太公兵法逸文 (*Jianxicun she congkan* 漸西村舍叢刊 ed.) 1a–b.

63. *Jingfa*, 200 (nos. 37–38); 201 (no. 44). The two-to-one ratio for *wen/wu* does not necessarily imply an unbalanced relationship. A true king still requires a due proportion of martiality, while lesser rulers may need a different ratio of elements—a ratio more favorable to *wu*.

64. *Jingfa*, 206 (nos. 65–66).

65. *Weiliaozi* 5.22a. Cf. *Chunqiu Guliang zhuan* 春秋穀梁傳 (Xiang 25): "In ancient times, although there were civil activities, there had to be martial preparation."

66. For a compendium of bibliographical data on the *Yi Zhoushu* (also called *Zhoushu* 周書), see Shen Yanguo 沈延國 and Yang Kuan,《逸周書》與《汲家周書》辨證, *Zhi yan* 制言 40 (May 1939), and Edward L. Shaughnessy, "*I Chou shu* 逸周書 (*Chou shu*)," in Loewe, *Early Chinese Texts*, 229–233. Shaughnessy notes in his article that his conclusions were based largely on the work of Taiwan scholar Huang Peirong 黃沛榮 (《周書》研究, PhD dissertation, National Taiwan University, 1976). For a recent translation and analysis of the military chapters of the *Yi Zhoushu*, see Robin McNeal, *Conquer and Govern: Early Chinese Military Texts from the Yi Zhou shu* (Honolulu: University of Hawai'i Press, 2012).

67. *Yi Zhoushu* (*Sibu congkan chubian* ed.) 2.1a–2b. In the "Da wu" 大武 chapter martiality is analyzed in even greater detail according to quasi-moral categories of military escalation.

68. *Yi Zhoushu* 2.4b–5b. For a discussion of this integration of *wen* and *wu* as evidenced in the "Wu shun" 武順 chapter of the *Yi Zhoushu*, see Robin McNeal, "The Body as Metaphor for the Civil and Martial Components of Empire in *Yi Zhou Shu*, chapter 32; with an Excursion on the Composition and Structure of the *Yi Zhou Shu*," *Journal of the American Oriental Society* 122, no. 1 (January–March 2002): 46–60.

69. A comparable analysis of the *wen/wu* problem in early China can be found in an article by Albert Galvany, ("La Dialéctica entre lo Civil y lo Militar en la China Antigua," *Estudios de Asia y África* 42, no. 3 [2007], 541–594). Galvany describes three different models of military thought: an "antagonist model," in which Confucian moral, civil principles are seen to be superior to violent, martial action in achieving peace and stability; "a complementary model," in which civil and martial means are seen to be part of natural cycles and equally important in preserving stability; and a "unifier model," in which civil and martial means are placed in equilibrium or are fused into a legalized structure in order to achieve general peace.

Chapter 2

1. It is difficult to identify this work precisely. The earliest appearance of titles similar to that referred to here is in the *Suishu* 隋書 "Jingji zhi" 經籍志

([Yiwen yinshu guan ed.] 34.12a). These works, none of which are extant, include the *Tai Gong yin mou* 太公陰謀, the *Tai Gong yin fu qian lu* 太公陰符 鈐錄, the *Tai Gong fufu yinyang mou* 太公伏符陰陽謀, plus seven other works attributed to or connected with Taigong Wang (Tai Gong of Qi). The citation for the *Tai Gong yin mou* contains an annotation by Tang dynasty commentators that works existed under this title during the Liang 梁 dynasty (502–557) but with varying numbers of volumes/chapters (*juan* 卷).

2. *Zhanguoce* 戰國策 (*Sibu congkan chubian* ed.) 3.4b–5b (trans. Crump, *Chan Kuo Ts'e*, 57–58).

3. Xiapi 下邳, located in present-day Suiningxian 睢寧縣, Jiangsu Province, was also the site of a major battle in the winter of 198 CE, near the formal end of the Han dynasty, between the forces of warlord Lü Bu 呂布 (d. 199) and the allied armies of Cao Cao 曹操 (155–220), noted general and commentator on the *Sunzi bingfa*, and Liu Bei 劉備 (161–223), founder of the Shu Han 蜀漢 kingdom.

4. The earliest known bibliographical reference to a work bearing the title *Tai Gong bingfa* 太公兵法 seems to be in the nonextant *Qilu* 七錄, compiled by Ruan Xiaoxu 阮孝緒 between 520 and 526 CE. The *Suishu* "Jingji zhi" (34.12a) also lists two versions by that title. However, the identity of any of these citations with the title mentioned in the *Shiji* cannot be determined.

5. *Shiji* 55.2a–3a, 55.12b–13a (trans. Burton Watson, *Records of the Grand Historian of China*. [New York and London: Columbia University Press, 1961], 1: 135–136, 150; translation slightly modified by author for style). Significantly, the military genius in the Zhang Liang story who turned himself into a yellow stone (*huang shi* 黃石) reappears in the Western Han in the name of an important military treatise, the *Huangshigong Sanlüe* 黃石公三略, which will be discussed in Chapter 5.

6. See Sarah Allan, "The Identities of Taigong Wang in Zhou and Han Literature," *Monumenta Serica* 32 (1972–1973): 57–99.

7. The term "Three Kings" (*san wang* 三王) usually refers to Yu 禹, the first king of Xia; Tang 湯, the first king of Shang; and the combination of King Wu 武王, the first reigning king of Zhou, and King Wen 文王, the founder of Zhou. In this case, where King Wen is an interlocutor, the identity of the intended third sage-sovereign is unclear.

8. The term "predispositions" (*qing* 情) has a special intention for military affairs, though still carrying a general philosophical sense. As will be indicated later in this study, predispositions are those particular concentrations of human vital energy (*qi*) that must be recognized by a general as part of his evaluation of enemy circumstances and friendly esprit. Because such concentrations are subtle, invisible, and latent, they constitute the manifestation or actualization of human will in a state of potency. To detect such predispositions is to know how others will use or not use their potency. Examples of the use of this concept can be found in early Chinese texts both military and nonmilitary. For an example of the former, see *Zhuangzi* 莊子 (Yiwen yinshuguan ed.) 1.15a–b; 2.11a.

9. *Liutao* 1.1a–2a.

10. See *Shiji* 41 (Fan Li 范蠡), 65 (Wu Qi 吳起, Sun Bin 孫臏), 80 (Yue Yi 樂毅, Yue Xian 樂閒).

11. See *Shiji* 73.7a–b.

12. See *Shiji* 73.5b–6a.

13. The association of the *Heguanzi* 鶡冠子 with Huang-Lao thought appears to be true in the main, even though portions of the received text of the *Heguanzi* may not have that origin. For a discussion of the filiation problem, see Carine Defoort, *The Pheasant Cap Master (He guan zi): A Rhetorical Reading* (Albany: State University of New York Press, 1997), 31–52. Also see R.P. Peerenboom, *Law and Morality in Ancient China*, 273–283.

14. This sense of psychical power (*shen* 神) in the military context resonates closely with portions of Daoist texts from the pre-Han era. The "Yangsheng zhu" 養生主 chapter of the *Zhuangzi*, for example, contains the following explanation from Cook Ding 庖丁 of his superior butchering skill: "I meet my task with *shen* and do not use my eyes" (2.2a). In the "Zai you" 在宥 chapter of the *Zhuangzi* we find a similar description of the true gentleman (*junzi* 君子), which relates directly to the ideal general of the military treatises: "Therefore, if the true gentleman will keep [the faculties lodged in] his five viscera unemployed, and not display his powers of seeing and hearing, while he is motionless as a representative of the dead, his dragon-like presence will be seen; while he is profoundly silent, the thunder [of his words] will resound; while his movements are [unseen] like those of a spirit (*shen dong* 神動), all Heavenly influences will follow them (*tian sui* 天隨)" (4.19b).

15. The Five Phases (*wuxing* 五行) theory, which developed from the pre-Han period onward, posited a natural mutual generation (*xiang sheng* 相生) and mutual overcoming (*xiang ke* 相克) of phenomena correlated variously with the five elements of wood, earth, water, fire, and metal. An introduction to this theory can be found in Joseph Needham, *Science and Civilisation in China*, vol. 2, *History of Scientific Thought* (Cambridge, UK: Cambridge University Press, 1956), 232–253. The Five Tones (*wuyin* 五音 or *wusheng* 五聲) are the five pitches of the traditional Chinese musical scale: *gong* 宫, *shang* 商, *jue* 角, *zhi* 徵, and *yu* 羽. These tones became important in Chinese military lore because a military commander could ostensibly use these pitches, when emanating from a foe's forces, to prognosticate the success or failure of his battle plans. The application of traditional music theory to warfare is further discussed in Chapter 3.

16. *Heguanzi* (*Sibu congkan chubian* ed.) c.4a–5a. The *Sun Bin bingfa* (97) also emphasizes the intangible factors in warfare: "If numerous troops meant victory, then we would only have to cast counters to wage battle. If wealth meant victory, then we would only have to measure grain to wage battle. If sharp weapons and strong armor meant victory, then it would be easy to know the victor. Thus the wealthy are still not safe and the poor are still not in peril; the numerous are still

not the victors and the few are still not the defeated. One decides who is victorious, defeated, safe or imperiled by the Way."

17. *Heguanzi* C.10b.

18. *Weiliaozi* 1.6b.

19. *Weiliaozi* 1.5a.

20. *Weiliaozi* 2.47a.

21. The *Weiliaozi* (3.6a) points out the necessity for the general to cultivate the Way in order for his potency to be effective: "Battle power lies in the consummation of the Way."

22. *Heguanzi* A.15a–b. A less developed cosmological argument is presented in *Zhuangzi* 6.22a.

23. *Heguanzi* B.5a.

24. Interesting in this regard is the biophysical analogy between the processing of energy and the transformation of vital energy (*qi*) in inanimate and animate systems, respectively, discussed by R.G.H. Siu in *Ch'i: A Neo-Taoist Approach to Life* (Cambridge, MA: MIT Press, 1974), 17–19, 22, 265–275.

25. *Sunzi bingfa* (*Sibu congkan chubian* ed.) 13.2b–4a (trans. Samuel B. Griffith, *Sun Tzu: The Art of War* [London: Oxford University Press, 1963], 144–145). The *Guiguzi* 鬼谷子, a work apparently of Zhanguo origin that will be discussed later, has a similar statement: "Thus it is said that the ruler's affairs are daily completed, and yet the people do not know; the ruler's armies are daily victorious, and yet the people show no awe. A sage plans [his actions] in secret, and therefore is called spirit-like; he completes them in full view, and therefore is called enlightened. . . . That the ruler's troops are daily victorious is because he constantly wages war without combat or expenditure, and yet the people do not know why their adversaries submit. They do not know why they show awe, and yet the world compares him to the spirit-like and the enlightened" ([*Sibu congkan chubian* ed.] 2.13b, 2.14a–b). The *Dengxizi* 鄧析子, although possibly authentic and of pre-Qin origin but probably containing additional material of a later date, is also useful here. While speaking of civil rulers, the "Zhuan ci" 轉辭 chapter of the *Dengxizi* describes an attitude and an inscrutability that compare closely to behavior in the sage-general: "An enlightened prince controls his people as though he were riding [in a carriage] at full speed and without reins; or treading on ice while shouldering a heavy burden. He shows them affection and yet stays aloof; stays aloof from them and yet shows affection. Thus, if he is reverent and prudent, blessings will come to him, but if he is prideful and extravagant, disaster will occur. A sage roams the whole world, managing and fashioning the dispositions of the myriad things. So serene he is, there are no punishments with whip or bludgeon; so quiescent he is, there are no voices of abuse or reprimand. And yet households are provided for, the people are satisfied, and the world is in great peace. Seeing what is clear and bright, he knows what is dark and obscure; he predicts what has not yet happened and espies what is not yet so. Hence, this is what is meant by the saying, 'spirit-like, it cannot be seen; abstruse, it cannot be heard' " ([*Sibu congkan chubian*

ed.] 9a–b). Adopted in this translation from the *Dengxizi* are the emendations suggested by Hellmut Wilhelm in "Schriften und Fragmente zur Entwicklung der staatsrechtlichen Theorie in der Chou-Zeit," *Monumenta Serica* 12 (1947), 41–96.

26. A famous passage in the *Sunzi bingfa* shows the centrality of the general as well as the importance of martial self-cultivation in the style of civil sages. Just as in the "Daxue" 大學 chapter of the *Liji* true government begins with the ruler, in the *Sunzi bingfa* victory begins in the mind and will of the military commander: "Anciently the skillful warriors first made themselves invincible and awaited the enemy's moment of vulnerability. Invincibility depends on one's self; the enemy's vulnerability on him" (4.1a–b; trans. Griffith, *Sun Tzu*, 85).

27. The term *shi* 勢 connotes here the potentialities present in the circumstances affecting a general's martial decision making. I have adopted the translation "circumstantial power" to refer to the real but subtle possibilities of a military situation, both physical and psychological, which can be manipulated to advantage by an astute commander. A useful discussion of the term *shi* in a military context can be found in François Jullien, *The Propensity of Things: Toward a History of Efficacy in China*, trans. Janet Lloyd (New York: Zone Books, 1995), 25–38.

28. *Sunzi bingfa* 6.19b–20b, 6.25b–32a (trans. Griffith, *Sun Tzu*, 98, 100).

29. *Guanzi* 管子 (*Sibu congkan chubian* ed.) 3.5a–b (trans. W. Allyn Rickett, *Kuan-tzu: A Repository of Early Chinese Thought* [Hong Kong: Hong Kong University Press, 1965], 1: 216; text rearranged by Rickett). The only chapters quoted from the *Guanzi* in this study are those that Luo Genze 羅根澤 (*Guanzi tan yuan* 管子探源 [Shanghai: Zhonghua shuju, 1931]) and/or W. Allyn Rickett in his commentary showed to be clearly or very probably pre-Han in origin. Translations other than those by Rickett were prepared with the aid of selected glosses by Guo Moruo 郭沫若 (1892–1978) in *Guanzi jijiao* 管子集校 (Beijing: Kexue chubanshe, 1956). It is worth mentioning in this regard a wood-slip text entitled *Wang bing* 王兵 found in tomb no. 1 at Yinqueshan, Shandong Province, in 1972. This text contains several passages on military strategy and tactics that closely match in content passages in various chapters of the received text of the *Guanzi*, including "Qi fa" 七法, "Bing fa" 兵法," "Can huan" 參患, "Di tu" 地圖, and "You guan" 幼官. For commentary on these resemblances, see Rickett, *Kuan-tzu*, 1: 24, 392, and Yinqueshan Han mu zhu jian zhengli xiaozu, 銀雀山漢墓竹簡整理小組, "Linyi Yinqueshan Han mu chutu *Wang bing* pian shiwen" 臨沂銀雀山 漢墓出土《王兵》篇釋文. *Wenwu* 1976 (12): 36–43.

30. *Sun Bin bingfa* (Beijing: Wenwu chubanshe, 1975), 121–122.

31. *Sun Bin bingfa*, 96.

32. *Sunzi bingfa* 10.18b–20a (trans. Griffith, *Sun Tzu*, 129). The need for Earthly potencies and Heavenly timing for the offense is also mentioned in *Yi Zhoushu* 2.5b.

33. The history of the *Guiguzi* text is discussed in the following: Yu Yan 俞棪, *Guiguzi xin zhu* 鬼谷子新注 (Shanghai: Shangwu yinshuguan, 1937); Liang Jiabin 梁嘉彬, "*Guiguzi* kao"《鬼谷子》考, *Dalu zazhi* 大陸雜誌 10, no. 4

(February 28, 1955): 12–15; Zhao Tiehan 趙鐵寒, "*Guiguzi* kao bian"《鬼谷子》考辨, *Dalu zazhi* 14, no. 5 (March 15, 1957): 3–7, 14, no. 6 (March 31, 1957): 20–25. Although the dating of the received version of the *Guiguz*i is still unresolved, the above commentators agreed, and other scholars from the Qing period and after have concurred, that the *Guiguzi* is basically a Zhanguo work into which various interpolations and addenda have since infiltrated. See Chen Puqing 陳蒲清, *Guiguzi xiang jie* 鬼谷子詳解 (Changsha: Yuelu shushe, 2005), 150–164. For purposes of this study, all chapters in the *Guiguz*i referring to military affairs have been accepted, with the exception of the "Ben jing yin fu" 本經陰符 section, which is in a different style and format and probably dates from the post-Han era.

34. *Guiguzi* 1.10a–b, 11a. Cf. *Guanzi* 13.6b–10b; *Dengxizi* 9b–10a; *Liutao* 2.10a–11a.

35. *Guiguzi* 1.15a, b. Cf. *Heguanzi* C.28a–30a.

36. *Guiguzi* 2.4b. The *Guiguzi* describes another method of persuasion that is also applicable to military confrontations, namely, *bai he* 捭闔. This method resembles the *fei qian* method in that one opens up (*bai*) the opponent by observing his likes and dislikes and by encouraging him to expose his weaknesses. Then you may close down (*he*) on him and take advantage of those weaknesses. See *Guiguzi* 1.1a–8b.

37. Cf. Satō Kenji 佐藤堅司, *Sonshi no taikeiteki kenkyū* 孫子の体系的研究 (Tokyo: Kazema shobo, 1963), 351–357. In his work on the *Guiguzi*, Chen Yinglüe 陳英略 not only made a clear connection between the persuasion techniques of the *Guiguzi* and military strategy, but also went on to discuss the relationship between ancient Chinese military thought and Huang-Lao philosophy. *Guiguzi shenji bingfa* 鬼谷子神機兵法 (Hong Kong: Xinli shuju, 1974?), 13. For a more recent investigation of the relationship between military strategy and persuasion tactics, see two articles by Albert Galvany: "Violencia y Persuasión: Los Fundamentos Estratégicos de la Sofistica en la China Antigua," *Estudios de Asia y África* 38, no. 2 (May–August 2003): 291–320; and "Sly Mouths and Silver Tongues: The Dynamics of Psychological Persuasion in Ancient China," *Extrême-Orient Extrême-Occident* 34 (2012): 15–40.

38. *Sun Bin bingfa*, 119.

39. *Shangjunshu* 3.7a (trans. Duyvendak, *Lord Shang*, 249; translation modified by author for style).

40. *Daodejing* 36 (trans. Lau, *Lao Tzu*, 95).

41. The modern scholar Benjamin E. Wallacker (1926–2011) suggested that the etymology of the term "regular" (*zheng* 正) may involve the character *ding* 丁, suggesting a "nailing down" of the enemy. See "Two Concepts in Early Chinese Military Thought," *Language* 42, no. 2 (1966): 297–298.

42. For an etymological analysis of irregular (*qi* 奇), see Benjamin E. Wallacker, "Two Concepts in Early Chinese Military Thought," 298–299. Wallacker saw among various cognate terms the idea of imbalance or asymmetry, and by extension to push or pull someone off balance.

43. *Sunzi bingfa* 5.3a, 5a–8a (trans. Griffith, *Sun Tzu*, 91–92; translation emended for accuracy and style).

44. *Sun Bin bingfa*, 122.

45. *Liutao* 3.21a.

46. *Sun Bin bingfa*, 122.

47. *Daodejing* 57.

48. Peter A. Boodberg, "The Art of War in Ancient China" (PhD dissertation, University of California at Berkeley, 1930), xxi.

49. *Cheng* 稱, 227 (no. 143) seems to refer to this more compartmentalized use of regular and irregular forces by a state ruler, rather than the complementary employment of regular and irregular forces on the battlefield: "Regular follows irregular, irregular follows regular, and the two are never found in the same domain."

50. *Sunzi bingfa* 6.10b–13a (trans. Griffith, *Sun Tzu*, 96–97).

51. *Sunzi bingfa* 7.26a–29b (trans. Griffith, *Sun Tzu*, 108–109; translation modified by author for clarity).

52. *Guanzi* 10.8a–b.

53. *Zhouyi* 周易 (*Xici zhuan* 繫辭傳) (*Sibu congkan chubian* ed.) 8.5a–b (trans. Richard Wilhelm/Cary F. Baynes, *The I Ching or Book of Changes* [Princeton, NJ: Princeton University Press, 1967], 342; translation slightly modified by author for consistency). See *Zhouyi* 8.4b for another passage on potency applied with timeliness.

54. *Sun Bin bingfa*, 104. The most fastidious observer of transitions points (*ji* 機) in military strategy may have been Fan Li, minister to King Goujian 勾踐王 of Yue 越 (r. 496–465 BCE). Fan Li was reportedly asked repeatedly by the king whether the time had come to take revenge on Wu for Yue's humiliating defeat at Kuaiji 會稽. Continually, however, Fan Li would reply that the conditions in Wu had still not reached the point at which Yue could retaliate and seize victory with ease, that is, with the least resistance. It was a matter, he said, of participating in harmony with Heaven and Earth, of observing the changes of *yin* and *yang* and their correlates. When the proper time for change did finally come, the Wu army, according to the chronicler, collapsed without difficulty. See *Guoyu* 21. It is important to point out that the *Guoyu* rendition asserts the importance of the correct moral transition point as much as the most advantageous transition point militarily for seizing victory. A similar explication of the principle is attributed to Dating Shi 大庭氏 in *Jing*, 223 (nos. 137–138).

55. See *Guanzi* 3.5a–b. Earlier in the same chapter of the *Guanzi* (3.2a) there is the phrase "the transition point between stability and danger" (*anwei zhi ji* 安危之機), which seems apposite here.

56. *Sunzi bingfa* 5.8a–10a (trans. Griffith, *Sun Tzu*, 92; translation modified by author for style). As in the case of psychical power (*shen* 神), the *Zhuangzi* contains useful civil analogues with regard to transition points (*ji*). In the "Ying diwang" 應帝王 chapter, where Liezi 列子 shows what he thinks to be a brilliant shaman to the sage Huzi 壺子, the term is used repeatedly in the sense of a trigger poised for

release, or the point of change when some inner capacity is about to be manifested. The shaman tries to physiognomize Huzi to determine his constant character, but Huzi continually changes appearances before him. The shaman becomes so confused by Huzi's transformations—first appearing as imminent death, then as imminent life, and finally as indefinable flux—that the shaman flees in madness. Huzi tells Liezi after meeting each time with the shaman what appearance he took on for the physiognomist. Initially, Huzi says: "Just now I appeared to him with Pattern of Earth—still and silent, nothing moving, nothing standing up. He probably saw in me the Workings (*ji*) of Virtue Closed Off." After the second meeting, Huzi says: "Just now I appeared to him as Heaven and Earth—no name or substance to it, but still the workings (*ji*) coming up from the heels. He probably saw in me the Workings (*ji*) of the Good One." And after the third encounter, Huzi relates: "Just now I appeared to him as the Great Vastness Where Nothing Wins Out. He probably saw in me the Workings (*ji*) of the Balanced Breaths" (3.21b–22b; trans. Burton Watson, *Chuang Tzu, Basic Writings* [New York: Columbia University Press, 1964], 93). The term *ji* takes on a combination of meanings here. On the one hand there is the image of automatic, mechanical succession, while on the other hand there is the notion of individual points of change leading inexorably to successive phases of being. In effect, Huzi posits an integration of space-time, based tacitly on the continual theme of vital energy (*qi*) in the *Zhuangzi*. Later portions of the *Zhuangzi* offer additional passages for comparison. The "Zhi le" 至樂 chapter, for example, speaks of the "ten thousand things all emerging at a nexus of change (*ji*), and all entering at a nexus of change" (6.25b). The "Qiu shui" 秋水 and "Tian yun" 天運 chapters, as well as the chronologically earlier "Dazong shi" 大宗師 chapter, also use *ji* either in the senses mentioned above or in the sense of a natural endowment (*tian ji* 天機) that works itself out in constantly changing ways. The "Tian yun" chapter varies by utilizing a musical analogy to speak of *ji*. In that analogy *ji* retains its function as a point of transition in endless change.

57. See *Heguanzi* A.18b–19a.

58. *Sun Bin bingfa*, 72.

59. *Sunzi bingfa* 5.11a–23b (trans. Griffith, *Sun Tzu*, 92–95).

60. *Heguanzi* C.10b.

61. *Guanzi* 6.11a.

62. *Weiliaozi* 1.15b–16a. The *Zhanguoce* supports this view of war: "So an enlightened ruler will not insist on the exhaustion of troops, the exposure of cities and great enmity from all, nor will the clear-sighted minister serve his lord by taking his strong troops and weakening them. That ruler and that minister will not need to move a single weapon and the lords will follow them, they will use soft words yet great riches will appear. So the enlightened ruler will do battle by not bringing out a single soldier, yet the enemy will be overcome. No assault towers will be used, but cities will surrender. The common citizen will never know it, but the king's business will be done. The enlightened will do things thus: his substance will be

used sparingly, few of his days will be wasted, and the benefits will be long-lasting. So I say all the Feudal Lords will wish to serve him who is last to move his troops" (4.47a–b; trans. Crump, *Chan Kuo Ts'e*, 201).

63. This principle, of course, also applies to government, as demonstrated in the *Daodejing*: "In ruling the people and in serving Heaven it is best for a ruler to be sparing. It is because he is sparing that he may be said to follow the way from the start; following the way from the start he may be said to accumulate an abundance of virtue; accumulating an abundance of virtue there is nothing he cannot overcome; when there is nothing he cannot overcome, no one knows his limit; when no one knows his limit he can possess a state; when he possesses the mother of a state he can then endure. This is called the way of deep roots and firm stems by which one lives to see many days" (59) (trans. Lau, *Lao Tzu*, 120). See the Heshang Gong 河上公 commentary on this passage, which refers to the retention of pure (*jing* 精) vital energy.

64. *Sunzi bingfa* 3.1b–7b, 11a–13b (trans. Griffith, *Sun Tzu*, 77–79). Also see *Guanzi* 6.10a: "Examine where movement and rest are necessary. Then success may be achieved without harm. Make known the difference between receiving and giving. Then territory may be obtained without fear. . . . Investigate the principles of what lies ahead and behind. Then the armed forces may be sent out without encountering trouble" (trans. Rickett, *Kuan-tzu*, 219; text rearranged by Rickett). Later in the same chapter of the *Guanzi* (6.11a) the restriction of conflict is further described: "To destroy the large and vanquish the strong is [the way] to achieve having only one [battle]. To throw them into disorder without resorting to opportunism, to gain ascendancy over them without resorting to deception, and to vanquish them without resorting to treachery is [the way] to realize having only one [battle]. . . . Incalculable strength, immeasurable force, unlimited spirit, and unfathomable power are the sources for having only one [battle]. To assemble like the seasonal rain and scatter like the whirlwind is to bring to an end the one [battle]" (trans. Rickett, *Kuan-tzu*, 230).

65. *Zhanguoce* 4.47b–48a (trans. Crump, *Chan Kuo Ts'e*, 201).

66. See Zhu Youzeng 朱右曾, comp., *Yi Zhoushu jiaoshi* 逸周書校釋 (Eguan shuchu, 1912), 11.6a; *Zhanguoce* 7.1a–b. The *Guanzi* (3.7a) also speaks of grasping and giving (*qu yu* 取與) as a means of overcoming the resistance of an interlocutor in persuasion.

67. *Sunzi bingfa* 7.40a–42a (trans. Griffith, *Sun Tzu*, 109–110).

Chapter 3

1. The transition from military rites (*junli* 軍禮) to military law (*junfa* 軍法) was probably not sudden. Judging from the infractions of proper martial behavior observed in the *Zuozhuan*, the substance of aristocratic etiquette differed

little from military law in the Zhanguo period. For example, under the thirty-third year of Lord Xi 僖公 of Lu (626 B.C.) in the *Zuozhuan* is the following passage: "In spring, the army of Qin was passing by the north gate of the [royal city of] Zhou, when the mailed men on the right and left of the chariots [merely] took off their helmets and descended, springing afterwards with a bound into the chariots—the three hundred of them. Wangsun Man 王孫滿 [grandson of King Xiang 襄王 of Zhou (d. 619 BCE)] was still quite young; but when he saw this, he said to the king: 'The army of Qin acts lightly and is unobservant of the ritual propriety (*li*); it is sure to be defeated. By acting so lightly, there must be little counsel in it, and by being unobservant of the ritual propriety, it will be heedless. When it enters a dangerous pass, and is heedless, being moreover without wise counsel, can it escape defeat?' " (trans. Legge, *Classics*, 5: 224; translation slightly modified by author for style). The shift may have indeed been already partially made, if one recalls the plight of Wei Jiang, who executed Yanggan, the brother of the marquis of Jin, for "throwing the ranks into confusion" (*Zuozhuan* [Xiang 3]). Although the basis for administering the severe punishment may have been military rites, the actual offense and penalty do not vary from those in penal law cited in the *Weiliaozi*. The difference seems to lie in social-philosophical attitudes toward undesirable martial behavior.

2. See *Zhouli* 7.1b; 3.21b–22a. The basic army structure presented under the latter reference is as follows: "Five men constitute a *wu* 伍; five *wu* constitute a *liang* 兩; four *liang* constitute a *zu* 卒; five *zu* constitute a *lü* 旅; five *lü* constitute a *shi* 師; five *shi* constitute a *jun* 軍." Also see *Zhouli* 4.23b for further connections between agricultural land and population subdivisions, on the one hand, and military organization, on the other.

3. For the *Shangshu*, see "Yin zheng" 胤征, "Gan shi" 甘誓 documents; for the *Shi*, see "Zhan bi Luo yi" 瞻彼洛矣, "Yu pu" 棫樸, and "Chang wu" 常武 odes; and for the *Zuozhuan*, see Xiang 14.

4. See Huang Jianshu 黃堅叔, *Zhongguo junzhi shi* 中國軍制史 (Changsha: Shangwu yinshuguan, 1941), 1: 71–118, and Xu Jingxian 徐景賢, "Chunqiu Jin jun zhi kao" 春秋晉軍制考, *Guo zhuan yuekan* 國專月刊 1, no. 5 (July 1935): 7–10. Cf. *Yuhai* 玉海 (Zhejiang shuju ed.) 136. For added documentation from the *Zuozhuan*, one can cite Xuan 12, which gives an internal organization for the Chu army that accords well with the *Zhouli* proportions, as well as the following statistics: (1) the term "three armies" (*sanjun* 三軍) appears twenty-one times in the text; (2) the term "left army" (*zuojun* 左軍) appears only once (Huan 5), but its commander (*zuoshi* 左師) is mentioned thirty-eight times; (3) the term "right army" (*youjun* 右軍) appears only twice (Huan 5, Ai 哀 11), but its commander (*youshi* 左師) is cited twenty-six times; (4) the term "center army" (*zhongjun* 中軍) appears forty-four times. The term "three armies" also appears once in the *Chunqiu* (Xiang 11).

5. *Guoyu* 6.5a–6b; *Guanzi* 1.12a–15a.

6. For example, the *Zuozhuan* (Huan 5) speaks of an attached fish (*yuli* 魚麗) formation, which the Western Jin 西晉 dynasty (265–316) commentator Du Yu 杜預 (222–284) interpreted to be a combined-arms team (infantry and chariots). Examples of harassing forces can be seen in Zhao 23 and Ai 17 of the *Zuozhuan*.

7. *Zuozhuan* (Zhao 30; Ai 5). Also, Zhao 昭 1 speaks of a three-five organization in an innovative battle order of infantry against chariots.

8. *Zuozhuan* (Xi 28; Xuan 12).

9. *Weiliaozi* 4.11b–12b. Figure 3.1 is based on this chapter for placement of insignia, but another chapter, "Bing jiao shang" 兵教 上, gives both different and additional information: "The left army wears badges on the left shoulder; the right army, on the right shoulder; the center army, on the chest. On the badges are written the man's *jia* 甲 and *shi* 士. On the front and back of each badge are five lines [providing this information]. Those with honor badges (*zunzhang* 尊章) [i.e., those of higher rank] are positioned at the head of the formation. Those next in rank show deference in graded manner" (5.12a–b).

10. *Guoyu* (19.8b–9a) presents a battle array for the Wu army that is ostensibly from the Chunqiu era but may represent a later tradition: "In setting forth the royal troops [i.e., the *zhongjun*] in battle order, one hundred men constitute a single line (*hang* 行), of which there are [also] one hundred. The commander of the line is in each case a *guanshi* 官師. He holds a gong, grasps a halberd [read as *ji* 戟, rather than as *ji* 稽], establishes his *feihu* 飛虎 [also read as *feihu* 肥胡] banner(s) and handles an adorned ox-horn shield. . . . Ten thousand men constitute a square (*fang* 方) formation. All are in white uniforms with white pennons (*qi* 旂), silk-colored armor, and white-feathered arrows; he grasps his *yue* 鉞 battleax, establishes his white banners (*qi* 旗), and takes up a position in the center formation. The left army is similar [except that] there are red uniforms, red *yu* 旟 pennants, cinnabar-colored armor, and vermilion-feathered arrows; [from a distance] it looks like fire. The right army is also similar, [except that] there are black uniforms, black banners, black armor, and arrows with crow-colored feathers; [from a distance] it looks like ink." It is significant that this schema does not accord with the correlation of colors and cardinal directions used by Zou Yan 鄒衍 (305–ca. 240 BCE) and his followers in the third century BCE.

11. *Weiliaozi* 4.1a.

12. *Weiliaozi* 3.65b–66a.

13. *Wuzi* (*Sibu congkan chubian* ed.) A.8a (trans. Griffith, *Sun Tzu*, 160). The *Sibu congkan chubian* edition of the *Wuzi* has *xuanwu* 玄武, rather than *xuangui* 玄龜. Cf. *Liji* 1.14b; *Huainanzi* 淮南子, 15.11b.

14. See *Shiji* 65.

15. Mount Chang 常 is probably a reference to Mount Heng 恆, located in present-day Shanxi Province. The character *chang* was used in the version translated here evidently to avoid the taboo of using the personal name of Emperor Wen 文帝 of Han.

16. *Sunzi bingfa* 11.26b. The term *shuairan* 率然 and its variant, *shuaier* 率爾, have, as compounds, the general meaning of "rapidly," "quick-like." However, Xu Shen (fl. second century CE) gave the meaning of *shuai* as "a hand-net for catching birds; the shape [of the character *shuai*] is that of a silken net with its rod-handles above and below." (See Ding Fubao, ed., *Shuowen jiezi gu lin*, 9: 5935.) This definition implies a net that one holds with both hands and wraps quickly around a prey, in a pincers movement. One might speculate whether this action may have become associated with the defenses of a certain mountain snake. For a fuller version of the legend of the pincers snake, see Dongfang Shuo 東方朔 (ca. 160–ca. 93 BCE), *Shenyijing* 神異經 (*Han Wei congshu* 漢魏叢書 ed.) 4b.

17. See *Sun Bin bingfa*, 89. Several of the chapter titles or prominent topics in the *Sun Bin bingfa* suggest a numerological proclivity—"Shi zhen" 十陣, "Shi wen" 十問, "Wu ming wu gong" 五名五恭, "Wu du jiu duo" 五度九奪 (title added by editor). The only exception is the "Ba zhen" 八陣 chapter, which discusses tripartite battle formations. Also indicative is the inclusion of the three sounds (*san sheng* 三聲)—drums, gongs, and horns—and the five colors (*wu cai* 五彩) of banners—green, red, yellow, white, and black—in the "Shi zhen" chapter. Aside from descriptions elsewhere, the *Liutao* also includes tripartite arrangements. Chapter titles include "San yi" 三疑 and "San zhen" 三陣, and the work itself is in six (2 x 3) sections.

18. Regarding the name of the formation translated as "dark wings," the "Shi zhen" chapter of the *Sun Bin bingfa* cites this formation title either as a combination of the character *xuan* 玄 and the character *xiang* 襄, or as a graph consisting of the character *xuan* and a second graph consisting of the character *xiang* 襄 below the character *yu* 羽. While the second graph in the combination has not been definitively deciphered, I have tentatively adopted the reading of the second graph as a variant of the character *yi* 翼. See also the translation by D.C. Lau and Roger T. Ames in *Sun Pin: The Art of Warfare*, 194–200.

19. The undeciphered text is a graph consisting of the character *quan* 犬 below the character *kou* 口.

20. *Sun Bin bingfa*, 83. See additional descriptions of formations in the "Wei wang wen" 威王問 chapter of the *Sun Bin bingfa* (42–43), and also descriptions of siege defense organization in the "Bei cheng men" 備城門, "Tong shuai" 同帥, and "Ying di ci" 迎敵祠 chapters of the *Mozi*. The *Tongdian* ([*Shi Tong* 十通 ed.] 148.776a–b) has a quotation attributed to Chunqiu-era general Tian Rangju concerning military organization, selection of soldiers to constitute a central command post (*zhonglei* 中壘), and area measures of ground to be used for such a headquarters and of terrain defensible by a 12,500-man army. Though multiples of five are maintained, the passage mentions a centrally commanded elite corps, *woqi* 握奇. Also, a set of eight formations (八陣 *ba zhen*) is discussed that does not, as far as is presently known, appear until probably the Eastern Han (25–220) (cf. *Hou Hanshu* 後漢書 53). This organization becomes prominent only in the

Woqijing 握奇經 (*Wojijing* 握機經), a text probably dating from Eastern Han or later, and in records concerning the noted general-statesman Zhuge Liang 諸葛亮 (181–234). The eight formations of the *Sun Bin bingfa* are only varied formations associated arbitrarily by the writer(s) of the work; they have little resemblance to the close-knit eight formations discussed in later times. Thus, the supposed quotation of Tian Rangju in the *Tongdian* probably does not date from the pre-Han period.

21. The "Jue dao" 絶道 chapter of the *Liutao* speaks of the positioning of reserve forces but gives little information on actual organization or deployment. On the other hand, the "Jun bing" 均兵 and "Zhanche" 戰車 chapters of the same work provide certain ratios among cavalry, infantry, and chariots according to battle terrain. The latter chapter also makes a variant interpretation of the term "three armies," using it to refer to the three combat branches, rather than the tripartite tactical division of Chunqiu times. This is additional evidence of a newer, practical, and nontraditional approach to deploying military units.

22. See *Liutao* 6.44b–45a, 47a–b. On this point, see Dong Dingming 董鼎銘, *Zhongguo bingyi shilüe* 中國兵役史略 (Taibei, 1962), 26.

23. See *Liutao* 5.40b–41a, 5.42a.

24. *Liutao* 5.41b.

25. *Liutao* 4.29b–30a.

26. *Liutao* 3.15a–16a.

27. *Liutao* 3.15a.

28. See *Liutao*, 4.32b–34a; *Weiliaozi* 4.4b; *Sun Bin bingfa*, 83–88.

29. *Wuzi* B.2b. The *Liji* ([*Sibu congkan chubian* ed.] 1.14b) speaks similarly of the use of banners with specific animal and bird designs to give information about geographical features encountered and the location of the army.

30. For a similar program of instruction, see *Liutao* 6.45b–46a; *Wuzi* A.7b. Also see *Weiliaozi* 5.11a.

31. To some extent this training procedure verifies that described in *Zhouli* 7.12b–17a, where troops are marched in formation between posts set up at prescribed distances and according to specific drum and gong signals. A somewhat different mode of military instruction from that described above is suggested in the *Wuzi*: "In training, cause your troops to form squares from circles, to sit down and get up, to move and to stop. Cause them to pass from left to right and from front to rear. Divide and concentrate them; unite and disperse them. When versed in all these varying circumstances, give them their weapons" (A.7b; trans. Griffith, *Sun Tzu*, 160).

32. *Sunzi bingfa* 11.29b–32a. Another example of this attitude can be found in the *Jingfa*, 195–196 (nos. 14–16), which describes a seven-year program of mass development, starting with sensitivity to local customs and ending with the promulgation of war fought by a loyal populace. Also see *Shiji* 92.7b, where General Han Xin 韓信 (fl. third century BCE) reportedly justified his placement of troops between Zhao forces and the Chi 泜 River during the Battle of Jingxing 井陘

(205 BCE) by claiming that his untried soldiers had no sense of horror as did elite soldiers (*shidafu* 士大夫) in the past, and thus would disobey orders and flee for safety unless placed in desperate situations.

33. See A.F.P. Hulsewé, *Remnants of Han Law* (Leiden: E.J. Brill, 1955).

34. *Weiliaozi* 3.62b–63a; 4.7b–8a; 5.24b–26a. For a discussion of the offenses listed in the *Weiliaozi*, see Weigand, *Staat und Militär*, 162–167. The *Liutao* also provides examples of severe retribution for disobedience to commands. The "Fen bing" 分兵 chapter indicates a method for a commander in chief to test his generals in order to gauge whether he can change his dispositions rapidly. He determines a time and place of battle and dispatches liaison officers belonging to his generals to convey this warning order to their respective superiors. Those generals who arrive before the set time are rewarded; those who arrive late are beheaded.

35. This severe approach to the application of military law, as well as an emphasis on strict organization and standardized insignia, can be seen in the wooden strips unearthed in 1978 from a tomb dating from the Western Han in Shangsunjiazhai 上孫家寨, Qinghai Province. Although the condition of the wooden strips is often poor, the content of these fragments clearly demonstrates the continuing importance of military law and military regulations in the post-Qin era. See descriptions and analyses of the Shangsunjiazhai wooden strips in: Qinghai sheng wenwu kaogu gongzuo dui 青海省文物考古工作隊, "Qinghai Datong xian Shangsunjiazhai yi yi wu hao Han mu" 青海大通縣上孫家寨一一五號漢墓, *Wenwu* 文物 1981 (2): 16–21; Guojia wenwu gu wenxian yanjiushi Datong Shansunjiazhai Han jian zhengli xiaozu 國家文物古文獻研究室大通上孫家漢簡整理小組, "Datong xian Shangsunjiazhai Han jian shiwen" 大通縣上孫家寨漢簡釋文, *Wenwu* 文物 1981 (2): 22–26; Zhu Guozhao 朱國炤, "Shangsunjiazhai mu jian chu tan" 上孫家寨木簡初探, *Wenwu* 文物 1981 (2): 27–34; Li Ling 李零, "Qinghai Datong xian Shangsunjiazhai Han jian xingzhi xiao yi" 青海 大通縣上孫家寨漢簡性質小議, *Kaogu* 考古 1983 (6): 549–553.

36. Cf. these penal laws with those of the Song period discussed by Herbert Franke in *Zum Militärstrafrecht im chinesischen Mittelalter* (München: Verlag der Bayerischen Akademie der Wissenschaften, 1970).

37. *Weiliaozi* 1.16a.

38. *Weiliaozi* 1.19b–20b.

39. For background on the composition of the *Lüshi chunqiu* 呂氏春秋, see D.C. Lau, "*Lü shih ch'un ch'iu* 呂氏春秋," in Loewe, *Early Chinese Texts*, 324–335, and John Knoblock and Jeffrey Riegel, introduction to *The Annals of Lü Buwei* (Stanford, CA: Stanford University Press, 2000).

40. Xihe 西河, or Xihe jun 西河郡, was in the Zhanguo state of Wei 魏.

41. *Lüshi chunqiu* (*Sibu congkan chubian* ed.) 25.12a. Cf. a similar story about Shang Yang in *Shiji* 68.4a. The modern scholar Guo Moruo (1892–1978) commented that this Wu Qi anecdote is probably a piece of fiction designed to illustrate a reputed trait of the official-general's policy. See "Shu Wu Qi" 述吳起

in *Xian Qin xueshuo shu lin* 先秦學說述林 (Yong'an: Dongnan chubanshe, 1945), 217–218.

42. *Guanzi* 2.3a–b. The stress in this passage is on the manifestation of public-mindedness (*gong* 公), as opposed to private-mindedness (*si* 私). The *Liutao* (3.19a), among other texts, similarly lauds military leaders who will punish the crimes of the most in favor and reward the achievements of the most not in favor. The *Guanzi* passage may also be compared to one in the *Shangjunshu*: "A sage knows the right principles which must be followed, and the right time and circumstances for action. Therefore, the rule which he exercises always leads to order, the people whom he employs in war are always brave, and the commands which he issues are always obeyed. In consequence, when his army marches out, it has no equal, and when his commands are issued, the whole empire submits" (4.11b; trans. Duyvendak, *Lord Shang*, 292).

43. *Guanzi* 6.4b.

44. *Jingfa*, 194–195 (nos. 9–10).

45. *Simafa* A.1a. Cf. *Shangjunshu* 4.8b.

46. *Shangjunshu* 1.13b–14a (trans. Duyvendak, *Lord Shang*, 204). Other chapters of the *Shangjunshu* offer complementary passages. The "Shuo min" 說民 chapter, for example, has the following statement: "Punishment produces force, force produces strength, strength produces awe, and awe produces virtue. Virtue has its origins in punishment" (2.2b). The "Kai sai" 開塞 chapter has a comparable statement: "This is my way of reverting to virtue by death penalties, and of making righteousness a corollary to violence" (2.11b). The "Jin ling" 靳令 chapter tells us in similar fashion: "Force produces strength, strength produces awesomeness, awesomeness produces virtue, and so virtue has its origin in force, which a sage-prince alone possesses. He therefore is able to transmit humaneness and righteousness to the empire" (3.10b) (trans. Duyvendak, *Lord Shang*, 210, 232, 259; the last translation slightly modified by author for style).

47. Both the *syncretist* and the *compartmentalist* approaches to military punishment were already evident in the period before Zhanguo. In the *Guoyu* (12.4a–b) we see the following account that illustrates this trend: "At the Battle of Yanling 鄢陵 [575 BCE], Jin attacked Zheng, and Jing [i.e., Chu] came to [Zheng's] aid. [Jin's] ministers wanted to go to battle, but Fan Wenzi 范文子 [a general and statesman of Jin] demurred, saying, 'I have heard that a lord prosecutes [the guilty among] his people and only afterwards does he conduct war outside [his borders]. In that way [his state] is harmonious within and awe-inspiring without. Now the blades and saws of the minister of punishments [used against offenders among the common people] are deteriorating by the day and axes and halberds are not being used [against wicked ministers]. If there are still no [due] punishments within, then it will be even more so without. War is a form of punishment—punishment for those who exceed [the limits of ethics]. Excess comes from high ministers and resentment from the common people. Thus by destroying resentment with kindness

and eliminating excess with forbearance, the lowly will have no resentment and the high-placed will not exceed [their duties]. Only then may you conduct war to punish those who do not submit from outside [your borders].' "

48. *Simafa* A.1a–b. Cf. *Zhouyi (Xici zhuan)* 8.5a: "The Master said: 'Danger arises when a man feels secure in his position. Destruction threatens when a man seeks to preserve his worldly estate. Confusion develops when a man has put everything in order. Therefore the superior man does not forget danger in his security, or ruin when he is well established, or confusion when his affairs are in order. In this way he gains personal safety and is able to protect the empire. In the *Changes* it is said: 'What if it should fail? What if it should fail?' " (trans. Wilhelm/Baynes, *Changes*, 341).

49. *Weiliaozi* 1.5a–b.

50. *Weiliaozi* 1.14a–b. Cf. *Shangjunshu* 1.6b–11b.

51. *Sun Bin bingfa*, 69.

52. See *Guanzi* 1.7b, 3.4b–5a, 21.1a. Cf. *Shangjunshu* 3.6a–b.

53. *Shangjunshu* 3.8b, 9a–b (trans. Duyvendak, *Lord Shang*, 253–254, 256; translation modified by author for style and accuracy). For a similar image, see *Lüshi chunqiu* 7.4a. Also see *Shangjunshu* 2.12a.

54. See *Zuozhuan* (Xuan 12); *Liutao* 4.30a; *Weiliaozi* 2.33a.

55. *Liutao* 3.17a.

56. *Weiliaozi* 2.30b–33b; *Weiliaozi* 2.37a.

57. *Sunzi bingfa* 1.2a–12b, 2.2b–12a.

58. Ray Huang (1918–2000), in his review of *Chinese Ways in Warfare*, edited by Frank A. Kierman Jr. and John K. Fairbank (*Journal of Asian Studies* 35, no. 2 [1976]: 312), pointed out that the prevalent distaste for martial activity in post–Western Han times meant that the institutions required for combat service support could not be effectively organized in times of war. Huang noted that successive imperial courts in China were never equipped with the necessary infrastructure and management wherewithal to control the machinery of government at all levels. Based on this observation, the relative lack of attention given to expeditionary supply planning in Chinese military treatises is a reflection of the chronic inability of Chinese imperial governments to create viable military logistical systems.

59. For a useful discussion of the use of prognostication methods in Chinese military strategy, see Robin D.S. Yates, "The History of Military Divination in China," *East Asian Science, Technology, and Medicine* 24 (2005): 15–43.

60. For background on Shang oracle-bone divination, see David N. Keightley, "The Shang: China's First Historical Dynasty," in *The Cambridge History of Ancient China: From the Origins of Civilization to 221 B.C.*, ed. Michael Loewe and Edward L. Shaughnessy (Cambridge, UK: Cambridge University Press, 1999), 236–255.

61. Keightley, *Sources of Shang History*, 77–78.

62. Ralph D. Sawyer, *The Tao of Spycraft: Intelligence Theory and Practice in Traditional China* (Boulder, CO: Westview Press, 1998), 76.

63. Tupu 菟圃 was located on the border of present-day Changyuanxian 長垣縣, Henan Province.

64. *Zuozhuan* (Xi 19; trans. Legge, *Classics*, 5: 177).

65. *Shiji* 27.6b. Cf. *Hanshu* 26.

66. *Shiji* 27.10a. The so-called Five Stars and their associations are as follows: *sui* 歲 (Jupiter, east, wood); *yinghuo* 熒火 (Mars, south, fire); *taibai* 太白 (Venus, west, metal); *chen* 辰 (Mercury, north, water); *zhen* 鎮 (Saturn, center, earth).

67. *Shiji* 27.12b.

68. *Liutao* 3.24b. Cf. *Hanshu* 1A.21b, *Tai Gong bingfa yiwen*, 17a.

69. *Shiji* 27.32b (trans. Sawyer, *Tao of Spycraft*, 535). For discussions of this vital energy prognostication technique as it was used during imperial times for both civil and military purposes, see Derk Bodde, "The Chinese Cosmic Magic Known as Watching for the Ethers," reprinted in *Essays on Chinese Civilization* (Princeton, NJ: Princeton University Press, 1981), 351–372; A.F.P. Hulsewé, "Watching the Vapors: An Ancient Chinese Technique of Prognostication," *Nachrichten der Gesellschaft für Natur- und Võlkerkunde Ostasiens/Hamburg* 125 (1979): 40–49; and Huang Yi-long and Chang Chih-ch'eng, "The Evolution and Decline of the Ancient Practice of Watching for the Ethers," *Chinese Science* 13 (1996): 82–106.

70. See Gu Tiefu 顧鐵符, "Mawangdui boshu *Tianwen qi xiang za zhan* neirong jian shu" 馬王堆帛書《天文氣象雜占》內容簡述, *Wenwu* 1978 (2): 1–4 (translated by Donald J. Harper, "A Summary of the Contents of the Ma-wang-tui Silk-scroll Book 'Assorted Astronomical and Meteorological Prognostications,'" *Chinese Studies in Archaeology* 1, no. 1 [1979]: 56–74). For a summary of Chinese scholarship on the *Tianwen qi xiang za zhan* up to 2007, see Wang Shujin 王樹金, "Mawangdui Han mu boshu *Tianwen qi xiang za zhan* yanjiu san shi nian," 馬王堆漢墓 帛書《天文氣象雜占》研究三十年 *Hunan sheng bowuguan guan kan* 湖南省博物館館刊 4 (2007): 31–42. Also see Michael Loewe, *Divination, Mythology, and Monarchy in Han China* (Cambridge, UK: Cambridge University Press, 1994), 61–84.

71. See *Shiji* 27.32–34b; *Hanshu* 26.43a–46a. A form of prognostication related to cloud omens was that involving wind. Accounts of wind prognostication in the *Shiji* and the *Hanshu*, which follow directly upon those for cloud prognostication, describe associations between wind direction and future agricultural and military events. Such wind prognostication, like other forms of prognostication based on meteorological events, almost certainly originated in the pre-Han period. See *Shiji* 27.34b–35b and *Hanshu* 26.46a–47a; also see Loewe, *Divination, Mythology, and Monarchy in Han China*, 191–213.

72. The connection between musical tones and martial activity existed in Sinitic culture for centuries prior to the Zhanguo era. There are references, for example, to the "Wu" 武 song-dance in a few *Shi* verses (e.g., "Wu" 武, "Zhuo" 酌, "Huan" 桓, "Lai" 賚), and there is a mention of *wu* choreography in the formal rites in honor of Kongzi 孔子 (Confucius) (551–479 BCE). According to

commentary on the *Shiji* by the Tang dynasty scholar Zhang Shoujie 張守節, this choreography was an abstract representation of King Wu of Zhou's military actions before his defeat of King Zhou of Shang. Also see Rao Zongyi 饒宗頤, "Jing Chu wenhua" 荊楚文化, *Zhongyang yanjiuyuan lishi yuyan yanjiusuo jikan* 41, no. 2 (1969): 273–315, esp. 280–282. In the Chunqiu period, Master Kuang 師曠, the noted blind music master from the state of Qi, appears in the *Zuozhuan* as an advisor on military affairs as interpreted through musical laws. See *Zuozhuan* (Xiang 18). In the *Zhouyi* there is the statement under hexagram seven, "army" (*shi* 師): "The army sets out according to *lü* 律." Although the usual translation of *lü* here is "proper order" or "rules," and the interpretation of an advisor in *Zuozhuan* also seems to be that of proper procedure, it appears from later writings, most notably the "Treatise on Pitch Pipes" ("Lü shu" 律書), the "Treatise on Music" ("Yue shu" 樂書), and Sima Qian's introduction ("Taishigong zixu" 太史公自序) in the *Shiji*, that the alternate, and perhaps principal, intention of the term was "pitch pipes." See *Shiji suoyin* 130.15b; *Shiji* 24.27a–28a. During the Tang dynasty, the scholar Sima Zhen 司馬貞 (679–732) commented that "The 'Treatise on Pitch Pipes' is [actually] a treatise on military affairs," and that the "Treatise on Music," referring presumably to ancient as well as Han times, speaks of certain musical sounds being stimulants to martial activity.

73. The term "Three Sovereigns" (*san huang* 三皇) is a reference to the earliest cultural heroes of Chinese antiquity. The identities of the Three Sovereigns vary among early Chinese texts, but most listings include Fu Xi 伏羲, the legendary inventor, along with his sister, Nü Wa 女媧, of hunting, fishing, and cooking, and Shen Nong 神農, the legendary progenitor of agriculture.

74. *Liutao* 3.23b–24a. A commentary by the Han scholar Zheng Xuan 鄭玄 (127–200) on the *Zhouli* gives a similar description of the meaning of musical resonances in a military context: "A military work (*bingshu* 兵書) says, 'The grand preceptor (*taishi* 太師) blows his pitch pipes to harmonize with the sounds [emitted]. If [the resounding tone is] *shang* 商, then the battle will result in a victory [for friendly forces], and the soldiers will be strong. If it is *jue* 角, then the army will be agitated and unsettled, and the hearts of the soldiers will be lost. If it is *gong* 宮, then the army will be harmonious and the soldiers will be of the same mind. If it is *zhi* 徵, then the general will be disturbed with feelings of anger and the soldiers will be fatigued. If it is *yu* 羽, then clearly the soldiers will be weak with little awesomeness" (6.14a).

75. See Lisa Raphals, "Divination in the *Han shu* Bibliographic Treatise," *Early China* 32 (2008–2009): 45–101; Tian Xudong, "'Bing yinyang jia' jige wenti de chubu yanjiu" 兵陰陽家幾個問題的初步研究, in *Gudai bingxue wenhua tan lun* 古代兵學文化探論 (Beijing: Zhongguo shehui kexue chubanshe, 2010), 90–102.

76. A work entitled *Didian* 地典 is listed in the *Hanshu* "Treatise on Literature" (30.62b).

77. Robin D.S. Yates, "The Yin-yang Texts from Yinqueshan: An Introduction and Partial Reconstruction, with Notes on their Significance in Relation to Huang-Lao Daoism," *Early China* 19 (1994): 86, 112.

78. Olivia Milburn, "*Gai lu*: A Translation and Commentary on a Yin-yang Military Text Excavated from Tomb M247, Zhangjiashan." *Early China* 33–34 (2010–2011): 108. For another discussion of the *Gai lu* (*He Lu*/*He Lü*), see Shao Hong 邵鴻, *Zhangjiashan Han jian Gai Lu yanjiu* 張家山漢簡《蓋廬》研究 (Beijing: Wenwu chubanshe, 2007), 5–26.

79. See Milburn, "*Gai lu*," 123–125. Guidance almost identical to that given here in the *Gai Lu* (*He Lu*/*He Lü*) appears in the "Bing lüe" chapter of the *Huainanzi*, compiled in the second century BCE. See *Huainanzi* 15.4b, 11b, 14b.

80. For a detailed examination of the *Xingde* texts, see Marc Kalinowski, "The *Xingde* 刑德 Texts of Mawangdui," trans. Phyllis Brooks, *Early China* 23–24 (1998–1999): 125–202.

81. *Lüshi chunqiu* 15.1a–2b.

82. *Sunzi bingfa* 13.18b–19a.

83. *Zuozhuan* (Huan 5).

84. *Zuozhuan* (Xi 15).

85. *Zuozhuan* (Xi 30).

86. *Sunzi bingfa* 13.4b–12a.

87. *Liutao* 3.20a–b.

88. *Liutao* 3.20b.

89. *Sunzi bingfa* 9 (trans. Griffith, *Sun Tzu*, 116–123; translations slightly modified by author for style).

90. *Wuzi* A.5a–b.

91. *Sun Bin bingfa*, 112–113. Three of the thirty-two items in the listing—the tenth, sixteenth, and twentieth—have been lost. Other examples of field observations for intelligence purposes can be seen in various chapters of the *Sunzi bingfa* ("Jiu bian" 九變, "Jun zheng" 軍爭), the *Liutao* ("Bing zheng" 兵徵, "Lei xu" 壘虛), and the *Sun Bin bingfa* ("Di bao" 地葆).

92. See *Shiji* 82.2b (trans. Sawyer, *Tao of Spycraft*, 105).

93. *Shiji* 82.2b–3a. For a comprehensive history of deception in military affairs from Chinese antiquity to modern times, including extended translations of relevant passages from period sources, see Ralph D. Sawyer, *The Tao of Deception: Unorthodox Warfare in Historic and Modern China* (New York: Basic Books, 2007).

94. *Liutao* 2.12a–13, 2.14a–b.

95. *Weiliaozi* 2.27b–28a.

96. *Weiliaozi* 1.1b–2b. See *Weiliaozi* 2.41a for additional disavowals of astrology and divination as valid military techniques.

97. See *Sunzi bingfa* 1.5b, 9.27a, 10.2a–6a.

98. *Sunzi bingfa* 6.33b.

99. *Wuzi* A.6b.

100. *Simafa* A.3b.

101. *Sun Bin bingfa*, 61. This chapter of the *Sun Bin bingfa* also has a reference to divination by wind direction, but there is no elaboration.

102. For evidence of further development of prognostication lore and its application to military intelligence in the imperial era, see Ralph D. Sawyer, "Military Prognostication," in *Military Culture in Imperial China*, ed. Nicola di Cosima (Cambridge, MA: Harvard University Press, 2009), 45–64, and Sawyer, *Tao of Spycraft*, 527–547. Also see Li Hansan 李漢三, *Xian Qin liang Han zhi yinyang wuxing xueshuo* 先秦兩漢之陰陽五行學說 (Taibei: Zhongding wenhua chuban gongsi, 1967); Xu Fuguan 徐復觀, *Yinyang wuxing guannian zhi yanbian ji ruogan youguan wenxian de chengli shidai yu jieshi de wenti* 陰陽五行觀念之演變及若干有關文獻的成立時代與解釋的問題 (Taibei: Minzhu pinglun she, 1961); Loewe, *Divination, Mythology, and Monarchy in Han China*, 160–213.

Chapter 4

1. It is widely accepted among modern scholars that there was probably no historical figure named Laozi, but that "Laozi" was a sobriquet given to an ostensible philosopher of the Chunqiu or Zhanguo eras, whose views were compiled by an unknown writer or writers to form the *Daodejing*. See William G. Boltz, "*Lao tzu Tao te ching* 老子道德經," in Loewe, *Early Chinese Texts*, 269–271.

2. *Daodejing* 30 (trans. Lau, *Lao Tzu*, 88). Cf. *Daodejing* 31. The "Zagua" 雜卦 commentary to the *Zhouyi*, hexagram seven (*shi* 師), reflects the *Daodejing* view: "The army means mourning." Also see the "Lie Yukou" 列御寇 chapter of the *Zhuangzi*: "The sage considers the inevitable as not inevitable and thus there is no war. The common man considers what is not inevitable as inevitable and thus there is frequent war. If one turns to war, it is to seek [self-aggrandizement]; by relying on war, one is lost."

3. *Daodejing* 68 (trans. Lau, *Lao Tzu*, 130).

4. *Daodejing* 50 (trans. Lau, *Lao Tzu*, 111). Also see *Daodejing* 67, 76.

5. See *Daodejing* 46.

6. For background on the dating and composition of the *Lunyu* 論語, see Anne Cheng, "*Lun yü* 論語," in Loewe, *Early Chinese Texts*, 313–323.

7. *Lunyu* (*Sibu congkan chubian* ed.) 7.12 (trans. Legge, *Classics*, 1: 198).

8. *Lunyu* 7.10.2–3 (trans. Legge, *Classics*, 1: 198).

9. *Lunyu* 13.29 (trans. Legge, *Classics*, 1: 275). The idea of seven years of instruction reminds one of a program referred to in *Jingfa*, 195–196 (nos. 14–16).

10. *Lunyu* 13.30 (trans. Legge, *Classics*, 1: 275). The sense of "to train" in the character *jiao* 教, though not consonant with Kongzi's predominantly civil attitude, is nevertheless relevant here and is apparent in the *Zuozhuan* (see, e.g., Xi

22 [*ming chi jiao zhan* 明耻教戰]; Cheng 7 [*jiao zhi zhanzhen* 教之戰陳]; Xiang 31 [*bi xiang jiaoxun yi weiyi ye* 必相教訓以威儀也]).

11. *Lunyu* 16.2.1 (trans. Legge, *Classics*, 1: 310; translation modified by author for style and accuracy).

12. *Lunyu* 15.1.1 (trans. Legge, *Classics*, 1: 294).

13. *Lunyu* 12.7.1–3 (trans. Legge, *Classics*, 1: 254; translation modified by author for style).

14. The received text of the *Yanzi chunqiu* 晏子春秋 is close in structure, and possibly in some of its content, to the *Yanzi* 晏子 compiled by Liu Xiang 劉向 (79–8 BCE) in the late Western Han period. See a discussion of the *Yanzi chunqiu* in Stephen W. Durrant, "*Yen tzu ch'un ch'iu*," in Loewe, *Early Chinese Texts*, 486–487.

15. *Yanzi chunqiu* (*Sibu congkan chubian* ed.) 3.5b–6a. For a similar exposition from Mengzi 孟子 to King Xuan 宣王 of Qi preceding the retaliation by the state of Yan for Qi's incursions into Yan territory, see *Mengzi* (*Sibu congkan chubian* ed.) 1B.11.

16. The text entitled *Cao Mo zhi zhen* (*Cao Mo's Battle Formations*), a bamboo-strip text acquired in 1994 from the Hong Kong antiques market by the Shanghai Museum, espouses a viewpoint similar to that presented in this passage from the *Yanzi chunqiu*. Evidently discovered in what was the state of Chu, the *Cao Mo zhi zhen* is cast as a conversation between Lord Zhuang 莊公 of Lu (r. 693–662 BCE) and Cao Mo 曹沫, a military strategist in the lord's employ. While the title of the work suggests that it is focused on military tactics and strategy, in fact *Cao Mo's Battle Formations* is equally concerned, if not more so, with the role of a ruler in ensuring a strong state and army. Similar to the argument given in the *Yanzi Spring and Autumn*, the main advice offered to Lord Zhuang in the *Cao Mo zhi zhen* is to avoid launching military offensives on a rival state without having first created in one's own state the proper sociopolitical conditions of government and the optimum leadership and order in the military forces. According to Cao Mo, offensive military ventures should be taken by a state only at the right time (*ji* 機) and only after the state's ruler has succeeded in forming close relations (*qin* 親) between himself and his people, achieved harmony (*he* 和) between the masses and the ruler's officials, and established righteousness (*yi* 義) as the moral basis for administering the state. For discussions of the structure and content of the *Cao Mo zhi zhen*, as well as the possible identity of Cao Mo, see Li Ling, *Cao Mo zhi zhen*, in Ma Chengyuan, *Shanghai bowuguan cang Zhanguo Chu zhu shu* 4: 239–242; Tian Xudong 田旭東, "Shi chuan yi jiu de Lu guo bingshu—*Cao Mo zhi zhen*" 失傳已久的魯國兵書—曹沫之陳, in *Gudai bingxue wenhua tan lun*, 46–54; and Ernest Caldwell, "Promoting Action in Warring States Political Philosophy: A First Look at the Chu Manuscript *Cao Mie's Battle Arrays*," *Early China* 37 (2014): 259–289. Caldwell indicates in his article that the title he adopts for the work—*Cao Mie zhi zhen* 曹蔑之陳—is based on the inscription on the back of strip no. 2 of the original bamboo-strip text as collated by Li Ling. Li

Ling interprets *mie* 蔑 to be *mo* 沫. See Ma Chengyuan, *Shanghai bowuguan cang Zhanguo Chu zhu shu*, 4: 245.

17. As background, the state of Song 宋 was formed through a territorial grant by King Cheng of Zhou (r. 1042/35–1006 BCE) to Weizi 微子, the oldest son of the penultimate ruler of the Shang, Di Yi 帝乙.

18. *Yanzi chunqiu* (*Sibu congkan chubian* ed.) 1.23b–24b.

19. *Mengzi* 7B.4.1 (trans. Legge, *Classics*, 2: 479).

20. *Mengzi* 4A.14.2–3 (trans. D.C. Lau, trans., *Mencius* (Hong Kong: Chinese University Press, 1984), 1: 149–150; translation slightly modified by author for style). Also see *Mengzi* 6B.9.2, in which Mengzi is quoted as claiming that the good ministers (*liang chen* 良臣) of his day were the "robbers of the people" (*min zei* 民賊) in former times. Mengzi's biography in *Shiji* 74 seems to attribute the impetus for his supposed writing of the *Mengzi* to his distaste for the excesses of martiality during his lifetime.

21. *Mengzi* 7B.4.2 (trans. Legge, *Classics*, 2: 479; translation slightly modified by author for style).

22. *Mengzi* 6B.8.8 (trans. Legge, *Classics*, 2: 440; translation slightly modified by author for style).

23. *Mengzi* 2A.3.2 (trans. Legge, *Classics*, 2: 196–197).

24. *Mengzi* 1B.10.1–3 (trans. Legge, *Classics*, 2: 169).

25. *Mengzi* 3B.5.5 (trans. Legge, *Classics*, 2: 273–274). Cf. *Shangshu*, "Wu cheng" 武成.

26. See *Mengzi* 1B.11.2, 3B.5.3–4, 7B.4.3.

27. *Mengzi* 2B.1.1–5 (trans. Legge, *Classics*, 2: 208–210; translation modified by author for style and consistency).

28. *Mengzi*, 2B.2 (trans. Legge, *Classics*, 2: 185–190; translation modified by author for style and accuracy).

29. The connection here with Zengzi 曾子, who was praised for his filial conduct, is important for another reason. As Zengzi is quoted in the *Liji*, the Ruist sense of courage is closely linked with filial deference (*xiao* 孝): "To go to war without courage is not filial" (14.11b). And yet to go to war at all, thereby threatening the body given by one's parents, would appear not to be filial. Mengzi seemed to avoid this contradiction in talking of Zengzi by concentrating on the moral mindset of an individual in adversity, rather than on family ethics.

30. An insightful discussion of Mengzi's views on this subject can be found in Benjamin I. Schwartz (1916–1999), *The World of Thought in Ancient China* (Cambridge, MA: Harvard University Press, 1985), 263–278.

31. *Mengzi* 6A.11, 1A.1, 4A.10.

32. For a useful overview of the history of the term *yibing* 義兵 from Zhanguo to Han times, see Mark Edward Lewis, "The Just War in Early China," in *The Ethics of War in Asian Civilization: A Comparative Perspective*, ed. Torkel Brekke (London and New York: Routledge, 2006), 185–200.

33. For background on the text of the *Xunzi* 荀子 and its component chapters, see Michael Loewe, "*Hsün tzu* 荀子," in Loewe, *Early Chinese Texts*, 178–188. Portions of the text of the "Yi bing" 議兵 chapter have been closely paraphrased in the *Han Shi waizhuan* 韓詩外傳 ([*Congshu jicheng* 叢書集成 ed.] 3.43–44), attributed to Han Ying 韓嬰 (fl. early second century BCE), and in the *Xinxu* ·新序 ([*Sibu congkan chubian* ed.] 3.1b–3b), compiled by Liu Xiang in the late first century BCE. For a translation of the portions in the *Han Shi waizhuan*, see James R. Hightower, *Han Shih Wai Chuan: Han Ying's Illustrations of the Didactic Application of the Classic of Songs* (Cambridge, MA: Harvard University Press, 1952), 120–122.

34. *Xunzi* (*Sibu congkan chubian* ed.) 10.2b (trans. Burton Watson, *Hsun Tzu, Basic Writings* [New York and London: Columbia University Press, 1963], 57; translation slightly modified by author for style).

35. See *Xunzi* 10.17b–18a.

36. See *Xunzi* 10.10a–b.

37. *Xunzi* 10.11a–b (trans. Watson, *Hsun Tzu*, 66).

38. *Xunzi* 10.11b (trans. Watson, *Hsun Tzu*, 67). Xunzi also hinted at his theory of mind in the "Yi bing" chapter of the *Xunxi*—that is, a ruler/general should cultivate an impassivity toward provocative events. By separating the emotion from the stimulant, one can purify the mind, that is, act on rational grounds and without second thoughts. He assumed, therefore, the ability in man to make moral choices based on clear criteria. "In knowledge, nothing is more important than discarding what is doubtful; in action, nothing is more important than avoiding mistakes; in undertakings, nothing is more important than to be without regret. Only make sure that you will not regret the undertaking, and then you need not worry about whether it will be successful or not" (*Xunzi* 10.10a [trans. Watson, *Hsun Tzu*, 65]).

39. See *Xunzi* 10.6a–7a.

40. Cf. *Zhuangzi* (Yiwen yinshuguan ed.) 5.18a: "Originating belongs to those in the higher position; details [of work] to those who are in the lower. The compendious decision belongs to the lord; the minutiae of execution belong to his ministers. The direction of the three armies (*sanjun* 三軍) with the five weapons (*wubing* 五兵) is but a trifling quality (*de zhi mo* 德之末)" (trans. James Legge, *The Sacred Books of China: Texts of Taoism*, in Sacred Books of the East, ed. F. Max Müller [London: Oxford University Press, 1927], 39: 334; translation slightly modified by author for style).

41. *Xunzi* 10.4b (trans. Watson, *Hsun Tzu*, 59; translation slightly modified by author for style).

42. Accounts of or information about Tian Dan 田單 of Qi, Zhuang Qiao 莊蹻 of Chu, Wei Yang 衛鞅 of Qin, and Miao Ji 繆蟣 of Yan can be found, respectively, in *Shiji* 82, 116, 68, and 89.

43. *Xunzi* 10.9a–10a (trans. Watson, *Hsun Tzu*, 64–65; translation slightly modified by author for style).

44. *Xunzi* 10.14b–15a (trans. Watson, *Hsun Tzu*, 70; translation slightly modified by author for style).

45. See *Xunzi* 10.15b.

46. *Xunzi* 10.22a.

47. Vitaly A. Rubin, *Individual and State in Ancient China: Essays on Four Chinese Philosophers*, trans. Steven I. Levine (New York: Columbia University Press, 1976), 37–45.

48. *Huainanzi* (21.7a) asserts this intellectual connection: "Mozi studied the doctrine of the Ruists and accepted Kongzi's methods."

49. The *Mozi* 墨子 is a work of uncertain date of composition, but it was probably compiled sometime before the Han dynasty. For background on the text of the *Mozi*, see A.C. Graham, "*Mo tzu* 墨子," in Loewe, *Early Chinese Texts*, 336–341. A complete English translation and analysis of the *Mozi* is available in Ian Johnston, trans., *Mozi: A Complete Translation* (Hong Kong: Chinese University Press, 2010).

50. *Mozi* (*Sibu congkan chubian* ed.) 13.10b–11b (trans. Yi-pao Mei, *The Ethical and Political Works of Motse* [London: Arthur Probsthain, 1929], 254–256; translation modified by author for accuracy and style).

51. *Mozi* 5.1a–2a (trans. Burton Watson, *Mo Tzu, Basic Writings* [New York and London: Columbia University Press, 1963], 50–51; translation slightly modified by author for style).

52. See *Mozi* 13.5a–b, 14a, 11.16b; *Lüshi chunqiu* 19.8b–9a, 1.12a–b; *Huainanzi* 20.10a.

53. *Mozi* 13.1a–b.

54. This socialist consciousness is evident in a passage in *Mozi* 5.14a–b, where Mozi gives some policy suggestions for averting aggression among states.

55. *Mozi* 5.11a (trans. Watson, *Mo Tzu*, 56).

56. As Feng Youlan (Fung Yu-lan) pointed out (*A Short History of Chinese Philosophy* [New York: Macmillan Company, 1948], 50–52), the knights-errant (*youxia* 游俠) of Zhanguo and early Han times can be compared to Mozi's disciples. Like Mozi's minions, knights-errant were men of martiality who professed obedience to a higher sense of righteousness. They gave their loyalties to local hegemons and/or small groups of like-minded knights-errant. Their decline after the success of the Han government to create an impersonal, universal state on the basis of Legalist-Ruist and Huang-Lao ideologies may indicate indirectly the chief reason for the failure of Mohism to endure as a viable political philosophy. There is further discussion of knights-errant in Chapter 5.

57. See *Xunzi* 12.22a; *Mengzi* 6B.4; *Zhuangzi* 10.18b–19a; *Hanfeizi* 19.8a.

58. See Feng, *History of Chinese Philosophy* [Princeton, NJ: Princeton University Press, 1952], 1: 133–143. Regarding Tuo Xiao 它囂 and Wei Mou 魏牟, also see *Xunzi* 3.12b: "There are those who give free rein to their passions, are satisfied with indulgence, and act like beasts. They are not qualified to develop

culture or conduct government. Nevertheless, their views have some foundation and their statements some reason, quite enough to deceive and confuse the ignorant masses. Such are Tuo Xiao and Wei Mou" (trans. Derk Bodde in Feng, *History*, 1: 140).

59. *Zhuangzi* 10.19a.

60. Jin Shoushen 金受申, *Jixia pai zhi yanjiu* 稷下派之研究 (Taibei: Commercial Press, 1971), 34–35.

61. *Xunzi* 12.18b.

62. Yin Wen 尹文, a philosopher of the late fourth and early third centuries BCE associated with the philosophers living at what became known as the "Jixia Academy" (*Jixia xuegong* 稷下學宮) in Linzi 臨淄, the capital of Qi, is generally linked with Songzi as being of like mind on philosophical matters. The evidence in favor of this close agreement is slim, however. Regarding the point made in the cited *Zhuangzi* passage, the received text of the *Yin Wen Zi* 尹文子, if judged to be largely genuine, agrees with Songzi's reputed belief in the value of correct names (*zheng ming* 正名) but does not mention delimiting desires or pacifism. A connection between Yin Wen and "not seeing insults as insults" is made in *Lüshi chunqiu* 16.19b–20a and *Gongsun Long Zi* 公孫龍子 (*Sibu beiyao* 四部備要 ed.) 2b, but the main point of these anecdotes is one of logic, not pacifism.

63. *Zhuangzi* 10.18a–19a (trans. Bodde in Feng, *History*, 1: 148).

64. *Xunzi* 12.22b (trans. Homer Dubs, *The Works of Hsuntze* [London: Arthur Probsthain, 1928], 209; translation modified by Derk Bodde). As clearly shown in the "Zheng lun" 正論 chapter of the *Xunzi*, Xunzi believed Songzi put too much emphasis on desire at the expense of virtue. Also see *Xunzi* 15.5a.

65. *Xunzi* 3.13b. For a discussion of direct connections between Songzi and Mozi, see Watanabe Hidekata 渡邊秀方, *Shina tetsugaku shi gairon* 支那哲學史概論 (Kyoto: Waseda daigaku shuppan bu, 1924), 217–218.

66. See *Mengzi* 6B.4.1–5.

67. Feng, *History*, 1: 150.

68. *Wuzi* A.2a (trans. Griffith, *Sun Tzu*, 152; translation slightly modified by author for style). Cf. the *Heguanzi* (A.15b–16b), which puts war second only to the welfare of man among the concerns of the sage and addresses war in moral terms.

69. *Wuzi* A.2b–3a. For comparable classifications of war, see *Jing*, 221 (nos. 126–127) and *Yi Zhoushu* 2.3a–4b.

70. *Sun Bin bingfa*, 107.

71. *Simafa* A.3b–4a.

72. *Liutao* 1.6a. Cf. *Zhanguoce* 3.57b–58a.

73. See Yinqueshan Han mu zhujian zhengli xiaozu 銀雀山漢墓竹簡整理小組, comp., *Yinqueshan Han mu zhujian Sunzi bingfa* 銀雀山漢墓竹簡孫子兵法 (Beijing: Wenwu chubanshe, 1976), 94–97. As a matter of historical fact, the states of Han 韓 and Wei 魏 were not conquered by the state of Zhao 趙 but by the state of Qin 秦 in 230 and 225 BCE, respectively.

74. *Sunzi bingfa* 10.14b–15a (trans. Griffith, *Sun Tzu*, 128). The Japanese scholar Kōno Osamu 河野收 ("Apudakushyon shuhō ni yoru *Sonshi* no shin kenkyū" アプダクツョン手法による孫子 の新研究, *Bōei daigakkō kiyō* 防衛大學校紀要 27 [1973]: 611–654) pointed out a certain altruism and compassion for the people and for soldiers in the *Sunzi bingfa*, along with the work's mixture of fatalism, positivism, materialism, monism, and affirmation of flux. For additional evidence of an *ethical* perspective in the military treatises, see *Weiliaozi* 2.36a and *Tai Gong bingfa yiwen*, 2a.

75. *Sun Bin bingfa*, 109.

Chapter 5

1. *Hanshu* 23.8b.

2. *Shiji* 97.7a–b (trans. Watson, *Records*, 1: 277–278; translation slightly modified by author).

3. *Shiji* 97.8b (trans. Watson, *Records*, 1: 279–280).

4. For a discussion of this Ruist idea of fiduciary community, see Tu Weiming, *Centrality and Commonality: An Essay on Chung-yung* (Honolulu: University of Hawai'i Press, 1976).

5. Yu Yingshi (Yu Ying-shih) 余英時, "Fan zhi lun yu Zhongguo zhengzhi chuantong" 反智論與中國政治傳統, *Ming bao yuekan* 明報月刊 12, no. 2 (February 1976), 2–8; 12, no. 3 (March 1976), 24–32 (esp. 28–32).

6. For Zhang Tang, see *Shiji* 122.5a–11a; *Hanshu* 59. For Dong Zhongshu, see *Chunqiu jueshi* 春秋決事 in *Yuhanshan fang ji yishu* 玉函山房輯佚書, compiled by Ma Guohan 馬國翰 (Taibei: Wenhai chubanshe, 1974), 2: 1180–1181, and Xu Fuguan 徐復觀, *Liang Han sixiang shi* 兩漢思想 (Hong Kong: Xianggang Zhongwen daxue, 1975), 2: 177–302.

7. For discussions of Ruism and law, see Étienne Balazs (*Le traité juridique des Souei-chou* [Leiden: E.J. Brill, 1954], 11–18) and Ch'u T'ung-tsu (*Law and Society in Traditional China* [Paris: Mouton, 1965], 267–279).

8. Zhou Shaoxian 周紹賢 ("Huang Lao sixiang zai Xi Han" 黃老思想在西漢, *Guoli Zhengzhi daxue xuebao* 國立政治大學學報 26 [December 1972]: 85–86) stated many years ago his belief that Tai Gong, when granted rule in Qi, governed by means of *daoshu* 道術, that is, the old learning of the region, which, according to Zhou, was the source of Huang-Lao, Yin-Yang, and *shenxian* 神仙 (later religious Daoism 道教) thought. He further asserted that Laozi was responsible for transmitting the previously undocumented concepts of the legendary Huangdi, and that the Huang school developed its own texts in the Zhanguo period, thereafter becoming a part of the Daoist school (*daojia* 道家). Zhou cited a man of Zhao, Yue Chengong 樂臣公, who migrated to Qi after the destruction

of the state of Zhao by Qin and there studied Huang-Lao thought, becoming its chief expositor. Yue Chengong's younger brother's son, He Gong 蓋公, inherited the tradition. References to the early development of Huang-Lao thought are also found in Tang Lan, "Mawangdui chutu *Laozi* yi ben qian yishu de yanjiu," 15–16.

9. See *Shiji* 54.6a (*Hanshu* 39.11a). Also see *Shiji* 54.7b (*Hanshu* 39.12a–b), where an example of Huang-Lao teaching by Cao Shen to Emperor Hui of Han 惠帝 (r. 195–188 BCE) is quoted.

10. *Shiji* 55.2a–3a; 56.10b.

11. Herrlee G. Creel, *Shen Pu-hai*, 246–261.

12. *Shiji* 121.6b–7b.

13. *Shiji* 49.6b. There was also during the reign of Emperor Jing of Han a Master Huang 黃子 (黃生), who was a teacher to Sima Qian's father, Sima Tan 司馬談 (*Shiji* 130.3a), and who engaged in debate with Ruist erudite Yuan Gu 轅固 (*Shiji* 121.6b–7a).

14. Zhou Shaoxian, "Huang Lao sixiang zai Xi Han," 85. This conclusion is strengthened by a passage from the *daojia* 道家 section of the bibliographic treatise in the *Suishu*: "From the time of Huangdi, sages and wise men, whenever they spoke of the Way, transmitted it to others; but for generations there was no master's doctrine [i.e., no master-disciple intellectual line]. In the Han period, for the first time, Cao Shen recommended He Gong as a capable expositor of Huang-Lao thought. Emperor Wen held it in reverence and it thence was transmitted, so that study of the Way [of Huang-Lao] flourished" (*Suishu* 34.5a–b).

15. One of the best known of these spokesmen was Ji An 汲黯 (d. 112 BCE), who is said to have served Emperor Wu vigorously and with integrity (see *Shiji* 120; *Hanshu* 50). He represents, however, something of an anomaly for the interpretation presented here of Han military thought, because of the seemingly ambivalent stances he took on public issues. Though an adherent of Huang-Lao thought, he is reported to have been an arrogant man, intimidating to his peers and impatient with people who disagreed with him. On the one hand, he was fond of knights-errant (*youxia*), but on the other hand, he argued in favor of the appeasement (*heqin* 和親) foreign policy adopted in Western Han to handle the Xiongnu and other nomadic peoples on Han's borders to the north. For other Han ministers influenced by Huang-Lao thought, see *Shiji* 120 (Zheng Dangshi 鄭當時), *Hou Hanshu* 60A (*liezhuan* 20A; Yang Hou 楊厚), *Hou Hanshu* 60A (Yang Hou 楊厚), *Hou Hanshu* 66 (Fan Sheng 范升), and *Hou Hanshu* 90A (Ma Rong 馬融).

16. See *Heguanzi* B.10b–15a.

17. *Heguanzi* B.15a.

18. *Heguanzi* A.20b.

19. See, e.g., Xu Peigen 徐培根 and Wei Rulin 魏汝霖, *Sun Bin bingfa zhushi* 孫臏兵法註釋 (Taibei: Liming wenhua shiye gongsi, 1976), 220.

20. *Hanshu* 30.65a.

21. *Shiji* 101; *Hanshu* 49.

22. *Hanshu* 49.9a–12a. For a comprehensive study of the rise of the Xiongnu on Han's northern frontier, as well as a discussion of the rise and fall of the Han appeasement (*heqin*) policy toward the Xiongnu, see Nicola Di Cosmo, *Ancient China and Its Enemies: The Rise of Nomadic Power in East Asian History* (Cambridge, UK: Cambridge University Press, 2004), esp. 161–252.

23. *Hanshu* 49.12a–16a.

24. *Xinshu* 新書 (*Sibu congkan chubian* ed.) 4.2a.

25. *Hanshu* 48.13a–b. Jia Yi also ascribed to the legendary Huangdi the notion that war must be initiated when circumstances demand it; otherwise, the opportunity for gain will be lost: "One must dry out things at midday; one must cut when knives are at hand" (*Hanshu* 48.11b; cf. *Liutao* 1.5b). The attribution to Huangdi may indicate some adaptation of Huang-Lao influence. Such an opinion is strengthened by the ideas Jia Yi forwarded for controlling potentially dangerous kings of Han states earlier in the same memorial (*Hanshu* 48.9a–11a).

26. See *Hanshu* 52.17a–19b.

27. Also see the memorials of Zhufu Yan 主父偃, Xu Yue 徐樂, and Yan An 嚴安 (*Shiji* 112), that of Xiahou Sheng 夏侯勝 (*Hanshu* 75.4a), and the statements of Ji Bu 季布 (*Shiji* 100.2b; *Hanshu* 37.2a).

28. Chang Ch'un-shu, "The Colonization of the Ho-hsi Region in the Former Han Period" (PhD dissertation, Harvard University, 1963), 27–28.

29. *Guanzi* 12.6b.

30. *Guanzi* 9.8a.

31. *Guanzi* 9.10b (trans. Rickett, *Kuan-tzu*, 1: 373).

32. *Xunzi* 10.13b–14a.

33. *Lüshi chunqiu* 7.10b–11a.

34. The Kuiqiu 葵丘 conference was an interstate meeting, held in 651 BCE in what is now Henan Province at the behest of Lord Huan of Qi, acting as hegemon (*ba*). The main topic of the meeting was the threat posed by the then rising power of Chu to the other states of the realm. See *Zuozhuan* (Xi 9), *Mengzi* 6B.7, and *Shuoyuan* 說苑 (*Sibu congkan chubian* ed.) 9.10a.

35. *Yantielun* (*Sibu congkan chubian* ed.) 8.10a-b. See the "Yao yi" 繇役 chapter for examples given by the Ruist erudites of virtue causing victory. Also, cf. a rebuttal by the worthies (*xianliang* 賢良) in *Yantielun* 7.3b–4a.

36. Cf. *Yantielun* 1.17a–b, 2.17a–b, 4.1b–2a.

37. See *Yantielun* 9.2a–b.

38. *Yantielun* 8.5a.

39. See *Yantielun* 9.5b–6a, 9.6b–7a, 9.8b, 2.1a.

40. *Yantielun* 9.3a–b.

41. *Shi*, "Yi" 抑 (trans. Legge, *Classics*, 4:511).

42. See *Chunqiu Guliang zhuan* (Xi 22); *Zuozhuan* (Xi 22).

43. *Yantielun* 8.10b–11a.

44. See *Hanfeizi* 19.2a. Also see *Huainanzi* 16.12b; *Shuoyuan* 15.1b–2a.

45. See *Zuozhuan* (Duke Ai 16.3); *Shiji* 33.20a.

46. *Yantielun* 8.12a. In the "Yao yi" chapter, Sang Hongyang, like Jia Yi, uses the butcher analogy, but in a *syncretist* way: "The butcher cuts [meat] according to its fibers so that it may be divided by slices of the hand. But when it comes to drawing out large sinews and penetrating bone, without using metal cleavers one cannot sever them. A sage-king accords with [the people's] nature to transform them, but when there are those who will not obey, then he will take up arms and punish them" (*Yantielun* 9.1a). For another discussion of the *Yantielun*, see Xu Fuguan, "*Yantielun* zhong de hehui wenhua wenti"《鹽鐵論》的社會文化問題, *Xinya xuebao* 新亞學報 11, no. 2 (1975): 337–419, esp. 368–380.

47. Another example of the importance of the concept of righteous war in the Western Han can be seen in a memorial by the official Wei Xiang 魏相 (d. 59 BCE) to Emperor Xuan 宣帝 (r. 74–49 BCE): "I have heard that when [a ruler] aids [a state] in disorder and executes the oppressive, [his army] is called righteous troops. He whose troops are righteous is a true king. When an enemy is invading us and we must raise an army, [this army] is called responding troops (*yingbing* 應兵). He whose troops are responding will overcome. When [a ruler] battles for a minor pretext and will not forbear his anger, [his army] is called enraged troops (*fenbing* 忿兵). He whose troops are enraged will be defeated. When [a ruler] gains another's territory and treasure, [his army] is called covetous troops (*tanbing* 貪兵). He whose troops are covetous will be destroyed. When [a ruler] relies on the great size of his state and boasts of the magnitude of his population in hopes of overawing his opponents, [his army] is called prideful troops (*jiaobing* 驕兵). He whose troops are prideful will be decimated. These five cases are not merely human situations, but [exemplify] the way of Heaven" (*Hanshu* 74.3a). Also see the memorial by Gan Yanshou 甘延壽 and Chen Tang 陳湯 justifying their attack in 36 BCE on the Xiongnu chieftain (*chanyu* 單于) Zhizhi 郅支 (*Hanshu* 70.10a).

48. Yu Ying-shih, *Trade and Expansion in Han China* (Berkeley and Los Angeles: University of California Press, 1967), 190.

49. Complementary to this intellectual change was an evolution in economic preparedness. In the course of Western Han, as exemplified by the shifts in the 135 and 81 BCE debates, one sees increasing use of economic as well as military means to avert foreign wars. Michael Loewe pointed out many years ago (*Records of Han Administration* [London: Cambridge University Press, 1967], 1: 52) that the Han military colonies in the northwest, Korea, and the southwest were essentially economic in nature, indicating a realization of the need for long-term and long-distance logistical planning—something that is absent in the military treatises. It would appear that the Han government, noting the demands of northern tribes for Chinese goods, was able to use commerce as a substitute for war, not only in its policy of appeasement, but also later for alleviating economic deficiencies and tensions in the tributary system.

50. *Shiji* 121.3a.

51. See Benjamin E. Wallacker, "Liu An, Second King of Huai-nan (180?–122 B.C.)," *Journal of the American Oriental Society* 92, no. 1 (1972): 36–51. Also see John S. Major, Sarah A. Queen, Andrew Seth Meyer, and Harold D. Roth, trans., eds., *The Huainanzi: A Guide to the Theory and Practice of Government in Early Han China* (New York: Columbia University Press, 2010), which contains a complete English translation of the work and analyses of each of its chapters.

52. *Huainanzi* 15.1a.

53. *Huainanzi* 15.1b.

54. *Huainanzi* 15.2b.

55. *Huainanzi* 15.3a.

56. *Huainanzi* 15.4a–b.

57. *Huainanzi* 15.4b.

58. *Huainanzi* 15.5a–b.

59. *Huainanzi* 15.15b.

60. *Huainanzi* 15.16b.

61. *Huainanzi* 15.16b.

62. An *ethical* emphasis in a basically *syncretist* argument can also be seen in other parts of the *Huainanzi*. The "Yao lüe" 要略 chapter, for example, makes the following statement: "Military strategy is the means for understanding the methods for battling to victory and of attacking and seizing [objectives], the circumstantial power provided by forms and key opportunities, and the rapid changes afforded by deception and wiliness. [The general] embodies the way of following and yielding, and grasps the doctrine of seizing the rear. In so doing, he knows that combat in ranks and fighting in separate units cannot be accomplished without virtue. If one genuinely understands the meaning [of these principles], then in advancing, retreating, or moving left and right, one will suffer no loss. Striking at points of danger and taking advantage of circumstantial power are considered [important] assets; purity and serenity are considered [important] regularities. By avoiding strong points and going for weak points, [overcoming] will be like driving a herd of sheep. This is how to speak of war." *Huainanzi* 21.3b. Also see Xu Fuguan, *Liang Han sixiang shi*, 2: 82, 152, for comments on the appearance of the *Huainanzi* before the Ruist rise to dominance at the Han court.

63. As earlier noted, the inclusion of the name Huangshigong in the title is an allusion to the legend of the meeting of Han general Zhang Liang with an old man at Xiapi, who gave Zhang the esoteric *Tai Gong bingfa* and later turned into a yellow stone at the foot of Mount Gucheng in Jibei. A translation of the *Shiji* version of this legend is given in Chapter 2. For a discussion of the dating of the *Sanlüe* 三略, see the comments of Huang Zhenhua 黃振華 in Li Ling, *Zhongguo bingshu ming zhu jin yi*, 184–187. Also see Xu Baolin 許保林, *Huangshigong Sanlüe qianshuo*黃石公三略淺說 (Beijing: Jiefangjun chubanshe, 1986).

64. *Sanlüe* (*Wujing qishu zhijie*, ed.), A.3b.

65. *Sanlüe*, B.33a–34a.

66. *Sanlüe*, C.44b–45a.

67. The authenticity of the received text of the *Wenzi* was long questioned by Chinese scholars, many of whom believed the work was a forgery written in post-Han times. The 1973 discovery in a Western Han tomb in Hebei Province of fragments of a *Wenzi* text closely resembling portions of the received text suggests, however, that a version of the *Wenzi* was circulating in the second century BCE. Thus, at least parts of the received text of *Wenzi* may now be considered a valid source of thought in Western Han times. The 1973 excavation occurred at the tomb of Liu Xiu 劉修, King Huai of Zhongshan (r. 69–54 BCE), in Bajiaolang 八角廊, Hebei Province. Comparing this excavated text with the already existing work by the same name, Chinese researchers have found that six sections of the excavated text also appear in the received text of the *Wenzi*, and that other passages in the excavated text do not appear in the known *Wenzi*. Moreover, close similarities exist between some passages in the excavated *Wenzi* bamboo strips and passages in the *Huainanzi*. See Jiang Guozhu 姜國柱, *Daojia yu bingjia* 道家與兵家 (Beijing: Xiyuan chubanshe, 1998), 38–51. More recently, Paul van Els has argued persuasively that the *Wenzi* fragments discovered in 1973 were composed probably in the latter part of Emperor Wen's reign (180–157 BCE), or at least before the death of Empress Dowager Dou in 135 BCE. He also points out connections between passages on warfare in the received text of the *Wenzi*—which he calculates was finalized sometime between 212 and 231 CE—and passages on warfare in the *Wenzi* fragments excavated in 1973. Paul van Els, "The *Wenzi*: Creation and Manipulation of a Chinese Philosophical Text" (PhD dissertation, Leiden University, 2006), 40–45, 86–95, 155–164.

68. *Wenzi* (*Qinding Siku quanshu* 欽定四庫全書 ed.) B.40a-b,

69. *Wenzi* B.53a–b.

70. See *Wenzi* A.49a–b; *Wuzi* A.2b–3a.

71. *Wenzi* B.61b.

72. See *Shangjun shu* 3.7b.

73. See Hsu Cho-yun, *Ancient China in Transition*, 72–77.

74. As evidence of this trend, Sima Qian recounted in the *Shiji* that Qin Shi Huangdi 秦始皇帝, in the thirty-third year of his reign (214 BCE), assembled an army of homeless men, displaced sons, and merchants (*wangren, zhuixu, guren* 亡人贅婿賈人) (*Shiji* 6.20b; 15.48a). Merchants were probably included pursuant to an existing policy to suppress the perceived extracting habits of tradespeople, but the rest were drafted undoubtedly from the marginal, unemployed elements of society who probably saw no other available vocation. These three groups also constituted three of the seven categories of disgraced persons (*qi ke zhe* 七科謫). On the latter, see Zhang Yan's 張晏 commentary in *Hanshu* 6.35a and *Shiji zhengyi* 123.16b. Also see Huang Jianshu, *Zhongguo junzhi shi*, 145–146.

75. See Lei Haizong, "Zhongguo de bing," 15.

76. See Lei Haizong, "Zhongguo de bing," 15.

77. For a discussion of the Western Han military system, see Sun Yutang 孫毓棠, "Xi Han de bing zhi" 西漢的兵制, *Zhongguo shehui jingji shi jikan* 中國社會經濟史集刊 5, no. 1 (March 1937): 1–74. For additional information as provided in excavated Han strip documents, see Lao Gan 勞榦, "Han dai bing zhi ji Han jian zhong de bing zhi" 漢代兵制及漢簡中的兵制, *Zhongyang yanjiuyuan lishi yuyan yanjiusuo jikan* 10 (1948): 23–55; Michael Loewe, *Records of Han Administration*, vol. 1.

78. See Lei Haizong, "Zhongguo de bing," 19–20, 22; Yu Ying-shih, *Trade and Expansion*, 96.

79. See *Hanshu* 1B.19b, 6.26a, 6.31a, 8.16b. Also see Lei Haizong, "Zhongguo de bing," 31; Sun Yutang, "Xi Han de bing zhi," 31–35. The makeup of Han wartime armies before Emperor Wu's time was not always the same. In the *Shiji* are reports, for example, that in Emperor Wen's time the army led by Li Guang 李廣 (d. 119 BCE) that penetrated the Xiao Pass and attacked a Xiongnu force consisted of "sons from good families" (*liangjia zi* 良家子) (*Shiji* 109.1a).

80. Cf. *Hanshu* 24B.12a, where the following passage occurs, dated ca. 120 BCE: "As laws became progressively strict [after Zhang Tang's revisions], a great number of officers (*li* 吏) were deprived [of their government standing] and dismissed from their posts; the armed forces were frequently sent into action; and the people for the most part bought exemption [from military and perhaps labor service, paying] as much as [the amounts required for purchase of] the ninth grade of honorary rank and/or the seventh grade of the order of military merit [both grades being exempt from military service]. Those who were recruited and mobilized for military service, officers [and privates (*shi* 士) alike], became the more rare" (trans. Nancy Lee Swann, *Food and Money in Ancient China* [Princeton, NJ: Princeton University Press, 1950], 272–273). Also see Yu Ying-shih, *Trade and Expansion*, 13–16.

81. See, for example, *Shiji* 92, *Hanshu* 34 (Han Xin); *Shiji* 56, *Hanshu* 40 (Chen Ping 陳平); *Shiji* 109, *Hanshu* 54 (Li Guang, Li Ling 李陵); *Shiji* 111 (Wei Qing 衛青, Huo Qubing 霍去病, Gongsun He 公孫賀, Zhang Cigong 張次公). Also see Michael Loewe, "The Campaigns of Han Wu-ti," in Kierman, *Chinese Ways in Warfare*, 67–122.

82. See a synopsis of battle losses in Homer Dubs, trans., *The History of the Former Han Dynasty* (Baltimore, MD: Waverly Press, 1938), 1: 13. Also see Chang Ch'un-shu, "Military Aspects of Han Wu-ti's Northern and Northwestern Campaigns," *Harvard Journal of Asiatic Studies* 26 (1966): 151–166. Lei Haizong noted many years ago that the Xiongnu threat lay not in its absolute insuperability, but in the relative incompetence of Han armies, the blame for which must be placed to some degree on inept generalship (see "Zhongguo de bing," 32). For a discussion of the lack of achievements among generals serving under Wei Qing and Huo Qubing, see *Shiji* 111.15b–19a.

83. *Shiji* 17.1b.

84. *Shiji* 57.9b; *Hanshu* 40.27b.

85. See Ch'u T'ung-tsu, *Han Social Structure*, ed. Jack L. Dull (Seattle and London: University of Washington Press, 1972), 168–174.

86. See Wang Yu-ch'uan, "An Outline of the Central Government of the Former Han Dynasty," *Harvard Journal of Asiatic Studies* 12 (1949): 166–173 (reprinted in *Studies of Governmental Institutions in Chinese History*, ed. John L. Bishop [Cambridge, MA: Harvard University Press, 1968], 34–41).

87. There were some exceptions. For example, the celebrated general Gan Yanshou was not of a consort family (see *Hanshu* 70). It also should be noted that many accounts of generals in this period do not specify how their original commissions were obtained.

88. As for the overall quality of training in military skills during this period, war games, known as *duyi* 都肄 and *dushi* 都試, are mentioned throughout the Han period. However, the variability in the occurrence of these games makes it difficult to tell whether these were regular events, designed to encourage military prowess. Neither is it easy to determine the content of the actual ceremonies or exercises and who participated in them. Annual archery competitions were apparently conducted at border stations in the north, but the nature and scope of these activities is difficult to gauge. It is therefore not possible with the data now available to say positively that military proficiency was consistently encouraged throughout the Western Han period. For a discussion of this issue, see Bodde, *Festivals in Classical China*, 349–359.

89. See *Hanshu* 30.65a, 99C.21b. For a useful article on efforts during Western Han to collect and categorize the military works then existing, see Tian Xudong, "Bingxue de jingdianhua yu xitonghua" 兵學的經典化與系統化, in *Gudai bingxue wenhua tan lun*, 158–165.

90. *Shiji* 124.1b (trans. Ch'u T'ung-tsu, *Han Social Structure*, 186).

91. James Crump theorized many years ago that the *Zhanguoce* is an anthology of debaters' rhetorical models (see *Intrigues: Studies of the Chan-kuo Ts'e* [Ann Arbor: University of Michigan Press, 1964]). If correct, this theory may explain why military strategy as found in the military treatises is not a common topic of discussion in the *Zhanguoce*. Those passages that do have relevance to military thought in the *Zhanguoce* emphasize verbal dexterity and appeasement rather than martial potency. The following excerpt may be representative: " 'We have wanted to be close to Wei 魏,' said the king [of Qin], 'but she is a country which changes frequently and I have not succeeded. May I ask how I can become close to her?' 'Use humble words and rich gifts to serve her,' replied Fan Ju 范雎. 'If that does not suffice, cede territories to tempt her. If that does not suffice, then raise troops and attack her' " (*Zhanguoce* 3.47b [trans. Crump, *Chan-Kuo Ts'e*, 106]). Also see Fan Ju's argument in *Shiji* 79.8a.

92. For a study of the emergence of knights-errant, including their ties to Ruism and Mohism, see Jian Zhao, "Historical Development of the *Xia* and its

Relationship with Other Social Groups in the Pre-Qin Period," *Journal of Asian History* 35 (2001): 59–91.

93. See *Shiji* 86.

94. *Hanfeizi* 19.3b–4a (trans. Watson, *Han Fei Tzu*, 105).

95. *Hanshu* 92.2a. For an essay on the evolution of the serviceman (*shi*) class from a group in Chunqiu times that had both civil and martial duties toward a bifurcation in Western Han between civil officials of Ruist affiliation and military elements such as knights-errant, see an article by the Chinese scholar Gu Jiegang 顧頡剛 (1893–1980), "Wushi yu wenshi zhi shuihua 武士與文士 之蛻化," in *Shi lin za shi chu bian* 史林雜識初編 (Beijing Zhonghua shuju, 1963), 85–91.

96. See Ch'u T'ung-tsu, *Han Social Structure*, 194. For another useful article on knights-errant during the Han, see Masubuchi Tatsuo, "The *Yu-hsia* and the Social Order in the Han Period," *Annals of the Hitotsubashi Academy* 3, no. 1 (1952): 84–101.

97. In the case of the harsh official (*kuli* 酷吏) Ning Cheng 寧成, the Ning family gained so much local power in Nanyang 南陽 after Ning Cheng's death that another harsh official, Yi Zong 義縱, had to be dispatched to neutralize the Nings (see *Shiji* 122.11b; *Hanshu* 90.6a–b).

98. Emperor Wu of Han was especially noted for his cruel treatment of powerful families and his frequent use of harsh officials (*kuli*). Among the thirteen harsh officials mentioned in *Hanshu* 90, nine lived during the reign of Emperor Wu. This statistic may, of course, be related to Ban Gu's critical attitude toward Emperor Wu. By comparison, Emperor Xuan was considered more moderate, governing with moral influence as much as with compulsion, but he, too, ordered harsh officials to rid troublesome districts of overbearing clans.

Epilogue

1. This compilation includes the *Sunzi bingfa*, the *Liutao*, the *Simafa*, the *Wuzi*, the *Weiliaozi*, the *Sanlüe*, and one post-Han work, the *Tang Taizong Li Weigong wendui* 唐太宗李衞公問對.

2. *Baihu tongyi* 白虎通義 (*Sibu congkan chubian* ed.) 4.1a–4a, 4.4b–8a.

3. *Qianfu lun* 潛夫論 (*Sibu congkan chubian* ed.) 5.7a–10a, 5.12b–13a, 5.14a–15a, 5.16b–19a.

4. See *Qunshu zhiyao* 群書治要 (*Congshu jicheng* ed.) 45.785.

5. See *Hou Hanshu* 49.17a–b.

6. See *Beitang shuchao* (Tianjin guji chubanshe ed.) 113.4a, 113.6b; 116.2a; 117.4a, 117.5a, 117.8a; *Taiping yulan* 太平御覽 (*Sibu congkan chubian* ed.) 271.6a–b; 273.3b.

7. For the *Bingyao* 兵要 and the *Junling* 軍令, see *Beitang shuchao* 113.8a; *Taiping yulan* 301.6a, 331.1a–3a, 337.6a, 339.2b, 340.5a, 341.4b, 526.6b; *Tongdian*

157.831a. For English translations of Zhuge Liang's attributed writings, see Ralph D. Sawyer, *Zhuge Liang: Strategy, Achievements, and Writings* (North Charleston, SC: CreateSpace Independent Publishing Program, 2014).

8. Brief mention should be made of commentary on military matters in the *Chunqiu fanlu* 春秋繁露, a work that has been traditionally ascribed to Western Han scholar-official Dong Zhongshu but whose authorship has been questioned ever since the Song dynasty. There is no consensus about the dating of the work as a whole or of individual chapters; a few commentators have asserted that Dong Zhongshu's ideas are represented faithfully in some chapters, while others point out anomalies suggesting that portions of the received text were inserted in post-Western Han times. A thorough discussion of the work's textual history can be found in Michael Loewe, *Dong Zhongshu, a 'Confucian' Heritage and the Chunqiu fanlu* (Leiden: Brill, 2011). For purposes of this study, the *Chunqiu fanlu* is worth citing as it contains ideas on military matters that resemble those circulating in Western Han, even though all or portions of the received text of the *Chunqiu fanlu* may have been compiled in the period after Western Han. In general, the received text supports the *compartmentalist* and *ethical* views that we saw ascending in the latter part of the Western Han period. This is evident in the "Fu zhi xiang" 服制像 chapter, which clearly places civility above martiality as the guiding principle for a secure state: "When martiality becomes [necessary] and yet is not used, this is how the sage exceeds others. Although he may wish to follow [a martial course], it is the last [alternative] he will choose. For being able to resist an enemy only after putting on armor is indeed not what is prized by a sage. . . . Thus, civility and virtue are to be prized, while awesomeness and martiality are of lesser importance. This is how the world is everlastingly unified" ([*Sibu congkan chubian* ed.], 6.1b). In the "Wuxing ni shun" 五行逆順 chapter we also see an emphasis on righteous war that was a recurrent theme in the Western Han period: "One does not overcome others in war carelessly; neither does one take territory without care. Only after it is a righteous duty does one act. . . . Thus, in mobilizing troops and raising armies one must accord with righteousness and ordering principle" (13.10a).

9. This phenomenon is also explored by Roger T. Ames in his study of the "Zhu shu" 主術 chapter of the *Huainanzi* (*The Art of Rulership: A Study in Ancient Chinese Political Thought* [Honolulu: University of Hawai'i, Press, 1983]).

10. For the question of how Chinese regimes have adapted early military thought to deal with geo-political threats in the imperial era, see, for example, Alastair Iain Johnston, *Cultural Realism: Strategic Culture and Grand Strategy in Chinese History* (Princeton, NJ: Princeton University Press, 1995).

Bibliography

Following is a listing of works cited in this study, as well as other publications that may help the reader better understand the evolution of military thought in China from earliest times into the post-Han era.

Allan, Sarah. "The Identities of Taigong Wang in Zhou and Han Literature." *Monumenta Serica* 32 (1972–1973): 57–99.

Ames, Roger T. *The Art of Rulership: A Study in Ancient Chinese Political Thought.* Honolulu: University of Hawai'i, Press, 1983.

———, trans. *Sun-tzu: The Art of Warfare.* New York: Ballantine Press, 1993.

Baihu tongyi 白虎通義 (*Baihu tong de lun* 白虎通德論). In *Sibu congkan chubian* 四部叢刊初編. Shanghai: Shangwu yinshuguan, 1919–1922.

Balazs, Étienne. *Le traité juridique des Souei-chou.* Leiden: E.J. Brill, 1954.

Balmforth, Edmund Elliott. "A Chinese Military Strategist of the Warring States: Sun Pin." PhD dissertation, Rutgers University, 1979.

Ban Gu 班固, and Ban Zhao 班昭. *Hanshu* 漢書 (*Hanshu bu zhu* 漢書補注). Taibei: Yiwen yinshuguan, 1955.

Blakeley, Barry B. "'On the Authenticity and Nature of the *Zuozhuan*' Revisited." *Early China* 29 (2004): 217–267.

Bodde, Derk. "Harmony and Conflict in Chinese Philosophy." In *Studies in Chinese Thought*, edited by Arthur Wright, 19–80. Chicago and London: University of Chicago Press, 1953.

———. *Festivals in Classical China.* Princeton, NJ: Princeton University Press, 1975.

———. "The Chinese Cosmic Magic Known as Watching for the Ethers." Reprinted in *Essays on Chinese Civilization*, 351–372. Princeton, NJ: Princeton University Press, 1981.

Boodberg, Peter A. "The Art of War in Ancient China." PhD dissertation, University of California at Berkeley, 1930.

Brooks, A. Taeko. "Heaven, *Li*, and the Formation of the *Zuozhuan* 左傳." *Oriens Extremus* 44 (2003–2004): 51–100.

Caldwell, Ernest. "Promoting Action in Warring States Political Philosophy: A First Look at the Chu Manuscript *Cao Mie's Battle Arrays*." *Early China* 37 (2014): 259–289.

Chang Ch'un-shu. "The Colonization of the Ho-hsi Region in the Former Han Period." PhD dissertation, Harvard University, 1963.

———. "Military Aspects of Han Wu-ti's Northern and Northwestern Campaigns." *Harvard Journal of Asiatic Studies* 26 (1966): 151–166.

Chen Puqing 陳蒲清, *Guiguzi xiang jie* 鬼谷子詳解. Changsha: Yuelu shushe, 2005.

Cheng Wu 程武. "Han chu Huang Lao sixiang he fajia luxian—Han Changsha Mawangdui san hao Han mu chutu boshu zhaji" 漢初黃老思想和法家路綫—漢長沙馬王堆三號漢墓出土帛書 扎記. *Wenwu* 文物 1974 (10): 43–47, 64.

Chen Yinglüe 陳英略. *Guiguzi shenji bingfa* 鬼谷子神機兵法. Hong Kong: Xinli shuju, [1974?].

Chunqiu fanlu 春秋繁露. In *Sibu congkan chubian* 四部叢刊初編. Shanghai: Shangwu yinshuguan, 1919–1922.

Chunqiu Gongyang zhuan 春秋公羊傳 (*Chunqiu Gongyang jing zhuan jie gu* 春秋公羊經傳解詁). In *Sibu congkan chubian* 四部叢刊初編. Shanghai: Shangwu yinshuguan, 1919–1922.

Chunqiu Guliang zhuan 春秋穀梁傳. In *Sibu congkan chubian* 四部叢刊初編. Shanghai: Shangwu yinshuguan, 1919–1922.

Chunqiu Zuozhuan 春秋左傳. In *Sibu congkan chubian* 四部叢刊初編. Shanghai: Shangwu yinshuguan, 1919–1922.

Ch'u T'ung-tsu. *Law and Society in Traditional China*. Paris: Mouton, 1965.

———. *Han Social Structure*, ed. Jack L. Dull. Seattle and London: University of Washington Press, 1972.

Creel, Herrlee G. "The *Fa-chia*: 'Legalists' or 'Administrators'?" in *Studies Presented to Tung Tso Pin on his Sixty-fifth Birthday, Zhongyang yanjiuyuan lishi yuyan yanjiusuo jikan* 中央研究院歷史語言研究所集刊, Extra Volume No. 4 (Taibei, 1961), 607–636.

———. *The Origins of Statecraft in China, Volume One: The Western Chou Empire*. Chicago and London: University of Chicago Press, 1970.

Crump, James. *Intrigues: Studies of the Chan-kuo Ts'e*. Ann Arbor: University of Michigan Press, 1964.

———, trans. *Chan Kuo Ts'e*. London: Oxford University Press, 1970.

Csikszentmihalyi, Mark, and Michael Nylan. "Constructing Lineages and Inventing Traditions through Exemplary Figures in Early China." *T'oung Pao* 89 (2003): 59–99.

Cui Shi 崔寔. *Zheng lun* 政論. In *Sibu congkan chubian* 四部叢刊初編 (*Qunshu zhiyao* 群書治要, *juan* 45). Shanghai: Shangwu yinshuguan, 1919–1922.

Daodejing 道德經 (*Laozi Daodejing* 老子道德經). In *Sibu congkan chubian* 四部叢刊初編. Shanghai: Shangwu yinshuguan, 1919–1922.

Defoort, Carine Defoort. *The Pheasant Cap Master (He guan zi): A Rhetorical Reading*. Albany: State University of New York Press, 1997.

Dengxizi 鄧析子. In *Sibu congkan chubian* 四部叢刊初編. Shanghai: Shangwu yinshuguan, 1919–1922.

Di Cosmo, Nicola. *Ancient China and Its Enemies: The Rise of Nomadic Power in East Asian History*. (Cambridge, UK: Cambridge University Press, 2004.

———, ed. *Military Culture in Imperial China*. Cambridge, MA: Harvard University Press, 2009.

Dingxian Han mu zhujian zhengli zu 定縣漢墓竹簡整理組, "Dingxian 40 hao Han mu chutu zhujian jian jie" 定縣40號漢墓出土竹簡簡介. *Wenwu* 1981 (8): 12.

Dong Dingming 董鼎銘. *Zhongguo bingyi shilüe* 中國兵役史略. Taibei, 1962.

Dongfang Shuo 東方朔. *Shenyijing* 神異經. In *Han Wei congshu* 漢魏叢書. Shanghai: Shangwu yinshuguan, 1925.

Dubs, Homer, trans. *The Works of Hsuntze*. London: Arthur Probsthain, 1928.

———, trans. *The History of the Former Han Dynasty*. 2 vols. Baltimore, MD: Waverly Press, 1938.

Du Weizhi 杜畏之. "Zhanquo shiqi junshi zhi yanjiu" 戰國時期軍事之研究. *Zhongshan wenhua jiaoyu guan jikan* 中山文化教育館季刊 3, no. 1 [1936]: 145–166.

Du You 杜佑. *Tongdian* 通典. In *Shi Tong* 十通. Taibei: Xinxing shuju, 1963.

Duyvendak, J.J.L, trans. *The Book of Lord Shang: A Classic of the Chinese School of Law*. Chicago: University of Chicago Press, 1963.

Erya 爾雅. In *Sibu congkan chubian* 四部叢刊初編. Shanghai: Shangwu yinshuguan, 1919–1922.

Fairbank, John K. "Introduction: Varieties of the Chinese Military Experience." In Kierman, *Chinese Ways in Warfare*, 1–26

Fan Ye 范曄. *Hou Hanshu* 後漢書 (*Hou Hanshu ji jie* 後漢書集解). Taibei: Yiwen yinshu guan, 1955.

Feng Youlan (Fung Yu-lan). *A Short History of Chinese Philosophy*. New York: Macmillan Company, 1948.

———. *History of Chinese Philosophy*. Translated by Derk Bodde. 2 vols. Princeton, NJ: Princeton University Press, 1952.

Franke, Herbert. *Zum Militärstrafrecht im chinesischen Mittelalter*. München: Verlag der Bayerischen Akademie der Wissenschaften, 1970.

Frantzell, Lennart. *Dr. Her's Comprehensive Essays on the Art of War, the Her Bor-shyh Bey Luenn*. Stockholm: Stockholms Universitet Institutionen för orientaliska språk, 1973), 166–170.

Fu Shaojie 傅紹傑. *Wuzi jin zhu jin yi* 吳子今註今譯. Taipei: Commercial Press, 1976.

Galvany, Albert. "Violencia y Persuasión: Los Fundamentos Estratégicos de la Sofistica en la China Antigua." *Estudios de Asia y África* 38, no. 2 (May–August 2003): 291–320.

———. "La Dialéctica entre lo Civil y lo Militar en la China Antigua." *Estudios de Asia y África* 42, no. 3 (2007): 541–594.

———."Sly Mouths and Silver Tongues: The Dynamics of Psychological Persuasion in Ancient China," *Extrême-Orient Extrême-Occident* 34 (2012): 15–40.

Gao Heng 高亨, and Dong Zhian 董治安. "*Shi da jing* chu lun"《十大經》初論, *Lishi yanjiu* 歷史 研究 1975 (1): 89–97.

Giles, Lionel, trans. *Sun Tzu on the Art of War*. London: Luzac and Company, 1910.

Gongsun Long zi 公孫龍子. In *Sibu beiyao* 四部備要. Shanghai: Zhonghua shuju, 1937.

Griffith, Samuel B., trans. *Sun Tzu: The Art of War*. London: Oxford University Press, 1963.

Guan Feng 關鋒. "*Sunzi* junshi zhexue sixiang yanjiu"《孫子》軍事哲學思想研究. *Zhexue yanjiu* 哲學研究 1957 (2): 70–90.

Guanzi 管子. In *Sibu congkan chubian* 四部叢刊初編. Shanghai: Shangwu yinshuguan, 1919–1922.

Guiguzi 鬼谷子. In *Sibu congkan chubian* 四部叢刊初編. Shanghai: Shangwu yinshuguan, 1919–1922.

Gu Jiegang 顧頡剛, "Wushi yu wenshi zhi shuihua" 武士與文士之蛻化. In *Shi lin za shi chu bian* 史林雜識初編, 85–91. Beijing Zhonghua shuju, 1963.

Guojia wenwu gu wenxian yanjiushi Datong Shansunjiazhai Han jian zhengli xiaozu 國家文物古文獻研究室大通上孫家漢簡整理小組, "Datong xian Shangsunjiazhai Han jian shiwen" 大通縣 上孫家寨漢簡釋文. *Wenwu* 文物 1981 (2): 22–26.

Guo Moruo 郭沫若. "Shu Wu Qi" 述吳起. In *Xian Qin xueshuo shu lin* 先秦學說述林, 217–218. Yong'an: Dongnan chubanshe, 1945.

———. *Guanzi jijiao* 管子集校. Beijing: Kexue chubanshe, 1956.

Guoyu 國語. In *Sibu congkan chubian* 四部叢刊初編. Shanghai: Shangwu yinshuguan, 1919–1922.

Gu Tiefu 顧鐵符. Mawangdui boshu *Tianwen qi xiang za zhan* neirong jian shu" 馬王堆帛書《天文氣象雜占》內容簡述. *Wenwu* 1978 (2): 1–4.

Han Fei. *Hanfeizi* 韓非子. In *Sibu congkan chubian* 四部叢刊初編. Shanghai: Shangwu yinshuguan, 1919–1922.

Han Ying 韓嬰, comp. *Han Shi waizhuan* 韓詩外傳. In *Congshu jicheng* 叢書集成. Shanghai: Shangwu yinshuguan, 1935–1937.

Harper, Donald J., trans. "A Summary of the Contents of the Ma-wang-tui Silk-scroll Book 'Assorted Astronomical and Meteorological Prognostications.'" *Chinese Studies in Archaeology* 1, no. 1 (1979): 56–74.

Heguanzi 鶡冠子. In *Sibu congkan chubian* 四部叢刊初編. Shanghai: Shangwu yinshuguan, 1919–1922.

Henricks, Robert G, trans. *Lao-Tzu Te-Tao Ching: A New Translation Based on the Recently Discovered Ma-wang-tui Texts*. New York: Ballantine Books, 1989.

Hightower, James R. *Han Shih Wai Chuan: Han Ying's Illustrations of the Didactic Application of the Classic of Songs*. Cambridge, MA: Harvard University Press, 1952.

Hsu Cho-yun. *Ancient China in Transition: An Analysis of Social Mobility, 722–22 B.C.* Stanford, CA: Stanford University Press, 1965.

Huainanzi 淮南子 (*Huainan hong lie jie* 淮南鴻烈解). In *Sibu congkan chubian* 四部叢刊初編. Shanghai: Shangwu yinshuguan, 1919–1922.

Huangdi sijing 黃帝四經. In *Boshu Laozi* 帛書老子. Taibei: He-Luo tushu chubanshe, 1975.

Huang Haoran 黃浩然. *Zhongguo gudai bingxue sixiang* 中國古代兵學思想. Huangpu chubanshe, 1959.

Huang Jianshu 黃堅叔. *Zhongguo junzhi shi* 中國軍制史. Changsha: Commercial Press, 1941.

Huang, Ray. Review of *Chinese Ways in Warfare*, edited by Frank A. Kierman Jr. and John K. Fairbank. *Journal of Asian Studies* 35, no. 2 (1976): 309–313.

Huang Yi-long, and Chang Chih-ch'eng. "The Evolution and Decline of the Ancient Practice of Watching for the Ethers." *Chinese Science* 13 (1996): 82–106.

Hulsewé, A.F.P. *Remnants of Han Law*. Leiden: E.J. Brill, 1955.

———. "Watching the Vapors: An Ancient Chinese Technique of Prognostication." *Nachrichten der Gesellschaft für Natur- und Völkerkunde Ostasiens/Hamburg* 125 (1979): 40–49.

Jiang Guozhu 姜國柱. *Daojia yu bingjia* 道家與兵家. Beijing: Xiyuan chubanshe, 1998.

———. *Zhongguo junshi sixiang tongshi* 中國軍事思想通史. 5 vols. Beijing: Zhongguo shehui kexue chubanshe, 2006.

Jin Shoushen 金受申. *Jixia pai zhi yanjiu* 稷下派之研究. Taibei: Commercial Press, 1971.

Johnston, Alastair Iain. *Cultural Realism: Strategic Culture and Grand Strategy in Chinese History*. Princeton, NJ: Princeton University Press, 1995.

Johnston, Ian, trans. *Mozi: A Complete Translation*. Hong Kong: Chinese University Press, 2010.

Jullien, François. *The Propensity of Things: Toward a History of Efficacy in China*. Translated by Janet Lloyd. New York: Zone Books, 1995.

Kalinowski, Marc. "The *Xingde* 刑德 Texts of Mawangdui." Translated by Phyllis Brooks. *Early China* 23–24 (1998–1999): 125–202.

Kang Li 康立, and Wei Jin 衛今. "Fajia luxian he Huang Lao sixiang—Han boshu *Jingfa*" 法家路綫 和黃老思想—漢帛書《經法》. *Wenwu* 文物 1975 (7): 1–7.

Keightley, David N. *Sources of Shang History: The Oracle-Bone Inscriptions of Bronze Age China*. Berkeley and Los Angeles: University of California Press, 1978.

Ke Shaomin 柯劭忞, comp. *Xin Yuan shi* 新元史. Taibei: Yiwen yinshu guan, 1955.

Kierman, Frank A. Jr., and John K. Fairbank, eds. *Chinese Ways in Warfare.* Cambridge MA: Harvard University Press, 1974

Kierman, Frank A. Jr. "Phases and Modes of Combat in Early China." In Kierman, *Chinese Ways in Warfare*, 27–66.

Kōno Osamu 河野收. "Apudakushyon shuhō ni yoru *Sonshi* no shin kenkyū" アプダクツョン手法による孫子の新研究. *Bōei daigakkō kiyō* 防衛大學校紀要 27 (1973): 611–654.

Lao Gan 勞榦. "Han dai bing zhi ji Han jian zhong de bing zhi" 漢代兵制及漢簡中的兵制, *Zhongyang yanjiuyuan lishi yuyan yanjiusuo jikan* 央研究院歷史語言研究所集刊 10 (1948): 23–55.

Lau, D.C., trans. *Lao Tzu, Tao Te Ching.* London: Penguin Books, 1963.

———. "Some Notes on the Sun Tzu." *Bulletin of the School of Oriental and African Studies* 28, no. 2 (1965): 319–335.

Lau, D.C., and Roger T. Ames, trans. *Sun Pin: The Art of Warfare.* New York: Ballantine Press, 1996.

Legge, James. *The Chinese Classics.* Taibei: Jinxue shuju, 1958; reprint of the last editions of Oxford University Press.

———. *The Text of Yi King.* Shanghai: China Modern Education Company, 1935.

Lei Haizong 雷海宗. "Zhongguo de bing" 中國的兵. *Shehui kexue* 社會科學 1, no. 1 (October 1935): 1–47.

Lewis, Mark Edward. *Sanctioned Violence in Early China.* Albany: State University of New York Press, 1990.

———. *The Early Chinese Empires: Qin and Han.* Cambridge, MA: Harvard University Press, 2007.

Liang Jiabin 梁嘉彬. "*Guiguzi* kao"《鬼谷子》考. *Dalu zazhi* 大陸雜誌 10, no. 4 (February 28, 1955): 12–15.

Li Fang 李昉, ed. *Taiping yulan* 太平御覽. In *Sibu congkan sanbian* 四部叢刊三編. Shanghai: Shangwu yinshuguan, 1936.

Li Feng. *Early China: A Social and Cultural History.* Cambridge, UK: Cambridge University Press, 2013.

Li Hansan 李漢三. *Xian Qin liang Han zhi yinyang wuxing xueshuo* 先秦兩漢之陰陽五行學說. Taibei: Zhongding wenhua chuban gongsi, 1967.

Liji 禮記 (*Zuan tu hu zhu Liji* 纂圖互註禮記). In *Sibu congkan chubian* 四部叢刊初編. Shanghai: Shangwu yinshuguan, 1919–1922.

Li Ling 李零, "Qinghai Datong xian Shangsunjiazhai Han jian xingzhi xiao yi" 青海大通縣 上孫家寨漢簡性質小議. *Kaogu* 考古 1983 (6): 549–553.

——— et al., comps. *Zhongguo bingshu ming zhu jin yi* 中國兵書名著今譯. Beijing: Junshi yiwen chubanshe, 1992.

———. "Shuoming" 說明, *Cao Mo zhi zhen* 曹沫之陳. In *Shanghai bowuguan cang Zhanguo Chu zhu shu* 上海博物館藏戰國楚竹書, edited by Ma Chengyuan 馬承源, 4: 239–242. Shanghai: Shanghai guji chubanshe 2001–.

Liu Shenning 劉申寧. *Zhongguo bingshu zongmu* 中國兵書總目. Beijing: Guofang daxue chubanshe, 1990.

Liutao 六韜. In *Sibu congkan chubian* 四部叢刊初編. Shanghai: Shangwu yinshuguan, 1919–1922.

Liu Xiang 劉向, comp. *Zhanguoce* 戰國策. In *Sibu congkan chubian* 四部叢刊初編. Shanghai: Shangwu yinshuguan, 1919–1922.

———, comp. *Shuoyuan* 說苑. In *Sibu congkan chubian* 四部叢刊初編. Shanghai: Shangwu yinshuguan, 1919–1922.

Liu Yuanyan 劉元彥. "*Lüshi chunqiu* lun yibing"《呂氏春秋》論義兵. *Zhexue yanjiu* 哲學研究 1963 (3): 70–76.

Liu Zhongping 劉仲平. *Weiliaozi jin zhu jin yi* 尉繚子今註今譯. Taipei: Commercial Press, 1975.

Loewe, Michael. *Records of Han Administration*. London: Cambridge University Press, 1967.

———. "The Campaigns of Han Wu-ti," in Kierman, *Chinese Ways in Warfare*, 67–122.

———, ed. *Early Chinese Texts: A Bibliographical* Guide. Berkeley, CA: Society for the Study of Early China, 1993.

———. *Divination, Mythology, and Monarchy in Han China*. Cambridge, UK: Cambridge University Press, 1994.

———. "The Western Han Army: Organization, Leadership, and Operation." In Di Cosmo, *Military Culture in Imperial China*, 65–89.

———. *Dong Zhongshu, a 'Confucian' Heritage and the Chunqiu fanlu*. Leiden: Brill, 2011.

Loewe, Michael, and Edward L. Shaughnessy, eds. *The Cambridge History of Ancient China, From the Origins of Civilization to 221 B.C.* Cambridge, UK: Cambridge University Press, 1999.

Lu Dajie 陸達節. *Lidai bingshu mulu* 歷代兵書目錄. Taibei: Guting shuwu, 1970.

Lunyu 論語.(*Lunyu ji jie* 論語集解). In *Sibu congkan chubian* 四部叢刊初編. Shanghai: Shangwu yinshuguan, 1919–1922.

Luo Genze 羅根澤. *Guanzi tan yuan* 管子探源. Shanghai: Zhonghua shuju, 1931.

Lüshi chunqiu 呂氏春秋. In *Sibu congkan chubian* 四部叢刊初編. Shanghai: Shangwu yinshuguan, 1919–1922.

Lu Xiuhu 陸修祜. "Qun jing jun xue shi" 羣經軍學事. *Guo zhuan yuekan* 5, no. 5 (June 1937).

Ma Guohan 馬國翰, comp. *Yuhanshan fang ji yishu* 玉函山房輯佚書. Taibei: Wenhai chubanshe, 1974.

Mair, Victor H., trans. *The Art of War: Sun Zi's Military Methods* (New York: Columbia University Press, 2007).

Major, John S., Sarah A. Queen, Andrew Seth Meyer, and Harold D. Roth, trans., eds. *The Huainanzi: A Guide to the Theory and Practice of Government in Early Han China*. New York: Columbia University Press, 2010.

Masubuchi Tatsuo. "The *Yu-hsia* and the Social Order in the Han period." *Annals of the Hitotsubashi Academy* 3, no. 1 (1952): 84–101.

Mattos, Gilbert Louis. *The Stone Drums of Ch'in*. PhD dissertation, University of Washington, 1973.

McNeal, Robin. "The Body as Metaphor for the Civil and Martial Components of Empire in *Yi Zhou Shu*, Chapter 32; with an Excursion on the Composition and Structure of the *Yi Zhou Shu*." *Journal of the American Oriental Society* 122, no. 1 (January–March 2002): 46–60.

———. *Conquer and Govern: Early Chinese Military Texts from the Yi Zhou shu*. Honolulu: University of Hawai'i Press, 2012.

Mengzi 孟子. In *Sibu congkan chubian* 四部叢刊初編. Shanghai: Shangwu yinshuguan, 1919–1922.

Milburn, Olivia. "*Gai lu*: A Translation and Commentary on a Yin-yang Military Text Excavated from Tomb M247, Zhangjiashan." *Early China* 33–34 (2010–2011): 101–140.

Mozi 墨子. In *Sibu congkan chubian* 四部叢刊初編. Shanghai: Shangwu yinshuguan, 1919–1922.

Needham, Joseph. *Science and Civilisation in China*. Vol. 2, *History of Scientific Thought*. Cambridge, UK: Cambridge University Press, 1956.

Needham, Joseph, and Robin D.S. Yates. *Science and Civilisation in China*. Vol. 5, part 6, *Military Technology: Missiles and Sieges*. Cambridge, UK: Cambridge University Press, 1994.

Niu Xianzhong 鈕先鐘. *Zhongguo zhanlüe sixiang shi* 中國戰略思想史. Taibei: Liming wenhua shiye youxian gongsi, 1992.

Ouyang Xiu 歐陽修. *Xin Tangshu* 新唐書. Taibei: Yiwen yinshuguan, 1955.

Ouyang Xun 歐陽詢 et al., comps. *Yiwen leiju* 藝文類聚. In *Qinding Siku quanshu* 欽定四庫全書. Taibei: Shijie shuju, 1985–1988.

Peerenboom, R.P. *Law and Morality in Ancient China: The Silk Manuscripts of Huang-Lao*. Albany: State University of New York Press, 1993.

Petersen, Jens Østergård. "What's in a Name? On the Sources concerning Sun Wu." *Asia Major*, 3rd ser. 5, no. 1 (1992): 1–31.

———. "Which Books Did the First Emperor of Ch'in Burn? On the Meaning of Pai Chia in Early Chinese Sources." *Monumenta Serica* 43 (1995):1–52.

Pines, Yuri. *Foundations of Confucian Thought: Intellectual Life in the Chunqiu Period (722–453 B.C.E.)*. Honolulu: University of Hawai'i Press, 2002.

Průšek, Jaroslav. "Quelques Remarques sur l'Art de la Guerre de Sun-tsï." *Archiv Orientální* 19 (1951): 407–427. Reprinted in *Chinese History and Literature*, 49–67. Dordrecht: D. Reidel Publishing Company, 1970.

Qian Dian 錢坫. *Shuowen jiezi jiaoquan* 說文解字斠詮 in *Shuowen jiezi gulin* 說文解字詁林, ed. Ding Fubao 丁福保. Taibei: Commercial Press, 1970.

Qinghai sheng wenwu kaogu gongzuo dui 青海省文物考古工作隊, "Qinghai Datong xian Shangsunjiazhai yi yi wu hao Han mu" 青海大通縣上孫家寨一一五號漢墓. *Wenwu* 文物 1981 (2): 16–21.

Rand, Christopher C. "Chinese Military Thought and Philosophical Taoism." *Monumenta Serica* 34 (1979–1980): 171–218.

———. "Li Ch'üan and Chinese Military Thought." *Harvard Journal of Asiatic Studies* 39, no. 1 (June 1979): 107–137.

Rao Zongyi 饒宗頤, "Jing Chu wenhua" 荊楚文化. *Zhongyang yanjiuyuan lishi yuyan yanjiusuo jikan* 41, no. 2 (1969): 273–315.

Raphals, Lisa. "Divination in the *Han shu* Bibliographic Treatise." *Early China* 32 (2008–2009): 45–101.

Rickett, W. Allyn, trans. *Kuan-tzu: A Repository of Early Chinese Thought.* 2 vols. Hong Kong: Hong Kong University Press, 1965

Riegel, Jeffrey K. "A Summary of Some Recent *Wenwu* and *Kaogu* Articles on Mawangdui Tombs Two and Three," *Early China* 1 (1975): 10–15.

Rubin, Vitaly A. *Individual and State in Ancient China: Essays on Four Chinese Philosophers*, tr. Steven I. Levine. New York: Columbia University Press, 1976.

Sanlüe 三略 (*Huangshigong Sanlüe* 黃石公三略). In *Wujing qishu zhijie* 武經七書直解. Nanjing, 1933.

Satō Kenji 佐藤堅司. *Sonshi no taikeiteki kenkyū* 孫子の体系的研究. Tokyo: Kazema shobo, 1963.

Sawyer, Ralph D. trans., *The Seven Military Classics of Ancient China*. Boulder, CO: Westview Press, 1993.

———, trans. *One Hundred Unorthodox Strategies*. Boulder, CO: Westview Press, 1996.

———. *The Tao of Spycraft: Intelligence Theory and Practice in Traditional China.* Boulder, CO: Westview Press, 1998.

———. *The Tao of Deception: Unorthodox Warfare in Historic and Modern China.* New York: Basic Books, 2007.

———. "Military Prognostication." In Di Cosmo, *Military Culture in Imperial China*, 45–64.

———. *Ancient Chinese Warfare*. New York: Basic Books, 2011.

———. *Zhuge Liang: Strategy, Achievements, and Writings*. North Charleston, SC: CreateSpace Independent Publishing Program, 2014.

Schaberg, David. *A Patterned Past: Form and Thought in Early Chinese Historiography.* Cambridge, MA: Harvard University Asia Center, 2001.

Schwartz, Benjamin I. *The World of Thought in Ancient China*. Cambridge, MA: Harvard University Press, 1985.

Shandong sheng bowuguan Linyi wenwu zu 山東省博物館臨沂文物組. "Shandong Linyi Xi Han mu faxian *Sunzi bingfa* he *Sun Bin bingfa* deng zhujian de jian bao" 山東臨沂西漢墓發現《孫子兵法》和《孫臏兵法》等竹簡的簡報. *Wenwu* 文物 1974 (2): 15–26.

Shangjunshu 商君書 (*Shangzi* 商子). In *Sibu congkan chubian* 四部叢刊初編. Shanghai: Shangwu yinshuguan, 1919–1922.

Shangshu 尚書. In *Sibu congkan chubian* 四部叢刊初編. Shanghai: Shangwu yinshuguan, 1919–1922.

Shao Hong 邵鴻. *Zhangjiashan Han jian Gai Lu yanjiu* 張家山漢簡《蓋廬》研究. Beijing: Wenwu chubanshe, 2007.

Shen Yanguo 沈延國, and Yang Kuan, "*Yi Zhoushu* yu *Jijia Zhoushu* bianzheng" 《逸周書》與《汲家周書》辨證. *Zhi yan* 制言 40 (May 1939).

Shi 詩 (*Mao Shi* 毛詩). In *Sibu congkan chubian* 四部叢刊初編. Shanghai: Shangwu yinshuguan, 1919–1922.

Shi Meiheng 史美珩. *Gudian binglüe* 古典兵略. Taibei: Hongye wenhua, 1997.

Simafa 司馬法. In *Sibu congkan chubian* 四部叢刊初編. Shanghai: Shangwu yinshuguan, 1919–1922.

Sima Qian 司馬遷 and Sima Tan 司馬談. *Shiji* 史記. Taibei: Yiwen yinshuguan, 1955.

Siu, R.G.H. *Ch'i: A Neo-Taoist Approach to Life*. Cambridge, MA: MIT Press, 1974.

Song Lian 宋濂 et al., comps. *Yuan shi* 元史. Taibei: Yiwen yinshuguan, 1955.

Sun Bin bingfa 孫臏兵法. Beijing: Wenwu chubanshe, 1975.

Sun Yutang 孫毓棠, "Xi Han de bing zhi" 西漢的兵制. *Zhongguo shehui jingji shi jikan* 中國社會經濟史集刊 5, no. 1 (March 1937): 1–74.

Sunzi bingfa 孫子兵法 (*Sunzi ji zhu* 孫子集注). In *Sibu congkan chubian* 四部叢刊初編. Shanghai: Shangwu yinshuguan, 1919–1922.

Tang Dapei 唐大沛, *Yi Zhoushu fenbian jushi* 逸周書分編句釋. Taibei: Xuesheng shuju, 1969.

Tang Lan 唐蘭. "*Huangdi si jing* chu tan"《黃帝四經》初探. *Wenwu* 文物 1974 (10): 48–52.

———. "Mawangdui chutu *Laozi* yi ben qian yishu de yanjiu" 馬王堆出土《老子》乙本卷前古佚書的研究. *Kaogu xuebao* 考古學報 1975 (1): 7–27.

Tang Taizong Li Weigong wendui 唐太宗李衛公問對. In *Wujing qishu zhijie*. Nanjing, 1933.

Tang Xin 湯新. "Fajia dui Huang Lao zhi xue de xishou he gaizao—Han Mawangdui boshu *Jingfa* deng pian" 法家對黃老之學的吸收和改造—漢馬王堆帛書《經法》等篇. *Wenwu* 文物 1975 (8): 18–22.

Thompson, Paul M. "The *Shen-tzu* [Shen Dao 慎倒] Fragments." PhD dissertation, University of Washington, 1970.

Tian Xudong 田旭東. *Gudai bingxue wenhua tan lun* 古代兵學文化探論. Beijing: Zhongguo shehui kexue chubanshe, 2010.

Tuotuo 脫脫 (Toghto) et al., comps. *Song shi* 宋史. Taibei: Yiwen yinshuguan, 1955.

Tuotuo 脫脫 (Toghto) et al., comps. *Jin shi* 金史. Taibei: Yiwen yinshuguan, 1955.

Tu Weiming. *Centrality and Commonality: An Essay on Chung-yung*. Honolulu: University of Hawai'i Press, 1976.

Twitchett, Denis, and Michael Loewe, eds. *The Cambridge History of China: Volume I, the Ch'in and Han Empires, 221 BC.–A.D. 220*. Cambridge, UK: Cambridge University Press, 1986.

van Els, Paul. "The *Wenzi*: Creation and Manipulation of a Chinese Philosophical Text." PhD dissertation, Leiden University, 2006.

Walker, Richard L. *The Multi-state System of Ancient China*. Hamden, CT: Shoe String Press, 1953.

Wallacker, Benjamin E. "Two Concepts in Early Chinese Military Thought." *Language* 42, no. 2 (1966): 295–299.

———. "Liu An, Second King of Huai-nan (180?–122 B.C.)." *Journal of the American Oriental Society* 92, no. 1 (1972): 36–51.

Wang, C.H. "Towards Defining a Chinese Heroism," *Journal of the American Oriental Society* 95, no. 1 (1975): 25–35.

Wang Fu 王符. *Qianfu lun* 潛夫論. In *Sibu congkan chubian* 四部叢刊初編. Shanghai: Shangwu yinshuguan, 1919–1922.

Wang Qinruo 王欽若 et al., comps. *Cefu yuangui* 冊府元龜. Taibei: Zhonghua shuju, 1967.

Wang Shujin 王樹金. "Mawangdui Han mu boshu *Tianwen qi xiang za zhan* yanjiu san shi nian" 馬王堆漢墓帛書《天文氣象雜占》研究三十年 *Hunan sheng bowuguan guan kan* 湖南省 博物館館刊 4 (2007): 31–42.

Wang Xianchen 王顯臣, and Xu Baolin 許保林. *Zhongguo gudai bingshu za tan* 中國古代兵書雜談. Beijing: Zhanshi chubanshe, 1983.

Wang Xiuzhi 王秀芝. *Huangshigong Sushu Sanlüe di yanjiu* 黃石公素書三略的研究. Taipei: Commercial Press, 1970.

Wang Yinglin 王應麟, comp. *Yuhai* 玉海. Hangzhou: Zhejiang shuju, 1883.

Wang Yu-ch'uan. "An Outline of the Central Government of the Former Han Dynasty." *Harvard Journal of Asiatic Studies* 12 (1949): 166–173.

Wang Zongyi 汪宗沂, comp. *Tai Gong bingfa yiwen* 太公兵法逸文. In *Jianxicun she congkan* 漸西村舍叢刊. Taibei: Yiwen yinshuguan, 1959.

Watanabe Hidekata 渡邊秀方. *Shina tetsugaku shi gairon* 支那哲學史概論. Kyoto: Waseda daigaku shuppan bu, 1924.

Watson, Burton, trans. *Records of the Grand Historian of China*. New York and London: Columbia University Press, 1961.

———, trans. *Mo Tzu, Basic Writings*. New York: Columbia University Press, 1963.

———, trans. *Chuang Tzu, Basic Writings*. New York: Columbia University Press, 1964.

———, trans. *Han Fei Tzu, Basic Writings*. New York: Columbia University Press, 1964.

Weigand, Jorg. *Staat und Militär im altchinesischen Militärtraktat Wei Liao Tzu*. Würzburg: Würzburg University, 1969.

Weiliaozi 尉繚子. In *Wujing qishu zhijie*. Nanjing, 1933.

Wei Rulin 魏汝霖. *Sunzi jin zhu jin yi* 孫子今註今譯. Taibei: Commercial Press, 1972.

Wei Rulin 魏汝霖, and Liu Zhongping 劉仲平. *Zhongguo junshi sixiang shi* 中國軍事思想史. Taibei: Guofang yanjiuyuan and Zhonghua dadian bianyin hui, 1968.

Wenzi 文子 (*Wenzi zuan yi* 文子纘義). In *Qinding Siku quanshu* 欽定四庫全書. Taibei: Shijie shuju, 1985–1988.

Wilhelm, Hellmut. "Schriften und Fragmente zur Entwicklung der staatsrechtlichen Theorie in der Chou-Zeit." *Monumenta Serica* 12 (1947): 41–96.

Wilhelm, Richard, and Cary F. Baynes, trans. *The I Ching, or Book of Changes*. Princeton, NJ: Princeton University Press, 1950.

Woqijing 握奇經 (*Feng hou Woqijing* 風后握奇經). Taibei: Xinxing shuju, 1970.

Wright, Quincy. *A Study of War*. Chicago: University of Chicago Press, 1942.

Wu Jiulong 吳九龍. *Yinqueshan Han jian shiwen* 銀雀山漢簡釋文. Beijing: Wenwu chubanshe, 1985.

Wuzi 吳子. In *Sibu congkan chubian* 四部叢刊初編. Shanghai: Shangwu yinshuguan, 1919–1922.

Xinshu 新書. In *Sibu congkan chubian* 四部叢刊初編. Shanghai: Shangwu yinshuguan, 1919–1922.

Xu Baolin 許保林. *Huangshigong Sanlüe qianshuo*黃石公三略淺說. Beijing: Jiefangjun chubanshe, 1986.

———. *Zhongguo bingshu tonglan* 中國兵書通覽. Beijing: Jiefangjun chubanshe, 1990.

Xu Fuguan 徐復觀. *Yinyang wuxing guannian zhi yanbian ji ruogan youguan wenxian di chengli shidai yu jieshi di wenti* 陰陽五行觀念之演變及若干有關文獻的成立時代與解釋的問題. Taibei: Minzhu pinglun she, 1961.

———. *Liang Han sixiang shi* 兩漢思想. 2 vols. Hong Kong: Xianggang Zhongwen daxue, 1975.

———. "*Yantielun* zhong de hehui wenhua wenti"《鹽鐵論》的社會文化問題. *Xinya xuebao* 新亞學報 11, no. 2 (1975): 337–419.

Xu Jingxian 徐景賢. "Chunqiu Jin jun zhi kao" 春秋晉軍制考. *Guo zhuan yuekan* 國專月刊 1, no. 5 (July 1935): 7–10.

Xunzi 荀子. In *Sibu congkan chubian* 四部叢刊初編. Shanghai: Shangwu yinshuguan, 1919–1922.

Xu Peigen 徐培根, and Wei Rulin 魏汝霖. *Sun Bin bingfa zhushi* 孫臏兵法註釋. Taibei: Liming wenhua shiye gongsi, 1976.

Yang Bing'an 楊丙安. *Shiyi jia zhu Sunzi jiaoli* 十一家注孫子校理. Beijing: Zhonghua shuju, 1999.

Yan Gengwang 嚴耕望. "Zhanguo xueshu dili yu rencai fenbu" 戰國學術地理與人才分佈. *Xinya shuyuan xueshu niankan* 新亞書院學術年刊 18 (1976), 10.

Yang Kuan 楊寬. *Zhanguo shi* 戰國史. Rev. ed. Taibei: Shangwu yinshuguan, 1997.

Yantielun 鹽鐵論. In *Sibu congkan chubian* 四部叢刊初編. Shanghai: Shangwu yinshuguan, 1919–1922.

Yanzi chunqiu 晏子春秋. In *Sibu congkan chubian* 四部叢刊初編. Shanghai: Shangwu yinshuguan, 1919–1922.

Yates, Robin D.S. "New Light on Ancient Chinese Military Texts: Notes on their Nature and Evolution, and the Development of Military Specialization in Warring States China." *T'oung Pao* 74 (1988): 211–248.

———. "The Yin-yang Texts from Yinqueshan: An Introduction and Partial Reconstruction, with Notes on their Significance in Relation to Huang-Lao Daoism." *Early China* 19 (1994): 75–144.

———, trans. *Five Lost Classics: Tao, Huang-Lao, and Yin-Yang in Han China*. New York: Ballantine Books, 1997.

———. "Early Modes on Interpretation of the Military Canons: The Case of the *Sunzi bingfa*." In *Interpretation and Intellectual Change: Chinese Hermeneutics in Historical Perspective*, edited by Ching-I Tu, 65–79. New Brunswick, NJ: Transaction, 2005.

———. "The History of Military Divination in China." *East Asian Science, Technology, and Medicine* 24 (2005): 15–43.

Yinqueshan Han mu zhujian zhengli xiaozu 銀雀山漢墓竹簡整理小組, comp. *Yinqueshan Han mu zhujian Sunzi bingfa* 銀雀山漢墓竹簡孫子兵法. Beijing: Wenwu chubanshe, 1976.

———. "Linyi Yinqueshan Han mu chutu *Wang bing* pian shiwen" 臨沂銀雀山漢墓出土《王兵》篇釋文. *Wenwu* 1976 (12): 36–43.

Yi Zhoushu 逸周書 (*Jizhong Zhoushu* 汲冢周書). In *Sibu congkan chubian* 四部叢刊初編. Shanghai: Shangwu yinshuguan, 1919–1922.

Yu Shinan 虞世南, comp. *Beitang shuchao* 北堂書鈔. Tianjin: Tianjin guji chubanshe, 1988.

Yu Yan 俞棪. *Guiguzi xin zhu* 鬼谷子新注. Shanghai: Commercial Press, 1937.

Yu Ying-shih (Yu Yingshi 余英時). *Trade and Expansion in Han China*. Berkeley and Los Angeles: University of California Press, 1967.

———. "Fan zhi lun yu Zhongguo zhengzhi chuantong" 反智論與中國政治傳統. *Ming bao yuekan* 明報月刊 12, no. 2 (February 1976), 2–8; 12, no. 3 (March 1976), 24–32.

Zeng Guoyuan 曾國垣. *Xian Qin zhanzheng zhexue* 先秦戰爭哲學. Taibei: Commercial Press, 1972.

Zhang Lie 張烈. "*Liutao* de chengshu ji qi neirong"《六韜》的成書及其內容. *Lishi yanjiu* 歷史 研究 1981 (3): 122–126.

Zhang Tingyu 張廷玉 et al., comps. *Ming shi* 明史. Taibei: Yiwen yinshuguan, 1955.

Zhangsun Wuji 長孫無忌 and Wei Zheng 魏徵, comps. *Suishu* 隋書. Taibei: Yiwen yinshuguan, 1955.

Zhao Erxun 趙爾巽 et al., comps. *Qing shi gao* 清史稿. Taibei: Yiwen yinshuguan, 1955.

Zhao, Jian, "Historical Development of the *Xia* and its Relationship with Other Social Groups in the Pre-Qin Period," *Journal of Asian History* 35 (2001): 59–91.

Zhao Tiehan 趙鐵寒. "*Guiguzi* kao bian"《鬼谷子》考辨. *Dalu zazhi* 14, no. 5 (March 15, 1957): 3–7, 14, no. 6 (March 31, 1957): 20–25.

Zheng Liangshu 鄭良樹. *Sunzi jiaobu* 孫子斠補. Taibei: Xuesheng shuju, 1974.

Zhongguo junshi shi bianxie zu 中國軍事史編寫組. *Zhongguo junshi shi* 中國軍事史, vol. 5 (*bingjia* 兵家). Beijing: Jiefangjun chubanshe, 1990.

Zhouli 周禮. In *Sibu congkan chubian* 四部叢刊初編. Shanghai: Shangwu yinshuguan, 1919–1922.

Zhou Shaoxian 周紹賢. "Huang Lao sixiang zai Xi Han" 黃老思想在西漢. *Guoli Zhengzhi daxue xuebao* 國立政治大學學報 26 (December 1972): 85–102.

Zhouyi 周易. In *Sibu congkan chubian* 四部叢刊初編. Shanghai: Shangwu yinshuguan, 1919–1922.

Zhuangzi 莊子 (*Nanhua zhenjing* 南華真經). Taibei: Yiwen yinshuguan, 1968.

Zhu Guozhao 朱國炤, "Shangsunjiazhai mu jian chu tan" 上孫家寨木簡初探. *Wenwu* 文物 1981 (2): 27–34.

Zhu Youzeng 朱右曾, comp. *Yi Zhoushu jiaoshi* 逸周書校釋. Eguan shuchu, 1912.

Index